TERMS & CONDITIONS

Table of Contents

SNACKS AND APPETIZERS 152

Chapter 1- Introduction

Fortunately, the Instant Pot has eliminated all of the obstacles to eating healthy home cooked meals every night of the week. The Instant Pot is your multi-tasking partner in the kitchen & enables you to serve a lot of kinds of elaborate meals with minimal time or effort. An Instant Pot comes with lots of advantages. It's just a single kitchen device but it's able to cover the work of many other devices.

It's a magical kitchen appliance that has multiple functions in one pot. An Instant Pot is a programmable pressure cooker that is equipped to function as a steamer, a slow cooker, a yogurt maker, a rice cooker, a sauté pan, a pressure cooker, & a warmer.

The stainless-steel interior of each Instant Pot is perfect for cooking. No other materials (like plastic or Teflon) are touching the food except the stainless steel. It is also very simply to clean.

The cookbook presented to you is a collection of recipes of various & incredibly tasty 300 super simply dishes. If you want to lose weight, the author has selected for you the easiest & tastiest Paleo diet recipes. Every recipe in this cookbook may be easily made at home in your Instant Pot.

Every recipe was created with love & inspiration. You may be sure that you'll love every meal you find here. There is no need any more to search for something special for the dinner, lunch, or breakfast. Even more, the main tasting & simply recipes for the snacks & appetizers were put in the cookbook. Just open this cookbook & find the recipe that will be appropriate particularly for you.

Chapter 2: All the Buttons on the Instant Pot

Is not it tempting to just take the Instant Pot out of its box, skip the directions, & then start loading food into it? Well, how hard may this really be? Put a lot of roast in, & the basically push the button, that's about it is not it?

Did you fill up the Instant Pot & then did you basically stare at the control panel with all the different buttons & try to figure out what the main setting is? Initially, it might have seemed really simple, but then what would happen if you press the poultry option & the chicken is fully frozen or if it's a little small? The default poultry setting is fifteen mints at very high pressure; would this setting do the trick? What if you want to boil some eggs? Is there a button for that as well? A little bit of experimenting or can be a lot will help you in getting a hang of things. A little bit of reading might also help. Well, this chapter will help you in getting started & save you from having to go on "experimenting" with the different functions. The Instant Pot has seven different functions that are present & these are yogurt maker, steamer, sautéing, slow cooker, rice cooker, pressure cooker & a warmer.

For the sake of convenience, these buttons have been divided into 3 different categories & these are as follows. The function button helps in activating 1 of the advertised functions that the Instant Pot performs. The present button is for starting a preset program. The utility button has to be used in combination with 1 or 2 of the other buttons.

Control Panel Buttons

Here is a list of all the buttons that are present on the Instant Pot & here's what happens when you push each of these buttons.

Meat/ Stew

This is a preprogrammed setting that has been designed for cooking meat & stews. It's set for a default time of 36 mints at a very high pressure. If you want to change the time, then pressing "Adjust" will help in increasing & decreasing the time accordingly. By pressing the Less button you'll be reducing the cooking time to twenty mints & by pressing the More button will increasing the cooking time to 46 mints. Pressing the Plus or the Minus buttons will help in navigating to any other time other than the one that has been programmed

Soup

This is a programed setting that has been designed for the purpose of cooking soup. This is a preset button. It's a default setting for half hour at a high pressure. If you want to change the time, then pressing "Adjust" will help in increasing & decreasing the time accordingly. By pressing the Less button you'll be reducing the cooking time to twenty mints & by pressing the More button will increasing the cooking time to 42 mints. Pressing the Plus or the Minus buttons will help in navigating to any other time other than the one that has been programmed. By pressing the Pressure button, you'll be able to change the pressure setting from high to low.

. By pressing the Pressure button, you'll be able to change the pressure setting from high to low.

Bean or Chili

This is a preprogrammed setting that has been designed for cooking beans & chili. It's set for a default time of half hour at a very high pressure. If you want to change the time, then pressing "Adjust" will help in increasing & decreasing the time accordingly. By pressing the Less button you'll be reducing the cooking time to 26 mints & by pressing the More button will increasing the cooking time to 42 mints. Pressing the Plus or the Minus buttons will help in navigating to any other time other than the one that has been programmed. By pressing the Pressure button, you'll be able to change the pressure setting from high to low.

Poultry

This is a preprogrammed setting that has been designed for cooking poultry. It's set for a default time of fifteen mints at a very high pressure. If you want to change the time, then pressing "Adjust" will help in increasing & decreasing the time accordingly. By pressing the Less button you'll be reducing the cooking time to five mints & by pressing the More button will increasing the cooking time to half hour. Pressing the Plus or the Minus buttons will help in navigating to any other time other than the one that has been programmed. By pressing the Pressure button, you'll be able to change the pressure setting from high to low.

Slow cook

This is a preprogrammed setting that has been designed for cook at a lower temperature and slowly. It's set for a default time of four hours at a normal temperature of about 200 degrees F. If you want to change the time, then pressing "Adjust" will help in increasing & decreasing the temperature accordingly. By pressing the "Less" button you'll be reducing the temperature at 190 degrees F & by pressing the More button will increasing temperature to 210 degrees F. Pressing the Plus or the Minus buttons will help in navigating to any other time other than the one that has been programmed. By pressing the Pressure button, you'll be able to change the pressure setting from high to low. The time can be varied by increments of half hour.

Sauté

This is a preprogrammed setting that has been designed for browning meat or stir-frying. This is a function button. It's set for a default time of 32 mints at a normal temperature of 320 degrees F. You'll be able to increase or decrease the temperature by pressing Adjust. You may navigate between the Less & the More options for decreasing the temperature to about 221 degrees F or increase it to 338 degrees F respectively. The cycle is preset for half hour & it cannot be altered. Don't place the lid on the Instant Pot in this function.

Plus

This is for adding time to any of the default or the preset time in a setting. This is a utility button & there is no default setting for this as such. You'll basically need to press it for increasing time.

Pressure

This is for the purpose of increasing or decreasing the pressure. It's a utility button. The default setting is for pressure between 10.2 to 11.6 psi while making use of this manually. This button is for changing pressure from high to low pressure.

Manual

This is for pressure-cooking food & it's a function button. The default setting is for half hour & by pressing the Plus or the Minus buttons you'll be able to increase or decrease the time. Pressure button helps in changing the pressure setting from high to low.

Minus

This is for reducing time to any of the default or the preset time in a setting. This is a utility button & there is no default setting for this as such. You'll basically need to press it for decreasing time.

Adjust

The temperature may be adjusted by using this function. It's also made use of for navigating to any of the other preset functions. This is a utility button. There are Normal, Less, & More modes for this setting.

Timer

The timer is for delaying the start of the cooking method & for timing the duration. This is a utility button. The default setting would be to start cooking after six hours. You may click on the Plus & the Minus options for adding another six hours to the cook.

Multigrain

This is a programmed setting that has been designed for cooking grains that are hard like split corn & wild rice. This is a preset function. The pressure is set at high & the default cooking time is 42 mints. If you want to change the time, then pressing "Adjust" will help in increasing & decreasing the time accordingly. By pressing the Less button you'll be reducing the cooking time to 22 mints & by pressing the More button will increasing the cooking time to 1 hour. Pressing the Plus or the Minus buttons will help in navigating to any other time other than the one that has been programmed. By pressing the Pressure button, you'll be able to change the pressure setting from high to low.

Porridge

This is a programmed setting that has been designed of grains that have a texture similar to that of porridge. The default time is set to 22 mints & it is set at a high pressure. If you want to change the time, then pressing "Adjust" will help in increasing & decreasing the time accordingly. By pressing the Less button you'll be reducing the cooking time to 16 mints & by pressing the More button will increasing the cooking time to half hour. Pressing the Plus or the Minus buttons will help in navigating to any other time other than the one that has been programmed. By pressing the Pressure button, you'll be able to change the pressure setting from high to low.

Rice

This is for cooking white rice or parboiled rice. This is a function setting & it has been set to a default of twelve mints at a low temperature. This is an automatic function & according to the moisture & the rice that is put in the container, the appliance would decide the time & pressure for the cooking process. You'll need to make sure that all the excess pressure has to be released.

Steam

This is for the purpose of steaming food with water or any other liquid. This is a function button. The default time is 10 mints at a high pressure. By pressing the Adjust option, you'll be able to increase or decrease the cook time. If you want to change the time, then pressing "Adjust" will help in increasing & decreasing the time accordingly. By pressing the Less button you'll be reducing the cooking time to three mints & by pressing the More button will increasing the cooking time to fifteen minutes. Pressing the Plus or the Minus buttons will help in navigating to any other time other than the one that has been programmed. By pressing the Pressure button, you'll be able to change the pressure setting from high to low.

Yogurt

This is for pasteurizing milk, making yogurt or Jiu Niang. It's a function button. The default setting is for eight hours & the temperature for incubation is between 100 to 115 degrees F. The Adjust button will help in increasing the incubation period to 1 day & you may navigate between Plus & Minus settings for boiling the milk for making yogurt. When you're making yogurt in small containers then you may steam it with the steam function for about a minute.

Keep warm or Cancel

The purpose of this button is to keep the food warm once it has been cooked. This is a function button. The default setting is for ten hours & it is set at a low temperature. You may increase or decrease the time limit in this function by pressing the Plus or Minus buttons. The time change may be made by ten hours. Once the pressure-cooking setting or the slow cooking setting has been completed, then this mode will be turned on automatically.

To sum it all up, all the buttons other than the Yogurt Sauté, , Slow Cook, Rice, & all the other utility buttons have a preset time & they've a default setting of high pressure.

Chapter 3: Instant Pot Safety Tips

When using any household appliance, you should always grab that manual & make sure you know how to safely operate the appliance.

- The Instant Pot cooks things at a very high-pressure rate & temperature, so you absolutely have to be careful.
- Do not leave the home when you're using the Instant Pot. While it may work like a slow cooker, this is no fix it & forget it appliance. When the appliance is going up to pressure, you easy need to keep an eye out to make sure things are working properly.
- Don't try to pressure fry anything in this appliance. KFC might do this, however, you do not have a commercial machine like KFC does... so just do not do it.
- Make sure to wear silicone gloves if you're doing a quick release.
- Don't use this appliance to steam your face. It was not meant for this purpose & you could get burned quite easily.
- Make sure you put at least 1 cup of water to maintain pressure. We cannot operate without water & neither may your pressure pot.
- Focus on what you're cooking when you fill the pressure pot. For eg., you would only fill the pot halfway with beans, pasta & oats. An excellent good rule of thumb is that if the food expands when you cook it, only fill it half way. For everything else, do not go above 2/3 full.
- Don't ever try to force the pressure cooker open. If it won't open, check to see if all of the steam has been released.
- Tilt the lid away from you when you're opening after cooking has completed.
- Pay very close attention to the Instant Pot's sealing ring. It should be cleaned properly & no food residue should be left on the ring. In case you see any cracks, cuts or damages, you'll need to replace the seal.

Chapter 4: Recipes

Breakfast Special Recipes

1. Energetic Creamy Chili Black Beans

Time for an iconic recipe.

Ingredients:

- 2 tablespoons canola oil
- Kosher salt, to taste
- About 1.5 medium onion, finely chopped
- 3 cups chicken / vegetable broth / plain water
- 1 medium green bell pepper, finely chopped
- 4 garlic cloves, grated finely
- 1/2 cup of chipotles in adobo, chopped coarsely
- About 1.5 tablespoon chili powder
- 1 tablespoon roasted cumin powder
- 1 cup black beans, soaked overnight

Directions:

1. First of all, please make sure you've all the ingredients available. Select Sauté and heat the Instant Pot.
2. Then once hot, Pour the oil.
3. Once hot, add in grated garlic, chopped onions and bell peppers and sauté for about 5 to 10 minutes.
4. This step is important. Add chili and cumin powders, stir well & toss in chipotles and coat well with the powders.
5. Now add beans, salt, broth and mix well. Secure the lid.
6. Cook properly on High for about 20 to 25 minutes on 'Manual' option.
7. Then once done, let the pressure release itself.
8. One thing remains to be done. Remove the lid & check if beans are cooked well.
9. Finally if not, cook properly for about 2 to 5 more minutes & serve hot.

Preparation Time: 5 to 10 minutes

Pressure Time: 15 to 20 minutes

Servings: 2

Delicious recipe is ready.

2. Funny Baked But Not Baked Beans

A style statement.

Ingredients:

- 1/4 cup finely chopped onion
- Salt, to taste
- 1 cup basic white beans, soaked and drained
- About 1 tablespoon dry mustard
- 1/2 tablespoon apple cider vinegar
- 2 teaspoons smoked paprika
- 1 bay leaf

- 1 cup veggie stock
- About 1.5 tablespoon Dijon mustard
- 2 tablespoons chopped dates
- 2 tablespoons tomato paste
- 1 tablespoon blackstrap molasses
- 1 teaspoon canola oil

Directions:

1. First of all, please make sure you've all the ingredients available. Set your Instant Pot to Saute.
2. Then pour in the oil. Once hot, add the chopped onion and saute for about 2 to 5 minutes or until fragrant.
3. Add the beans, mustard, paprika & the bay leaf. Stir well.
4. This step is important. Mix in the veggie stock. Secure the lid and cook properly for about 15 to 20 minutes on High Pressure.
5. Now allow the pressure to release naturally (8-10 minutes).
6. Remove the lid & test the texture of the beans.
7. If they are not cooked through or aren't soft enough to squish, then cook properly for about 2 to 5 more minutes (add water/stock if needed).
8. Then discard the bay leaf. Mix in the chopped dates, molasses, tomato paste, mustard and vinegar.
9. One thing remains to be done. Mix well. Season with salt.
10. Finally select Saute and let simmer for about 2 to 5 minutes. Serve.

Preparation Time: 5 to 10 minutes

Pressure Time: 15 to 20 minutes

Servings: 2

Have you made it yet?

3. Scrumptious Crustless Kale and Tomato Quiche

Who wants to try this one?

Ingredients:

- 1 cup chopped Kale
- 1 1/2 cups Water
- About 3.5 tbsp Milk
- Pinch of Black Pepper
- 5 Eggs
- 1/4 cup grated Parmesan Cheese
- About 1.5 tsp Garlic Salt
- 1/2 Tomato, sliced
- About 1.5 Green Onion (Chopped)
- 1/2 cup diced Tomatoes

Directions:

1. First of all, please make sure you've all the ingredients available. Pour the water into the Instant Pot & lower the trivet.
2. Now grease a baking dish that can fit inside your Instant Pot with some cooking spray.
3. Place the kale, diced tomatoes, & green onions in it.
4. Then sprinkle the cheese over & arrange the tomato slices on top.
5. One thing remains to be done. Choose the MANUAL cooking mode & cook properly on HIGH for about 20 to 25 minutes.

6. Finally press CANCEL and wait for about 10 to 15 minutes before doing a quick pressure release.

Total Time: 35 to 40 Minutes

Serves: 2

The next big recipe…

4. Astonishing Breakfast Quinoa

Certainly a show stopper.

Ingredients:

- 1/8 tsp cinnamon
- 3/4 cup quinoa (Rinsed)
- About 1.5 tsp maple syrup
- 1 1/8 cup water
- About 1/2 tsp vanilla
- Salt

Directions:

1. First of all, please make sure you've all the ingredients available. Add cinnamon, quinoa, maple syrup, salt, vanilla, and water to cooker.
2. Now choose high pressure and set a minute cooking time.
3. Once finished, turn it off and let it set 10 to 15 minutes.
4. Release the remaining pressure.
5. One thing remains to be done. Then ease the lid off.
6. Finally fluff the mix and sever with almonds, berries, & milk.

I use to have it during my exams.

5. Excellent Spanish Casserole

You can make this very easily.

Ingredients:

- 8 oz. cheddar cheese
- About 2.5 tbsp olive oil
- 8 oz. mozzarella cheese
- Black pepper
- 1 onion (Chopped)
- 4 eggs, whisked
- About 1/2 tsp
- 1 yellow bell pepper (Chopped)
- 1/4 tsp salt
- 1 cup spinach (Chopped)

Directions:

1. First of all, please make sure you've all the ingredients available. In a bowl add eggs, spinach, bell pepper, mozzarella cheese, cheddar cheese, & onion, mix well.
2. Now season with salt & pepper.
3. Grease Instant Pot with olive oil.
4. Transfer spinach mixture to Instant Pot & cover with lid.
5. One thing remains to be done. Then leave to cook properly for about 25 to 30 minutes on SLOW cook mode.
6. Finally serve hot & enjoy.

Prep + Cooking Time: 50 to 55 minutes

Servings: 2

Ready, set, go….

6. Legendary Chorizo Pepper Jack Frittata

A little different, a little extra ordinary.

Ingredients:

- 4 Eggs
- 1 1/2 cups Water
- About 2.5 tbsp Sour Cream
- Pinch of Pepper
- 1/4 cup grated Pepper Jack Cheese
- Pinch of Salt
- About 1 tsp dried Parsley
- 1/3 cup ground Chorizo

Directions:

1. First of all, please make sure you've all the ingredients available. Pour the water into your IP and lower the trivet.
2. Now grease a round smaller baking pan with cooking spray.
3. In a bowl, whisk together the eggs, parsley, salt, pepper, & sour cream.
4. This step is important. Stir in the chorizo.
5. Then pour the mixture into the greased pan.
6. Sprinkle the cheese over.
7. Cover the baking pan with aluminum foil & place inside the Instant Pot.
8. Then close the lid and choose MANUAL.
9. One thing remains to be done. Cook properly on LOW for about 15 to 20 minutes.
10. Finally release the pressure quickly.

Total Time: 25 to 30 Minutes

Serves: 2

Legend overload...

7. Awesome Steamed Artichokes

Most fantastic recipe ever.

Ingredients:

- Lemon 1
- Paprika to taste
- Mayonnaise 28g
- Dijon mustard 5g
- Medium Artichokes about 2.5

Directions:

1. First of all, please make sure you've all the ingredients available. Add 240ml of water to the instant cooker pot & carefully lower the steamer basket inside.
2. Now place artichokes facing upwards & then spritz any remaining lemon on top of each.
3. This step is important. Select a cooking time for about 10 to 15 minutes at high pressure.
4. When time is up, open the pressure cooker with the natural release method.
5. One thing remains to be done. Then mix mayonnaise with mustard & place in a small dipping container, & then sprinkle with paprika.
6. Finally serve warm and enjoy the taste.

Preparation Time: 25 to 30 minutes

Total Servings: 2

Nostalgic feeling…

Nutritional Information:

Calories from Fat: 34

Protein:2g

Fat: 5g

Sugar: 0g

Saturated Fat: 4.8g

Fiber: 3.5g

Cholesterol: 31mg

Total Carbohydrates: 7.1g

Calories: 77.5

8. Quick Breakfast cheesecake ramekins

Jumpstart your taste. ?

Ingredients:

- About 1.5 tablespoon almond flour
- 2 cups cottage cheese
- 2 egg yolks
- About 1.5 teaspoon vanilla extract
- 1/2 cup brown sugar
- 1 tablespoon butter

Directions:

1. First of all, please make sure you've all the ingredients available. Put the egg yolks in the bowl & sprinkle them with the brown sugar and vanilla extract.
2. Now take the mixer and mix the mixture till it gets lemon color.
3. Add almond flour & stir it carefully with the help of the wooden spoon.
4. This step is important. Place the cottage cheese in the blender & blend it until smooth.
5. Now add the lemon color egg yolk mixture in the blender and blend it for about 2 to 5 minutes on the high speed.
6. Add butter in every ramekin & then put the cottage cheese mixture there.
7. Then cover the ramekins with the foil & place them in the instant pot.
8. Cook the dish at the steam mode for about 15 to 20 minutes.
9. One thing remains to be done. When the time is over – remove the ramekins from the instant pot & discard the foil immediately.
10. Finally chill the meal gently & serve it.

Prep time: 5 to 10 minutes

Cooking time: 15 to 20 minutes

Servings: 2

Simplicity is best.

Nutritional information:

Calories 519

Protein 19

Fat 16.1

Fiber 0

Carbs 75.05

9. Wonderful Vegetable Omelet

Oh yeah. This is the recipe I was waiting for.

Ingredients:

- 1/2 cup broccoli florets
- 2 tablespoons cheese (Grated)
- About 1.5 clove garlic (Minced)
- 2 tablespoons each of tomatoes, onions and parsley to top
- 1/2 small yellow onion (Chopped)
- About 1 red bell pepper (Chopped)
- A pinch garlic powder
- A pinch chili powder
- Salt to taste
- Pepper to taste
- 3 eggs

Directions:

1. First of all, please make sure you've all the ingredients available. Whisk whites until fluffy. Add yolks & whisk again.
2. Then add vegetables and seasonings.
3. Spray the instant pot container with cooking spray.

4. Pour eggs over it.
5. Now close the lid. Press 'Steam' button & set timer for about 5 to 10 minutes.
6. One thing remains to be done. When the timer goes off, remove omelet on to a plate.
7. Finally cut into 2 halves & serve with toppings and cheese.

Legendary taste.

10. Elegant Beef and Cheese Quiche

Light taste.

Ingredients:

- About 4.5 tablespoons fresh milk
- 1/2 cup chopped onion
- A pinch of salt
- 1/2 cup grated mozzarella cheese
- A pinch of black pepper
- About 1.5 cup ground beef
- 3 fresh eggs

Directions:

1. First of all, please make sure you've all the ingredients available. Place a trivet in a pressure cooker then add 1-1/2 cups of water.
2. Now prepare a medium soufflé dish then grease with cooking oil. Set aside.
3. Crack the eggs then place in a bowl.
4. This step is important. Add salt, fresh milk, & black pepper then whisk until fluffy.

5. Add the mozzarella cheese, ground beef, & chopped onion into the egg mixture then stir well.

6. Then pour the mixture into the prepared soufflé dish & cover with aluminum foil.

7. Place in the pressure cooker then cover with the lid properly.

8. Now cook properly for about 30 to 35 minutes on high pressure and once it is done, turn it off & quick release the pressure cooker.

9. One thing remains to be done. Open the lid carefully then remove the dish from the pressure cooker.

10. Finally discard the aluminum foil then serve & enjoy.

Ready in about 45 to 50 minutes

Servings 2

As the name suggests....

11. Rich Almond and Apricot Oatmeal

Magical...

Ingredients:

- 1 tsp Vanilla Extract
- 1 tbsp Maple Syrup
- About 2.5 tbsp Almond Meal
- 1 tbsp chopped Almonds
- 2 cups Water
- 1 cup Rolled Oats
- About 2.5 Large Apricots (Chopped)

Directions:

1. First of all, please make sure you've all the ingredients available.

Combine everything but the chopped almonds in your Instant Pot.

2. Now close and lock the lid.

3. Choose MANUAL and cook properly on HIGH for about 2 to 5 minutes.

4. One thing remains to be done. Then do a quick pressure release.

5. Finally divide between two serving bowls & top with chopped almonds.

Right on track.

12. Titanic Cheesy Bacon Egg Strata

Believe me...

Ingredients:

- 1 cup tap water
- Salt and pepper, to taste
- About 1.5 tablespoon coconut oil, virgin
- 2 medium, free-range eggs, beaten
- 1 cup milk
- 4 tablespoons cheddar cheese (Grated)
- 2 cups whole bread, sliced in 1 inch cubes
- About 2.5 bacon slices, sautéed and browned in a skillet, drained & chopped into smaller pieces

Directions:

1. First of all, please make sure you've all the ingredients available. Pour the water into your Instant Pot & place a steam rack on top.

2. Now grease a 6-inch baking dish with coconut oil.

3. Take a medium mixing bowl & whisk in the eggs, milk, salt and pepper.
4. This step is important. Stir in the bread cubes & let sit for a couple of minutes.
5. Add in the chopped bacon & cheese.
6. Then mix well and transfer everything into the baking dish.
7. Next, place the baking dish on the steam rack.
8. Cover the lid of the Instant Pot.
9. Now hit the 'Manual' and cook properly for about 15 to 20 minutes on high pressure.
10. One thing remains to be done. Once cooked, let it depressurize naturally.
11. Finally remove the dish, top with some cheese & broil for about 2 to 5 minutes until the cheese melts.

Preparation Time: 15 to 20 minutes

Pressure Time: 15 to 20 minutes

Servings: 2

Always kept wondering how it was made… One day I sat beside my chef and got it.

13. Tasty Baked But Not Baked Beans

Stylish.

Ingredients:

- 1/4 cup finely chopped onion
- Salt, to taste
- 1 cup basic white beans, soaked and drained
- About 1 tablespoon dry mustard
- 2 teaspoons smoked paprika
- 1/2 tablespoon apple cider vinegar
- 1 bay leaf
- 1 cup veggie stock
- 2 tablespoons chopped dates
- About 1.5 tablespoon Dijon mustard
- 2 tablespoons tomato paste
- 1 tablespoon blackstrap molasses
- 1 teaspoon canola oil

Directions:

1. First of all, please make sure you've all the ingredients available. Set your Instant Pot to Saute.
2. Then pour the oil. Once hot, add the chopped onion & sauté for about 2 to 5 minutes or until fragrant.
3. Add the beans, mustard, paprika and the bay leaf. Stir well.
4. Mix in the veggie stock.
5. This step is important. Secure the lid and cook properly for about 15 to 20 minutes on High Pressure.
6. Now allow the pressure to release naturally (5 to 10 minutes).
7. Remove the lid and test the texture of the beans.
8. If they are not cooked through or aren't soft enough to squish, then cook properly for about 2 to 5 more minutes (add water/stock if needed).
9. Then discard the bay leaf. Mix in the chopped dates, molasses, tomato paste, mustard and vinegar.

10. One thing remains to be done. Mix well. Season with salt.
11. Finally select Saute and let simmer for about 2 to 5 minutes. Serve.

Preparation Time: 5 to 10 minutes

Pressure Time: 15 to 20 minutes

Servings: 2

I bet you'll find it amazing…

14. Yummy Feta and Leafy Green Egg Cups

A simple recipe which you will like.

Ingredients:

- 2 tbsp shredded Mozzarella Cheese
- 1 cup Water
- About 2.5 tbsp chopped Tomatoes
- 1/3 cup chopped Leafy Greens (Chard, Spinach, Kale…)
- Pinch of Pepper
- About 2.5 tbsp crumbled Feta Cheese
- 2 Eggs

Directions:

1. First of all, please make sure you've all the ingredients available. Pour the water into the Instant Pot.
2. Now take two silicone ramekins & divide the leafy greens between them.
3. Whisk together the eggs & pepper, in a bowl.
4. This step is important. Stir the remaining ingredients.
5. Then pour the egg mixture into the ramekins.

6. Place the ramekins inside the IP, on the rack.
7. Close & lock the lid.
8. Now cook properly on HIGH for about 5 to 10 minutes.
9. One thing remains to be done. Release the pressure quickly.
10. Finally serve & enjoy!

Total Time: 15 to 20 Minutes

Serves: 2

A fine recipe, it just works.

15. Unique Instant Refried Beans

Yummy, definitely yummy.

Ingredients:

To prepare the salsa:

- 1 medium onion (Minced)
- About 1/2 teaspoon minced jalapeno
- 2 garlic cloves (Minced)
- 1 medium tomato, finely chopped

To prepare the beans:

- 2 garlic cloves (Minced)
- 2 tablespoons freshly chopped cilantro
- About 1 tablespoon ground cumin
- 1/4 teaspoon chili powder
- Dash of salt
- About 1 teaspoon dried oregano
- 3/4 cups black beans
- 1 sprig Mexican tea

- 1 1/4 cup water
- 1 piece (1-inch) seaweed, preferably kombu
- 1 medium onion (Diced)

Directions:

1. First of all, please make sure you've all the ingredients available. To prepare the salsa, combine all the salsa ingredients together in a mixing bowl: Onion, garlic, tomato, and chile. Set aside.
2. Now to prepare the beans, set your Instant Pot to Sauté.
3. Add the diced onion & dry saute for about a minute.
4. This step is important. Add the garlic, ground cumin, chili, chili powder and oregano. Cook for a minute more, stirring occasionally.
5. Mix in the black beans, water, seaweed and the Mexican tea.
6. Then secure the lid and cook properly for about 30 to 35 minutes on High Pressure.
7. Allow the pressure to release naturally.
8. Remove the lid and test to make sure the beans are cooked well. If not, cook properly for about 2 to 5 minutes more.
9. Discard the kombu using tongs and Mexican tea.
10. Now add the prepared salsa on top.
11. Without stirring or anything, simply put the lid back on, select Manual and cook properly for about 5 to 10 minutes on High Pressure.
12. One thing remains to be done. Using an immersion blender, blend the beans according to your desired texture.
13. Finally season with salt & garnish with freshly chopped cilantro. Serve warm!

Preparation Time: 5 to 10 minutes

Pressure Time: 20 to 25 minutes

Servings: 2

Don't wait, eat it!!

16. Ultimate Hard Boiled Egg

Just make it once and you will keep making it!!

Ingredients:

- 1 cup water
- eggs, however many you want

Directions:

1. First of all, please make sure you've all the ingredients available. Pour water in the pot, & ease eggs in the steamer basket.
2. Now close and seal lid. Set cooking time to about 5 to 10 minutes, high pressure.
3. The cooker will take 5 to 10 minutes to get to the correct pressure, and then will cook properly for about 2 to 5 minutes.
4. One thing remains to be done. Then let pressure reduce for about 5 to 10 minutes & then use quick release.
5. Finally put the eggs in cold water. Then peel & enjoy.

I've always loved them. Plus they can be eaten anytime!!

17. Iconic Spread Of Eggplant And Olive

Good luck!!

Ingredients:

- 2 pound of eggplant
- Extra virgin olive oil
- 3 to 4 garlic cloves with their skin on
- 1 tsp of salt
- Sprigs of fresh thyme
- About 1 cup of water
- 1/4 cup of black pitted black olives
- 1/4 a cup of lemon juice
- About 1.5 tbsp of tahini
- 4 tbsp of olive oil

Directions:

1. First of all, please make sure you've all the ingredients available. Peel off the eggplants in alternative stripes of skin and no skin.
2. Now slice up the biggest possible chunk & cover up the bottom of the cooker.
3. Rest of the plant can be chopped up roughly In your preheated Instant Pot, add some olive oil & once heated, place the large chunks of eggplant face down trying to caramelize the side for about 5 to 10 minutes.
4. This step is important. Once done, throw in your Garlic Cloves making sure that their skin is still on.
5. Then flip over the eggplants & add the remaining chopped up pieces of eggplant alongside water and salt.
6. Close the lid and let it cook properly for about 2 to 5 minutes at HIGH pressure.
7. Once done, release the pressure naturally.
8. Now take the inner pot to a sink & discard the brown liquid.
9. Take out the garlic cloves & gently remove the skin.
10. One thing remains to be done. Pour in the lemon juice, Tahini, all of the garlic cloves and black olives into an immersion blender & puree everything.
11. Finally pour the mixture & serve it with some fresh thyme sprinkled around with a dash of olive oil.

Prep + Cooking Time: 20 to 25 minutes

Servings: 2

Oh yeah!!

18. Awesome Prosciutto Mozzarella Egg Muffins

Stupidly simple...

Ingredients:

- About 3.5 tbsp shredded Mozzarella Cheese
- 1 1/2 cups Water
- 3 Eggs
- Pinch of Pepper
- Pinch of dried Basil
- Pinch of Garlic Powder
- 4 Prosciutto Slices (Diced)

- About 1/2 Green Onion (Chopped)

Directions:

1. First of all, please make sure you've all the ingredients available. In a bowl, whisk the eggs along with the pepper, garlic powder, and basil.
2. Now divide the onion, prosciutto, and mozzarella, between 2 silicone muffin cups.
3. This step is important. Pour the egg mixture over.
4. Pour the water into the IP & lower the rack.
5. Then place the muffin cups inside & close the lid.
6. Choose MANUAL and cook properly on HIGH for about 10 to 15 minutes.
7. One thing remains to be done. Release the pressure quickly.
8. Finally serve & enjoy!

Total Time: 20 to 25 Minutes

Serves: 2

Be unique, be extraordinary...

19. Super Scotch Country Eggs

Something is special!!

Ingredients:

- Country style ground sausage 255g
- Water 150ml
- Vegetable oil 10g
- Large eggs 2

Directions:

1. First of all, please make sure you've all the ingredients available. Place your steamer basket in your instant pot cooker; add 240ml of water along with eggs.
2. Now select 5 to 10 minutes cooking time.
3. When the timer beeps, select a quick pressure release & carefully remove the lid.
4. This step is important. Remove the steamer basket from the pressure cooker pot. Put eggs in cold water to cool.
5. When the eggs are cool, remove the shells. Divide the sausage into four equal pieces.
6. Then flatten each piece into a flat round.
7. Place the hard-boiled egg in the center & gently wrap the sausage around the egg.
8. Heat your instant cooking pot on sauté or browning.
9. Now when the pot is hot, add oil & brown the scotch eggs on four sides.
10. Remove the scotch eggs from the pot & add 240ml water.
11. One thing remains to be done. Put a rack in the instant cooking pot & place the scotch eggs on the rack.
12. Finally select high pressure for about to 10 minutes. When the pressure is released, carefully remove and enjoy the taste.

Preparation Time: 30 to 35 minutes

Total Servings: 2

If you're a legend, then make this one.

Nutritional Information:

Calories from Fat: 485

Protein:25.9g

Fat: 53.9g

Sugar: 2.1g

Saturated Fat: 13.5g

Fiber: 0.9g

Cholesterol: 323mg

Carbohydrates: 16.6

Calories: 659

20. Scrumptious Bacon muffins

Being lucky is definitely better.

Ingredients:

- 1 teaspoon salt
- 5 oz. bacon
- About 1 teaspoon baking soda
- 1 tablespoon lemon juice
- 1/4 cup fresh dill
- 1 teaspoon cilantro
- About 4.5 tablespoon butter
- 1 cup flour
- 1 egg

Directions:

1. First of all, please make sure you've all the ingredients available. Beat the egg in the mixer bowl.
2. Now add salt, baking soda, butter, lemon juice, cilantro, and flour.
3. Start to mix the mixture.
4. Wash the fresh dill & chop it.
5. This step is important. Sprinkle the mixed mixture with the chopped dill and mix it for about 2 minutes more.
6. Now chop the bacon into the small pieces.
7. Add the chopped bacon in the mixed dough & stir it carefully with the help of the spatula.
8. When the dough is cooked – leave it for about 5 to 10 minutes to rest.
9. Then after this, pour the dough in the muffin forms & fill only the 1/2 part of every muffin form.
10. Place the muffin forms in the instant pot.
11. Close the lid and set the high-pressure mode.
12. Then cook the muffins for about 10 to 15 minutes.
13. One thing remains to be done. Release the pressure from the instant pot & check if the muffins are cooked.
14. Finally cool the muffins gently and serve them.

Prep time: 10 to 15 minutes

Cooking time: 10 to 15 minutes

Servings: 2

Mystery is unveiled!!

Nutritional information:

Fat 49.4

Fiber 4

Protein 19

Carbs 53.31

Calories 718

21. Funny Quinoa Veggie Porridge

The speed matters...

Ingredients:

- 1 stalk celery (Chopped)
- Miso to serve
- About 1.5 onion (Chopped)
- 1 carrot, peeled (Chopped)
- 1 small piece kombu sea vegetable
- 1/2 cup squash (Chopped)
- About 2.5 green onions (Sliced)
- 1/4 cup quinoa (Rinsed)

Directions:

1. First of all, please make sure you've all the ingredients available. Then add all the ingredients into the instant pot & stir.
2. Close the lid. Press 'Slow cook' button and set timer for about 2 to 3 hours.

3. Finally when the timer goes off, add miso, stir & serve.

Be super

22. Energetic Scallions and Eggs Rice Porridge

Deserved!!

Ingredients:

- 1 cup Chicken Broth
- About 1.5 tbsp Olive Oil
- 1 cup Water
- 2 Eggs
- 1 tsp Soy Sauce
- 2 Scallions (Diced)
- About 1.5 tsp Sugar
- 1/4 cup White Rice

Directions:

1. First of all, please make sure you've all the ingredients available. Place the water, salt, broth, sugar, and rice, in your Instant Pot.
2. Then stir to combine and close the lid.
3. Cook properly on PORRIDGE for about 30 to 35 minutes.
4. This step is important. Release the pressure quickly and transfer to a bowl.
5. Wipe the IP clean & add the olive oil in it.
6. Now Set it to SAUTE & cook the scallions properly for a minute.

7. Add the eggs and soy sauce and scramble well.
8. Cook until the eggs are set.
9. One thing remains to be done. Stir in the rice and cook properly for about 2 to 5 minutes, or until thickened.
10. Finally serve & enjoy!

Total Time: 45 to 50 Minutes

Serves: 2

Long way to go…

23. Charming Strawberry Lemon Oats

Cooking level infinite….

Ingredients:

- 1 cup oats
- About 2.5 tablespoons chia seeds
- 2 cups water
- 3 teaspoons sugar
- 1/2 cup fresh strawberries
- About 1.5 teaspoon lemon zest
- 11/2 teaspoons margarine

Directions:

1. First of all, please make sure you've all the ingredients available. Put margarine in a pressure cooker pot then choose the sauté button.
2. Then once it is melted, add the oats then stir for approximately 2 to 5 minutes—the oats will smell nutty.
3. This step is important. Pour water into the pot together with sugar and lemon zest then cover with the lid and cook properly for about 5 to 10 minutes on high pressure.
4. Now once it is done, carefully release the pressure cooker, open the lid then add strawberry & chia seeds.
5. One thing remains to be done. Cook uncovered for about 5 to 10 minutes then transfer the oats to a serving cup.
6. Finally serve & enjoy immediately.

Uber fantastic!!

24. Reliable Quick n Easy Pumpkin-Spice Oats

For those who are not ordinary, try this one.

Ingredients:

- 1 cup vanilla-flavored milk (of your choice)
- About 4.5 tablespoons toasted and chopped pecans/walnuts
- Pinch of salt
- 1/2 teaspoon grated nutmeg
- 1/4 teaspoon ground cardamom
- Maple syrup
- 1 stick cinnamon
- 1/4 cup dried cranberries
- About 1.5 teaspoon pumpkin pie spice
- 2/3 cup steel-cut oats
- 1/2 cup pumpkin puree
- 1 cup water

Directions:

1. First of all, please make sure you've all the ingredients available. Pour the water and milk in your Instant Pot.
2. Now mix in the salt, cardamom, nutmeg, cinnamon and cranberries. Stir.
3. Add the pumpkin puree & the steel cuts oats. Do not stir.
4. Secure the lid. Select Manual and cook properly for about 2 to 5 minutes on High Pressure.
5. This step is important. Allow the pressure to release naturally.
6. Then remove the lid and stir the mixture.
7. If the texture is too thin, simply replace the lid & allow to sit for about 5 to 10 minutes. (Be careful while removing the lid as the water droplets might fall)
8. Now discard the cinnamon sticks.
9. One thing remains to be done. Stir in the pumpkin spice & maple syrup.
10. Finally transfer to a serving bowl. Top with toasted nuts & serve.

Preparation Time: 2 to 5 minutes

Pressure Time: 5 to 10 minutes

Servings: 2

Be amazed ?

25. Dashing White Bean Rosemary Dip

Wow, just wow!!

Ingredients:

- 3 cups plain water
- About 1.5 teaspoon rosemary leaves
- 4 large cloves garlic (Chopped)
- 1 tablespoon extra virgin olive oil + more to garnish
- About 1.5 tablespoon lemon juice
- 1 teaspoon Kosher salt
- 1/2 teaspoon freshly ground black pepper
- 1 cup Great Northern White Beans, washed

Directions:

1. First of all, please make sure you've all the ingredients available. Add oil, beans, salt, onions, garlic, pepper and water into the pot.
2. Then stir & secure the lid.
3. Set to Manual & cook properly on HIGH for about 35 to 40 minutes.
4. This step is important. Turn off the pot and let depressurize naturally for about 10 to 15 minutes.
5. Now reserve about 1 cup of liquid from pot & drain the beans into a food processor & puree until smooth.
6. One thing remains to be done. Add cooking liquid to puree until creamy & Pourto a bowl.
7. Finally add rosemary & lemon juice, season, mix, drizzle a bit more oil and serve.

Preparation Time: 5 to 10 minutes

Pressure Time: 35 to 40 minutes

Servings: 2

Show time!!

26. Reliable Vegan Sausage

Feast for you!!

Ingredients:

To prepare the spices:

- About 1 teaspoon smoked paprika
- 2 teaspoons Italian seasoning
- Pinch of ground fennel

To prepare the sausage mixture:

- 1 cup common mushroom (Diced)
- About 1.5 tablespoon soy sauce
- 1 small-medium onion, finely diced
- 1 tablespoon vinegar
- 2 garlic cloves (Minced)
- 3/4 cup black-eyed peas, soaked and drained
- 1/2 cup veggie stock/water
- About 1.5 tablespoon tomato paste
- 1/3 cup all-purpose flour
- 1 tablespoon nutritional yeast
- 1 tablespoon olive oil

Directions:

1. First of all, please make sure you've all the ingredients available. Mix all the spices ingredients in a mixing bowl & set aside.

2. Now select Saute and preheat your Instant Pot.
3. Throw in the chopped mushrooms & onions. Dry sauté for about 2 to 5 minutes.
4. Add the garlic and sauté for about 2 minutes.
5. This step is important. Stir in the drained beans. Add water and stir.
6. Then secure the lid. Select Manual & cook properly for about 5 to 10 minutes on High Pressure.
7. Allow the pressure to release naturally.
8. Remove the lid and test if the beans are well cooked.
9. If not, cook properly for about 2 to 5 minutes (add water if needed).
10. Now transfer the content to a bowl.
11. Once cooled, mash the beans using a fork. Stir in the previously prepped spice mixture, all-purpose flour, nutritional yeast, tomato paste, vinegar and soy sauce.
12. Blend everything up and allow to sit for about 5 to 10 minutes.
13. Then divide the mixture into 4 separate portions.
14. Roll each portion into a sausage link shape & wrap with foil.
15. Now drain your Instant Pot. Add 1 cup of tap water. Mount a rack & place a steamer inside.
16. Distribute the foiled sausages in the basket.
17. Then secure the lid, select Manual & cook properly for about 10 to 15 minutes on High Pressure. Allow the pressure to release naturally.
18. One thing remains to be done. Remove the lid and keep in the fridge for about 3 to 4 hours to set.

19. Finally when done, remove put under the broiler & broil for about 2 to 5 minutes on each side to make it crispy.

Preparation Time: 2 to 5 minutes

Pressure Time: 5 to 10 minutes

Servings: 2

Being super is a matter of recipe… ?

27. Charming Poached Eggs with Hash

Being a legend.

Ingredients:

- About 1.5 tbsp chopped cilantro
- 1 cup cubed potatoes
- 1/2 cup onion (Diced)
- 1 sliced jalapeno
- 2 eggs
- About 2.5 tbsp butter
- 1 tbsp cooked, chopped bacon
- 1 tsp taco seasoning

Directions:

1. First of all, please make sure you've all the ingredients available. Pour cup water in pot, & put the trivet in.
2. Then put the bowl with potatoes in trivet.
3. Close and seal vent.
4. Set to high for about 2 to 5 minutes.
5. Chop the jalapeno, bacon, cilantro, and onion.
6. This step is important. When potatoes are done, quick release them.

7. Now remove potatoes & set aside.
8. Take out the trivet and pour out water.
9. Set to sauté and let heat. Add butter & cook onions properly until see through.
10. Then add bacon, cilantro, pepper, potatoes, & seasoning and mix well together.
11. Create a crater in the middle of the potatoes.
12. Crack the eggs into the hole in the hash.
13. One thing remains to be done. Close and seal lid and cook properly for a minute on high. Quick release when done.
14. Finally the eggs should have a poached consistency. Lift the hash out of the pot & sprinkle with cilantro.

When you're fantastic, this is best!!

28. Energetic Hard-Boiled Eggs (S&F)

Being rich is a plus point ?

Ingredients:

- 1 cup of water
- 12 large white eggs

Directions:

1. First of all, please make sure you've all the ingredients available. In the Instant Pot Pour down about 1 cup of water into the bowl.
2. Then place stainless steamer basket inside the pot.

3. Place the eggs in the steamer basket.
4. Boil 5 to 10 minutes on manual HIGH pressure
5. One thing remains to be done. Now release the pressure through the quick release valve.
6. Finally open up the lid & take out the eggs using tongs & dunk them into a bowl of cold water.

Prep + Cooking Time: 10 to 15 minutes

Servings: 2

Amazing cooking starts here...

29. Funny Butter Liver Spread
Don't forget this one...

Ingredients:

- Chopped onion about 1.5
- Salt and pepper to taste
- Bay leaf 1
- Vinegar 10g
- Vegetable butter 10g
- Anchovies about 2.5 (which are stored in oil)
- Capers 10g
- Chicken liver 150g

Directions:

1. First of all, please make sure you've all the ingredients available. Set your instant pot cooker to sauté mode and add olive oil, onions with a little salt & pepper, then add the chicken livers and bay leaf.
2. Then select instant pot cooker timer to about 5 to 10 minutes.

3. After 5 to 10 minutes, open the lid and add red wine and mix well with a wooden spoon.
4. Again, set your instant pot cooker timer for about 5 to 10 minutes at high pressure by selecting a natural release, remove and discard the bay leaf and add the anchovies & capers.
5. One thing remains to be done. Now blend the contents using a blender, add seasoning, vegetable butter & mix well until it mixed well.
6. Finally transfer to a serving container & sprinkle with your favorite fresh herbs.

Preparation Time: 15 to 20 minutes

Total Servings: 2

Sizzle your taste buds...

Nutritional Information:

Calories from Fat: 87

Sugar: 2.1g

Protein: 7.1g

Fat: 9.7g

Saturated Fat: 5.6g

Cholesterol: 158mg

Fiber: 0.6g

Carbohydrates: 4.2g

Calories: 139

30. Scrumptious breakfast potato casserole

Legends are born in…

Ingredients:

- 1 carrot
- About 1.5 onion
- 1/2 cup broccoli
- 8 oz. Cheddar cheese
- 1 tablespoon bread crumbs
- 1 tablespoon butter
- 1/2 cup parsley
- About 1 teaspoon salt
- 2 tablespoon sour cream
- 1 potato

Directions:

1. First of all, please make sure you've all the ingredients available. Peel the carrot & cut it into the small strips.
2. Then chop the broccoli finely.
3. Grate Cheddar cheese.
4. Chop the parsley & peel the onion.
5. This step is important. Slice the onion & peel the potato.
6. Grate the potato and sprinkle it with the salt & sour cream.
7. Now take the instant pot form & spread it with the butter.
8. After this, make the layer of the grated potato.
9. Sprinkle the potato layer with the chopped broccoli & carrot strips.
10. Add the sliced onion & Cheddar cheese.
11. Then combine the sour cream with the chopped parsley & cover the casserole with the mixture.
12. Then sprinkle the dish with the breadcrumbs.
13. Transfer the casserole to the instant pot & adjust the time to about 25 to 30 minutes.
14. Now cook the dish at the pressure mode.
15. One thing remains to be done. When the casserole is cooked – it should be chilled well.
16. Finally cut it into pieces & serve it.

Prep time: 10 to 15 minutes

Cooking time: 25 to 30 minutes

Servings: 2

Jaw dropping!!

Nutritional information:

Calories 511

Fiber 7

Fat 18.3

Carbs 65.6

Protein 23

31. Mushroom and Egg Breakfast
Speed defines it…

Ingredients:

- 1 green bell pepper (Chopped)
- Cilantro to sprinkle
- About 2.5 tablespoons olive oil
- 2 garlic cloves (Chopped)
- Pepper to taste
- 1 teaspoon chili flakes
- 1 cup portabella mushrooms (Sliced)
- Salt to taste
- 1 cup shiitake mushrooms (Sliced)
- 2 eggs, beaten
- About 1.5 red onion (Chopped)

Directions:

1. First of all, please make sure you've all the ingredients available. Press 'Sauté' button. Add the onions, oil, and garlic to a pot and sauté until brown.
2. Then add the chili flakes, mushrooms, bell pepper, salt and pepper & mix until. Press 'Cancel' button.
3. One thing remains to be done. Now add eggs and stir.
4. Finally close the lid. Press 'Manual' button & timer for about 5 to 10 minutes. Sprinkle cilantro and serve.

Mystery with this recipe or rather a chemistry with it.

32. Wonderful Pumpkin Cake with Cinnamon Sauce

Awesomeness fully loaded…

Ingredients:

- 3 tablespoons palm sugar
- 1 cup raisins
- About 3.5 tablespoons butter
- 3/4 cup pumpkin puree
- 1 teaspoon pumpkin pie spice
- 6 tablespoons yogurt
- 1 teaspoon vanilla extract
- About 2.5 teaspoons cinnamon
- 1 cup wheat flour
- 2 tablespoons multi-purpose flour
- 1 teaspoon baking powder
- 6 fresh eggs

Sauce

- 3 tablespoons honey
- 1/4 teaspoon vanilla extract
- About 1.5 teaspoon cinnamon
- 3/4 cup plain yogurt

Directions:

1. First of all, please make sure you've all the ingredients available. Place butter in a saucepan over low heat.
2. Now once it melts, remove from heat then set aside.
3. Prepare a 7-inch spring form pan then grease with cooking spray.
4. Place eggs and sugar in a mixing bowl then using an electric mixer beat them until smooth and fluffy.
5. This step is important. Add pumpkin puree together with yogurt & vanilla extract. Continue beating until combined well.
6. Then in a separate bowl, place the flour, baking powder & pumpkin pie spice then stir well.

7. Add the flour mixture into the liquid mixture then slowly stir using a wooden spatula.

8. Fold in the raisins then pour the batter into the prepared spring form pan.

9. Now pour one cup of water into a pressure cooker and put a trivet in it.

10. Place the spring form pan on the trivet then cover the pressure cooker properly.

11. Select the high-pressure menu then cook properly for about 30 to 35 minutes.

12. Now meanwhile, combine all of the sauce ingredients in a bowl then stir well.

13. Once the cake is cooked, naturally release the pressure cooker.

14. One thing remains to be done. After 10 to 15 minutes, open the lid, remove the cake, and let it cool for a few minutes.

15. Finally transfer the cake to a serving dish then drizzle the cinnamon sauce on top. Serve & enjoy.

Ready in about 30 to 35 minutes

Servings 2

Now the wait is over for hungry people.

33. Elegant Sweet & Savory Congee

Magical, isn't it?

Ingredients:

- 2 cups chicken broth
- About 1.5 tablespoon soy sauce
- 2 cups tap water
- 1 tablespoon brown sugar
- 4 green onions, finely chopped
- 1/2 teaspoon sea salt
- About 1.5 tablespoon coconut oil
- 4 medium, free range eggs
- 1/2 cup basmati (white, long-grain) rice, washed and drained

Directions:

1. First of all, please make sure you've all the ingredients available. Distribute the ingredients – rice, chicken broth, brown sugar and sea salt into your Instant Pot. Stir to mix.

2. Now secure the lid, select Manual and cook properly for about 25 to 30 minutes on high pressure.

3. In the meantime, heat the coconut oil in a large non-stick skillet.

4. This step is important. Once hot, crack the eggs open & Pourto the skillet; one egg on each quarter circle.

5. Then cover and cook properly for about 2 to 5 minutes under low-medium or until the whites are crispy & yolks are still runny.

6. Sprinkle salt and pepper.

7. Once the instant pot completes the cooking, turn it off or hit 'Cancel'.

8. One thing remains to be done. Now let it depressurize naturally for about 15 to 20 minutes.

9. Finally top up with finely chopped soy sauce, green onions, & cooked egg. Serve.

Preparation Time: 5 to 10 minutes

Pressure Time: 25 to 30 minutes

Servings: 2

Yeah, it is a vintage recipe.

34. Rich Easy Adzuki Beans

Always the upper hand…

Ingredients:

- 1 cup water/veggie stock
- About 1 cup adzuki beans
- 1 small piece seaweed (kombu)

Directions:

1. First of all, please make sure you've all the ingredients available. Add the beans, water/stock and kombu in your Instant Pot.
2. Then secure the lid and cook properly for about 10 to 15 minutes on High Pressure.
3. Allow the pressure to release naturally (5 to 10 minutes).
4. Now make sure the beans are well cooked.
5. One thing remains to be done. If not, cook properly for about 2 to 5 minutes more in the same settings.
6. Finally remove the lid. Transfer to a serving bowl & serve.

Preparation Time: 2 to 5 minutes

Pressure Time: 10 to 15

Servings: 2

Now you're happy…?

35. Titanic Easy Adzuki Beans
Classic style…

Ingredients:

- 1 cup water/veggie stock
- 3/4 cup adzuki beans
- About 1.5 small piece seaweed (kombu)

Directions:

1. First of all, please make sure you've all the ingredients available. Add the beans, water/stock & kombu in your Instant Pot.
2. Then secure the lid and cook properly for about 10 to 15 minutes on High Pressure.
3. Allow the pressure to release naturally (5 to 10 minutes).
4. Make sure the beans are well cooked.
5. One thing remains to be done. Now if not, cook properly for about 2 to 5 minutes more in the same settings.
6. Finally remove the lid. Transfer to a serving bowl & serve.

Preparation Time: 2 to 5 minutes

Pressure Time: 10 to 15

Servings: 2

Arrive in style with this recipe.

36. Tasty Fruit Yogurt

Ironic in taste…

Ingredients:

- 2 tbsp dry milk powder
- About 2.5 tbsp sugar
- 2 2/3 cup milk
- 2 pint jars
- 1 cup chopped fruit

Directions:

1. First of all, please make sure you've all the ingredients available. Pour 1 1/2 cup water in pot. Place in grate.
2. Now pour 1 1/3 cup milk in both jars. Loose lid and put in pot.
3. Set pressure cycle, and set time to about 2 to 5 minutes.
4. This step is important. Release pressure & remove jars; cool.
5. Then add in culture to milk.
6. Put 1 tbsp sugar, dry milk, & yogurt culture to both jars. Stir together.
7. Now mix in 1/2 cup fruit to both jars. Don't over fill.
8. One thing remains to be done. Lid jars, & place in pot. Set yogurt, 12 hours.
9. Finally refrigerate when done.

Looking forward to this one!!

37. Yummy Soft-Boiled Egg (S&F)

Used to eat this one a lot.

Ingredients:

- About 1.5 cup of water
- Salt and pepper to taste
- 2 toasted English muffins
- 4 eggs

Directions:

1. First of all, please make sure you've all the ingredients available. Pour 1 cup of water into the Instant Pot & insert the steamer basket.
2. Then put four canning lids into the basket before placing the eggs on top of them, so they stay separated.
3. This step is important. Secure the lid.
4. Press the STEAM setting & choose 2 to 5 minutes.
5. Now when ready, quick-release the steam valve.
6. Take out the eggs using tongs & dunk them into a bowl of cold water.
7. Wait 2 minutes.
8. One thing remains to be done. Peel & serve with one egg per half of a toasted English muffin.
9. Finally season with salt & pepper.

There it is.

38. Unique Spicy Apple Butter

Tasty dish just one step away!!

Ingredients:

- Water 245ml
- Pumpkin pie spice 5g
- Cinnamon 5g
- Raw honey 15g
- Nutmeg 2g
- Apples 2

Directions:

1. First of all, please make sure you've all the ingredients available. At first, fill your instant pot with apples & add 240ml water.
2. Now adjust your instant pot to steam setting and set the timer for 4 minutes.
3. This step is important. When it finishes, leave it for about 10 to 15 minutes or until pressure releases naturally.
4. Open the lid and using a blender, blend the apples until it reaches the consistency of butter.
5. Then add cinnamon, raw honey to taste.
6. Additionally, you can add nutmeg & pumpkin pie spice for extra taste.
7. One thing remains to be done. Fill the apple butter in a jar and water bath for about 25 to 30 minutes.
8. Finally delicious apple butter is ready; you can spread over pancakes or waffles & enjoy the taste.

Preparation Time: 45 to 50 minutes

Total Servings: 2

I was waiting for this one.

Nutritional Information:

Calories from Fat: 0g

Protein: 1g

Fat: 0g

Saturated Fat: 0g

Cholesterol: 0g

Sugar: 8.3g

Carbohydrates: 9g

Calories: 34

Fiber: 0.5g

39. Ultimate Breakfast quiche

I know, this is amazing!!

Ingredients:

- 1/2 cup shrimps
- About 1.5 teaspoon minced garlic
- 5 oz. Parmesan cheese
- 1 tablespoon olive oil
- 1 teaspoon salt
- 1 egg
- 1/4 cup green peas
- 1 sweet green pepper
- 1/4 cup sweet corn
- About 1/2 teaspoon ground black pepper
- 3 tablespoon flour
- 1/2 teaspoon oregano
- 1/2 teaspoon cayenne pepper
- 1 cup red onion
- 1/2 cup milk

Directions:

1. First of all, please make sure you've all the ingredients available. Chop the shrimps & sprinkle them with the ground black pepper.
2. Now grate Parmesan cheese.
3. Beat the egg in the bowl & add salt.
4. Whisk the mixture.
5. This step is important. Then sprinkle the egg mixture with the grated cheese, green peas, shrimps, sweet corn, and oregano.
6. Then add olive oil, cayenne pepper, & minced garlic.
7. Discard the seeds from the green pepper.
8. Chop the green pepper finely.
9. Add the chopped pepper in the mixture.
10. Now add flour.
11. After this, dice the onion & add in the mixture too.
12. Churn the mass well with the help of the plastic spatula.
13. Then transfer the mass in the instant pot & flatten it well to make the quiche texture smooth.
14. One thing remains to be done. Close the instant pot lid & cook the dish properly at the steam mode for about 30 to 35 minutes.
15. Finally after the dish is cooked – remove it from the instant pot and chill.

Prep time: 10 to 15 minutes

Cooking time: 30 to 35 minutes

Servings: 2

Silently, you were waiting for this one. Don't lie… ?

Nutritional information:

Fat 34.4

Calories 611

Carbs 39.53

Fiber 4

Protein 37

40. Iconic Banana and Coconut Milk Steel-Cut Oatmeal

Make it quickly.

Ingredients:

For the oatmeal:

- About 3.5 tablespoons water
- A pinch of salt
- 12 ounces light coconut milk
- 2 teaspoons brown sugar or to taste
- 1/4 teaspoon vanilla extract
- 3/4 cup steel-cut oats
- About 1.5 teaspoon butter, chopped (optional)
- 1/4 teaspoon ground cinnamon
- 1 teaspoon ground flaxseed
- A pinch nutmeg
- 3/4 cup ripe banana slices

For topping:

- About 2.5 teaspoons shredded coconut, toasted

33

- Maple syrup as required
- 2 tablespoons walnuts (Chopped)
- Few banana slices

Directions:

1. First of all, please make sure you've all the ingredients available. Add all the ingredients of the oatmeal into the instant pot & stir.
2. Now close the lid. Press 'Slow cook' option & set timer for about 2 to 3 hours.
3. Stir and serve in bowls.
4. Then add more milk if required.
5. One thing remains to be done. Place banana slices over it.
6. Finally sprinkle coconut & walnuts. Drizzle maple syrup and serve.

Supreme level.

41. Awesome Cheese Grits
Sincere efforts will be awesome.

Ingredients:

- 2 cups milk
- Pinch of sea salt and black pepper powder, to taste
- 1 cup water
- 1/2 cup cheddar cheese (Shredded)
- About 2.5 tablespoons butter
- 2 cups old fashion grits

Directions:

1. First of all, please make sure you've all the ingredients available. Mix the

ingredients: cornmeal, butter, water, salt and pepper into your Instant Pot.
2. Now hit the 'Manual' and cook properly for about 15 to 20 minutes on low pressure.
3. One thing remains to be done. Then once cooked, let depressurize naturally for about 10 to 15 minutes, then release manually.
4. Finally sprinkle the cheese & whisk continuously until smooth. Serve.

Preparation Time: 5 to 10 minutes

Pressure Time: 15 to 20 minutes

Servings: 2

Let's dive in...

42. Super Indian Dahl Stew
Your friends and family are waiting. Hurry!!

Ingredients:

- 1/4 onion (Diced)
- Salt, to taste
- 2 large garlic cloves (Minced)
- About 1 tablespoon berbere spice powder
- 2 cups vegetable stock or water
- 1/2 cup diced tomato
- 1/2 cup red lentils (rinsed)
- About 1.5 tablespoon olive oil

Directions:

1. First of all, please make sure you've all the ingredients available. Set your Instant Pot to Sauté.

2. Now pour in the oil. Add the chopped onion and sauté for about 2 to 5 minutes or until fragrant.

3. Add the garlic & cook properly for about 2 minutes.

4. This step is important. Mix in the berbere powder.

5. Then add the diced lentils, tomato, & stock/water and stir everything up.

6. Secure the lid. Select Manual and cook properly for about 10 to 15 minutes on High Pressure.

7. Now allow the pressure to release naturally.

8. Remove the lid. Check for doneness.

9. One thing remains to be done. If not cook properly for about 2 to 5 minutes more.

10. Finally season with salt. Serve warm.

Royal taste…

43. Delightful Applesauce

We all are legends in some ways.

Ingredients:

- 1/2 cup water
- 6 apples, cored and peeled
- About 1.5 tbsp lemon juice
- 1/4 tsp salt

Directions:

1. First of all, please make sure you've all the ingredients available. Combine everything in cooker. Close and seal lid.

2. Now cook properly 3 to 4 hours on high, stir twice while cooking.

3. One thing remains to be done. Then once finished, puree the sauce & season with cinnamon if desired.

4. Finally cool & store in air tight container.

Prepare yourself for this…

44. Fantastic Eggplant Paste

Looking forward to healthy life.

Ingredients:

- Eggplant 305g
- Fresh extra virgin olive oil (topping)
- Garlic 2 cloves
- Fresh thyme 10g
- Salt 2g
- Water 110ml
- Black olives 10g
- Lemon juice 10ml
- Tahini 1g
- Olive oil 55g

Directions:

1. First of all, please make sure you've all the ingredients available. At first, remove the skin of eggplant using peeler and slice into big chunks as possible to fill the bottom of instant pot cooker.

2. Now keep the instant pot cooker on medium heat & add the olive oil.

3. This step is important. When the oil has heated, carefully add the chunks of eggplant and fry until it is caramelized on one side, approximately it will take 5 to 10 minutes, and add garlic cloves

without removing the skin, salt, and water.

4. Set your instant pot cooker timer to about 2 to 5 minutes at high pressure.

5. Then when it is finished, remove the extra water (brown liquid) from the cooker.

6. One thing remains to be done. Add the tahini, lemon juice, cooked & garlic cloves and black olives and blend everything together using and blender.

7. Finally pour into the serving dish & sprinkle with fresh thyme, remaining black olives & a dash of fresh olive oil before serving.

Preparation Time: 20 to 25 minutes

Total Servings: 2

Astonishing!!

Nutritional Information:

Calories from Fat: 34

Protein: 2g

Fat: 11.7g

Saturated Fat: 1.8g

Sugar: 5.6g

Cholesterol: 0mg

Carbohydrates: 16.8g

Calories: 155.5

Fiber: 4.5g

45. Great Egg-tomato cups

Grab it!!

Ingredients:

- 2 tomatoes
- 1 teaspoon cream
- About 1.5 teaspoon chives
- 1 teaspoon salt
- 1/4 teaspoon butter
- About 1 teaspoon ground black pepper
- 1/2 teaspoon cilantro
- 2 eggs

Directions:

1. First of all, please make sure you've all the ingredients available. Combine the chives & salt together.

2. Then add ground black pepper & cilantro.

3. Stir the mixture well.

4. After this, make the cups from the tomatoes: cut the "hats" and remove the meat from them.

5. This step is important. Combine the butter and sour cream together & whisk the mixture.

6. Now put the small amount of the butter-sour cream mixture in every tomato "cup".

7. Beat the eggs in the tomato "cups" & transfer the tomatoes to the instant pot.
8. Then cook the dish at the pressure mode for about 5 to 10 minutes.
9. One thing remains to be done. When the dish is cooked - open the instant pot and let the tomatoes rest for about 2 to 5 minutes.
10. Finally serve dish immediately.

Prep time: 10 to 15 minutes

Cooking time: 5 to 10 minutes

Servings: 2

Freshness loaded!!

Nutritional information:

Fat 10.9 fiber

Calories 166

Protein 10

Carbs 6.98

46. Happy Minty Green Lentil

Dreams are good!! So dream about this one or else make it…

Ingredients:

- 1 medium onion (Chopped)
- Salt and pepper, to taste
- 1/2 cup green lentils (Rinsed)
- 3/4 cup veggie stock/water

- About 1 teaspoon cumin powder
- 1 medium carrot (Grated)
- 2 tablespoons fresh mint (Chopped)
- 1 tablespoon lemon juice
- 2 tablespoons fresh cilantro
- About 1 teaspoon grated lemon zest
- 1 teaspoon olive oil

Directions:

1. First of all, please make sure you've all the ingredients available. Select Saute and preheat your Instant Pot. Pour oil.
2. Now add the chopped onion & sauté for a minute.
3. Mix in the green lentils and water. Stir.
4. This step is important. Secure the lid and cook properly for about 5 to 10 minutes on High Pressure.
5. Allow the pressure to release naturally.
6. Then remove the lid and test for doneness. If the lentils are not cooked well, cook properly for about 2 minutes in the same procedure.
7. One thing remains to be done. Remove the lid and allow to cool.
8. Finally mix in all the remaining ingredients & stir well to mix. Serve.

Preparation Time: 2 to 5 minutes

Pressure Time: 5 to 10

Servings: 2

Something is defintely different.

47. Lucky Chinese Style Tea Eggs

This is epic. Take a look!!

Ingredients:

- Soy Sauce 25g
- Water 280ml
- Lemon zest 10g
- Bay leaves 2
- Black tea bags 1
- Juniper berries 15g
- Powdered cloves 5g
- Black peppercorns 10g
- Hard-boiled eggs 2

Directions:

1. First of all, please make sure you've all the ingredients available. Crack the shell of the hard-boiled egg using a teaspoon (just tap them) and set aside.
2. Now take one separate pan; add all of the ingredients including 240ml of water except the soy sauce.
3. This step is important. Bring to a boil, and then add the soy sauce, eggs & any additional water (if necessary).
4. Then cover it with tin foil. Prepare your instant pot cooker by adding 240ml of water, & placing a steamer basket inside it.
5. Set your instant pot cooker timer for about 20 to 25 minutes. When the time is up, remove tin foil & let cool further.
6. One thing remains to be done. Serve with shell and let your guests peel it & enjoy the taste.
7. Finally optional: eggs can be stored in the refrigerator in a plastic bag or darkened even further stored in the tea mixture.

Preparation Time: 30 to 35 minutes

Total Servings: 2

Life of a legend begins here.

Nutritional Information:

Calories from Fat: 45

Fat: 5g

Fiber: 0.3g

Saturated Fat: 1.6g

Calories: 76

Cholesterol: 186mg

Carbohydrates: 1.2g

Sugar: 0.4g

Protein: 6.6g

48. Vintage Slow-Cooked Hot Granola

Funny but definitely yummy!!

Ingredients:

- 2 tbsp pumpkin seeds
- Pinch of salt
- About 1.5 tbsp sunflower seeds
- 8fl oz milk

- 1 tbsp whole linseeds
- 20 almonds (Chopped)
- 16fl oz pure apple juice
- 10 walnuts (Chopped)
- 10 pecans (Chopped)
- About 1.5 tsp cinnamon
- 12 dried apricots (Chopped)
- 10 dates (Chopped)
- Small handful of dried cranberries
- 1 1/2 cups oats (any kind)

Directions:

1. First of all, please make sure you've all the ingredients available. Place all ingredients, (yup, all of them), plus a very small pinch of salt into your Instant Pot, stir to combine.
2. Then secure the lid onto the pot & press the SLOW COOK button, adjust the temperature to LOW & set the time to about 7 to 8 hours.
3. Make sure the steam valve is set to "vent".
4. Now once the pot beeps, quick-release the steam & remove the lid.
5. One thing remains to be done. Stir the granola, if it's too thick for your liking you can add a bit more milk or apple juice.
6. Finally serve with cold milk or yoghurt.

Time: approximately 7 to 8 hours

Now that's something!!

49. Best Black Beans, and Greens Mix

Can you make it? Yes, why not?

Ingredients:

- 1 3-inch strip seaweed (kombu)
- 2 cups salad greens, washed and dried
- 1 cup veggie stock/water
- 1/4 cup chopped green onions
- About 1.5 teaspoon olive oil
- 1 tablespoon lime juice
- 1/4 cup leek (Chopped)
- 3/4 cup common mushrooms (Sliced)
- 1 teaspoon soy sauce
- About 1.5 teaspoon grated lime zest
- 1/2 teaspoon ginger (Grated)
- 2 garlic cloves (Minced)
- 3/4 cup black beans

Directions:

1. First of all, please make sure you've all the ingredients available. Mix the black beans, seaweed, & stock in your Instant Pot.
2. Now secure the lid. Select Manual & cook properly for about 10 to 15 minutes on High Pressure.
3. Allow the pressure to release naturally. Remove the lid.
4. Test the beans for doneness, if not well-cooked, cook properly for about 2 to 5 more minutes using the same procedure.
5. This step is important. Discard the kombu and transfer the content to a bowl & set aside.
6. Then drain the IP & set it to Saute. Pour in the olive oil. Once hot, add the leek and mushrooms.
7. Saute for about 2 to 5 minutes.

8. Mix in the rest of the ingredients - soy sauce, grated ginger, and garlic.
9. Pour 4 tablespoons stock and stir well to combine.
10. Now secure the lid. Select Manual and cook properly for about 2 to 5 minutes on High Pressure.
11. Allow the pressure to release naturally.
12. Remove the lid and quickly throw in the greens.
13. Then if the content is dry, add about 4 tablespoons of stock.
14. Secure the lid, select Manual and cook properly for about 2 minutes on High Pressure.
15. This time do a quick pressure release.
16. Now remove the lid and transfer the content to a serving bowl.
17. One thing remains to be done. Add the beans. Sprinkle the lime juice & zest and green onions.
18. Finally season with salt & serve on top of salad greens.

Preparation Time: 5 to 10 minutes

Pressure Time: 10 to 15 minutes

Servings: 2

Good days!!

50. Nostalgic Pastry-Free Bacon, Egg, and Goat Cheese Tarts

I am interested!!

Ingredients:

- 4 bacon rashers, chopped into small pieces
- 8 cupcake cases
- About 2.5 oz goat cheese, crumbled into small pieces
- Salt and pepper, to taste
- 3 eggs, lightly beaten

Directions:

1. First of all, please make sure you've all the ingredients available. With a fork, stir together the eggs, bacon pieces, pepper, goat cheese, and salt (only use a tiny pinch of salt as bacon & goat cheese are quite salty).
2. Now pour 2 cups of water into the Instant Pot & place a rack into the pot (above the water).
3. This step is important. Pour the egg mixture into 8 cupcake cases & very carefully place them onto the rack in the pot.
4. Then secure the lid onto the pot & press the STEAM button, keep the time at the default 10 to 15 minutes.
5. Once the pot beeps, quick-release the pressure & remove the lid.
6. One thing remains to be done. Carefully remove the tarts from the pot & leave them to cool before eating.
7. Finally freeze leftover tarts in an airtight container in the freezer for up to 3 months.

Time: approximately 15 to 20 minutes

This never goes out of style.

51. Mighty Peanut Butter and Apricot Breakfast Muffins

Now be a legend!!

Ingredients:

- 2 tbsp honey
- About 8 to 12 cupcake cases
- 6fl oz milk
- 2 eggs, lightly beaten
- 12 dried apricots, chopped into small pieces
- 1 1/2 cups plain flour
- 1/2 cup peanut butter (any kind)
- About 1.5 tsp baking powder

Directions:

1. First of all, please make sure you've all the ingredients available. Place the peanut butter and honey in a microwave-safe bowl, then into the microwave & heat for about 20 to 30 seconds to make it a bit easier to stir.
2. Now add the milk and eggs to the peanut butter &7 honey and whisk until combined and smooth.
3. This step is important. Sift the flour and baking powder into a large bowl & add the wet ingredients, stir very gently until just combined, don't over mix, don't worry if it looks a bit lumpy!
4. Pour 2 cups of water into the Instant Pot & place a rack into the pot (above the water).
5. Then pour the muffin mixture and apricot pieces into 8 to 12 cupcake cases (depending on the size of your cases, don't fill more than three quarters) & very carefully place them onto the rack in the pot.
6. Secure the lid onto the pot and press the STEAM button, keep the time at the default 10 to 15 minutes.
7. One thing remains to be done. Once the pot beeps, quick-release the pressure & remove the lid.
8. Finally carefully remove the muffins from the pot & leave them to cool before eating.

Time: approximately 15 to 20 minutes

Simple yet fantastic!!

52. King sized Marinated Artichokes

It is a brand new day.... Ever listened to this one!!

Ingredients:

- Fresh lemon juice 15g
- Water 280ml
- Balsamic vinegar 5g
- Fresh ground black pepper 5g
- Olive oil 25ml
- Dried oregano 5g
- Sea salt 5g
- Garlic 2 cloves
- Large artichokes 2

Directions:

1. First of all, please make sure you've all the ingredients available. At first, wash artichokes under cold water & cut off the top inch of the artichoke.
2. Now place your artichokes in the inner pot of the instant pot cooker with 480ml of water.

3. Select steam mode and reduce cooking time to about 5 to 10 minutes.
4. This step is important. On the other side prepare the marinade by mixing lemon juice, garlic, olive oil, oregano, salt, balsamic vinegar, and pepper in a small jar; mix well until it incorporates all ingredients and set aside.
5. Then remove the artichokes from the pot & cut into half.
6. Remove the center cone of purple prickly leaves.
7. One thing remains to be done. Sprinkle the marinade over the warm artichoke & let it sit for about 30 to 35 minutes to overnight.
8. Finally when ready to serve, grill for about 2 to 5 minutes and serve.

Awesome, isn't it?

Nutritional Information:

Carbohydrates: 19.3g

Fiber: 8.9g

Calories: 205

Calories from Fat: 124

Sugar: 2g

Protein: 5.5g

Fat: 13.8g

Fat: 2.9g

Cholesterol:0mg

53. Crazy Broccoli n Chickpea Mix

Luxury tasty dish for you!!

Ingredients:

To prepare the mix:

- 2 garlic cloves (Minced)
- Salt and red pepper powder, to taste
- 1-inch seaweed (kombu)
- 1/2 cup veggie stock
- About 2.5 tablespoons freshly chopped cilantro
- 2 cups broccoli florets
- 1 medium onion (Sliced)
- 1/2 cup chickpeas, soaked and drained

Dressing

- 1 tablespoon red wine vinegar
- About 1.5 teaspoon white miso
- 2 teaspoons Dijon mustard
- 1 tablespoon extra-virgin olive oil
- 1 teaspoon minced fresh garlic
- About 1.5 tablespoon fresh lemon juice

Directions:

1. First of all, please make sure you've all the ingredients available. Combine the seaweed, chickpeas, garlic and stock/water in your Instant Pot.
2. Now secure the lid. Select Manual and cook properly for about 10 to 15 minutes on High Pressure.

3. This step is important. Allow the pressure to release naturally.
4. Remove the lid and quickly add the broccoli. Secure it back.
5. Then select Manual and cook properly for about 2 minutes on Low Pressure.
6. One thing remains to be done. Do a quick release. Discard the seaweed & transfer everything into a serving bowl.
7. Finally add the cilantro, onion, salt and pepper & stir. Serve.

Preparation Time: 5 to 10 minutes

Pressure Time: 10 to 15 minutes

Servings: 2

Get ready to make it my way!!

54. Pinnacle Vanilla Date Oatmeal

The best combo ever!!

Ingredients:

- 24fl oz milk (or 12floz water and 12floz milk)
- Pinch of salt
- About 2.5 tsp vanilla extract
- 8 dates, chopped into small pieces
- 1 3/4 cups rolled oats (I use whole oats but you can use any you have)

Directions:

1. First of all, please make sure you've all the ingredients available. Place the oats, dates, milk (and water if using), vanilla, and a good pinch of

salt into your Instant Pot, stir to combine.
2. Then secure the lid onto the pot & press the MANUAL button, cook properly on LOW pressure for about 15 to 20 minutes.
3. One thing remains to be done. Once the pot beeps, quick-release the pressure & remove the lid, stir the oatmeal.
4. Finally serve with sliced bananas and a drizzle of maple syrup, or fresh berries & a dollop of yogurt (it's all up to you, great creative).

Time: approximately 20 to 25 minutes

Something is new here!!

55. Perfect Mango Banana Pancakes

A little work here but will be worth it.

Ingredients:

- 1 1/4 cups plain flour
- 6fl oz coconut milk
- About 1.5 tsp baking powder
- 1 egg, lightly beaten
- 2 bananas, mashed
- About 1.5 ripe mango, peeled, flesh cut into small chunks
- Coconut oil

Directions:

1. First of all, please make sure you've all the ingredients available. Drizzle some coconut oil into your Instant Pot & press the SAUTE button, keep the temperature at NORMAL,

prepare the batter as the pot heats up.

2. Then sift the flour and baking powder into a bowl.
3. Stir together the mashed bananas, egg, mango pieces, & coconut milk in a small bowl.
4. Now add the wet ingredients to the flour & baking powder, gently stir until just combined, don't over mix.
5. One thing remains to be done. Drop large spoonsful of mixture into the hot pot & cook properly until bubbles appear, flip the pancakes over & cook the other side properly until golden.
6. Finally stack them up, top them with fresh fruit & yoghurt, and enjoy!

Time: approximately 20 to 15 minutes

Try it...

56. Dashing Bacon Egg Muffins
This is different, isn't it?

Ingredients:

- Water 255ml
- Lemon pepper 5g
- Cooked bacon slices 2
- Chopped green onion half
- Large eggs 2

Directions:

1. First of all, please make sure you've all the ingredients available. At first, place a steamer basket inside instant pot cooker & add 360ml water.
2. Now slowly break eggs into a large & add lemon pepper, beat well until it looks nice texture.
3. This step is important. Divide bacon and green onion evenly between the 4 silicone muffin cups.
4. Pour the beaten eggs into each muffin cup.
5. Then place muffin cups slowly in a steamer basket & set the timer for 8 minutes.
6. One thing remains to be done. When the timer beeps, wait for natural pressure release (approximately 2 to 5 minutes) & lift out the steamer basket, and remove muffin cups.
7. Finally serve immediately with extra cream on top.

Yeah, this is a new variation.

Nutritional Information:

Protein: 15.6g

Sugar: 2.9g

Calories: 147

Fiber: 1.3g

Calories from Fat: 52

Fat: 3.8g

Carbohydrates: 5g

Saturated Fat: 1.1g

Cholesterol: 157mg

57. Reliable Honey Poached Pears
Classic, isn't it?

Ingredients:

- Water 2 cups
- Bartlett pears 2
- White vinegar 1 cups
- Cinnamon sticks 3
- Lemon 1

Honey Sauce:

- Coconut milk 65ml
- Maple syrup 20ml
- Coconut oil 25ml
- Raw honey 50g

Directions:

1. First of all, please make sure you've all the ingredients available. At first, add honey, water, cinnamon sticks and wine, to your instant pot cooker & select a warm option to make hot syrup.
2. Now on the other hand, peel the pears, & squeeze lemon juice.
3. Slowly drop pears into hot syrup and cook properly for about 2 to 5 minutes on high pressure.
4. Then after 2 to 5 minutes, carefully remove the pears with a slotted spoon and add syrup on pears.
5. One thing remains to be done. To prepare the honey sauce for pears, put honey in saucepan d bring to boil, when it hot, add oil, coconut milk, maple syrup.
6. Finally before serving, cut the bottom of pears (to make it stand on the plate) & pour the warm honey sauce over. Enjoy the taste.

Different yet fantastic in many ways.

Nutritional Information:

Protein: 4g

Saturated Fat: 2.1g

Sugar: 45.4g

Fiber: 6.2g

Calories: 400

Calories from Fat: 43

Carbohydrates: 65.2g

Fat: 4.8g

58. Charming Pearl Onions

Yeah, direct from the heaven; yeah?

Ingredients:

- Water 105ml
- Coconut flour 10g
- Bay leaf 1
- Salt to taste
- Honey 10g
- Balsamic Vinegar 25ml
- Cipolline 200g

Directions:

1. First of all, please make sure you've all the ingredients available. At first, cut the both ends of the onions and clean.
2. Then place the onions in instant pot cooker & add 125ml of water, salt and bay leaf to taste.
3. Adjust cooker timer for about 5 to 10 minutes on low pressure.

4. This step is important. On the other hand, make the sweet and sour sauce for onions.
5. Now take small saucepan; add vinegar, honey, and flour.
6. Bring to boil on low heat, stir with a wooden spoon to avoid lumps (approximately it will take 30 to 40 seconds).
7. One thing remains to be done. Add this sweet and sour sauce into the cooker & mix with the baby onions.
8. Finally serve immediately & enjoy the taste.

What's so typical or different here?

Nutritional Information:

Calories: 168

Fiber: 2.6g

Fat: 11.8g

Saturated Fat: 7.4g

Sugar: 6.9g

Cholesterol: 31mg

Protein: 2.4g

Carbohydrates: 14.6g

Calories from Fat: 106

Lunch Special Recipes

59. Nostalgic Pork Coarse Roast

I've always loved them. Plus they can be eaten anytime!!

Ingredients:

- Salt 2g
- Onion powder 2g
- Apple juice 40ml
- Garlic powder 2g
- Chili powder 3g
- Water 144ml
- Pork sirloin tip roast 350g
- Coarse black pepper 2g
- Vegetable oil 14g

Directions:

1. First of all, please make sure you've all the ingredients available. In a small bowl, add spices & rub that spice mixture all over pork roast.
2. Then add oil to your instant pot cooker & select browning option.
3. This step is important. When oil is hot, add pork & roast until it turns to golden brown on both sides.
4. Then add the water, apple juice to the pressure cooker pot.
5. One thing remains to be done. Close the lid & set the timer for about 25 to 30 minutes.
6. Finally when beep sounds, wait for natural press release (approximately 5 to 10 minutes) & serve hot.

Preparation Time: 30 to 35 minutes

Total Servings: 2

Just make it once and you will keep making it!!

Nutritional Information:

Calories from Fat: 171

Fat: 19g

Protein: 23.2g

Saturated Fat: 8g

Cholesterol: 92mg

Sugar: 16.2g

Carbohydrates: 32.6g

Calories: 406

Fiber: 1.4g

60. Mighty Green Onion Chicken

Don't wait, eat it!!

Ingredients:

- Oil 17g
- Chicken 905g
- Garnish: Green onions

Sauce:

- Light soy sauce 105ml
- Bay leaves 4

- Filipino vinegar 44ml
- Red chili 1
- Fish sauce 14g
- Sugar 14g
- Ground black peppercorn 4g
- Crushed garlic cloves 13
- Chopped small white onion 1
- Filipino soy sauce 60ml

Directions:

1. First of all, please make sure you've all the ingredients available. At first, mix vinegar, soy sauces (Filipino and light), fish sauce and sugar in a medium bowl.
2. Then add oil to instant pot cooker on sauté mode, brown the chicken for about 2 to 5 minutes when skin turns to golden color then remove the chicken from the pot & keep aside.
3. Sauté onion, garlic until it fragrant then, add red chili, red chili, ground black peppercorn, & bay leaves for about 30 to 35 seconds.
4. One thing remains to be done. Then add the sauce mixture.
5. Finally set timer for about 5 to 10 minutes at high pressure with the natural pressure release.

Preparation Time: 35 to 40 inutes

Total Servings: 2

Yummy, definitely yummy.

Nutritional Information:

Calories from Fat: 277

Protein: 44.5g

Fat: 30.7g

Saturated Fat: 8.3g

Sugar: 0.2g

Cholesterol: 188mg

Carbohydrates: 2.2g

Calories: 520

Fiber: 0.3g

61. King sized Italian Tenderloin Pork

A fine recipe, it just works.

Ingredients:

- Olive oil 13g
- Black pepper to taste
- Crushed tomatoes 150g
- Kosher salt 2g
- Roasted red peppers 54g
- Chopped fresh parsley 5g
- Fresh thyme 5g
- Bay leaves 1
- Tenderloin pork 110g

Directions:

1. First of all, please make sure you've all the ingredients available. At first, season your pork with salt & pepper to nice taste.
2. Now select sauté button and add oil, garlic & sauté until turns to golden brown (approximately 2 minutes), remove using a slotted spoon.
3. Add pork and cook properly until it turns brown on each side (about 2 minutes).

4. Add the remaining all ingredients but reserve half of the parsley for garnish.
5. Then set cooker at high pressure for about 45 to 50 minutes, wait for the natural release.
6. One thing remains to be done. When it finished, remove bay leaves, shred the pork using forks & top with remaining parsley.
7. Finally serve over your favorite pasta.

Preparation Time: 55 to 60 minutes

Total Servings: 2

A simple recipe which you will like.

Nutritional Information:

Calories from Fat: 34

Protein: 11g

Fat:1.5g

Saturated Fat: 0.5g

Cholesterol: 33mg

Sugar: 3g

Carbohydrates: 6.5g

Calories: 93

Fiber: 0g

62. Energetic Yummy Barbecue Beef

This is different, isn't it?

Ingredients:

- Chopped onion half
- Bay leaves 1
- Lime juice 10ml
- Chipotles 24g (mixed in adobo sauce)
- Oil 5g
- Ground cumin 7g
- Ground oregano 5g
- Black pepper to taste
- Ground cloves 3g
- Water 150ml
- Beef 350g (bottom roast)
- Garlic 2 cloves
- Salt 2g

Directions:

1. First of all, please make sure you've all the ingredients available. At first, put your ingredients like onion, oregano, garlic, cloves, cumin, lime juice, chipotles and water in a mixer & make a thick paste out of it.
2. Now on the other hand, trim all the fat off meat & your beef into 3-inch pieces.
3. This step is important. Season with salt & black pepper for subtle, delicious taste.
4. Then select sauté button on the cooker; add oil and slowly add beef pieces & brown all sides, approximately 5 to 10 minutes.
5. One thing remains to be done. Add the paste and bay leave in the pot & set the cooking timer to about 60 to 65 minutes on the high pressure until the meat is tender and easily shreds with a fork.

6. Finally once it is done, remove the bay leaf & add salt, cumin and enjoy the taste.

Preparation Time: 80 to 85 minutes

Total Servings: 2

Yeah, this is a new variation.

Nutritional Information:

Calories from Fat: 65

Protein: 24g

Fat: 4.5g

Saturated Fat: 2.3g

Sugar: 0g

Cholesterol: 44mg

Calories: 153

Carbohydrates: 2g

63. Reliable Lime Chicken Sauce

Classic, isn't it?

Ingredients:

- Lime juice 13ml
- Fresh cilantro 14g
- Fish sauce 4g
- Olive oil 15g
- Fresh mint 5g
- Coconut milk 14g

- Chicken thighs 450g (skinless and boneless)
- Grated fresh ginger 7g

Directions:

1. First of all, please make sure you've all the ingredients available. At first, rinse your chicken breasts & trim any excess fat.
2. Then put in bottom of the instant pot cooker.
3. In a mason jar, combine all remaining ingredients & shake well.
4. This step is important. Add this mixture to the chicken.
5. Now select poultry option in your instant pot setting & reduce time to about 10 to 15 minutes.
6. One thing remains to be done. Use the quick release lid setting when done.
7. Finally drain excess liquid & enjoy the taste.

Preparation Time: 20 to 25 minutes

Total Servings: 2

Different yet fantastic in many ways.

Nutritional Information:

Calories from Fat:96

Protein: 27.7g

Fat:10.7g

Saturated Fat: 4.5g

Sugar: 0.6g

Cholesterol: 84mg

Sodium: 555mg

Fiber: 0.3g

Potassium: 341mg

Carbohydrates: 2.6g

Calories: 220

64. Dashing Barbeque Chicken Curry
Yeah, direct from the heaven; yeah?

Ingredients:

- Ground paprika 4g
- Vinegar 15g
- Salt and pepper to taste
- Chile or hot sauce 23ml
- Minced onion 30g
- Water 70ml
- Chicken thighs 200g (skinless and boneless)

Directions:

1. First of all, please make sure you've all the ingredients available. At first, heat your instant pot cooker over medium heat and cook chicken until browned approximately 10 to 15 minutes.
2. Then sprinkle pepper, salt, and paprika on chicken for extra taste.
3. In a separate bowl, add water, onion, vinegar, hot sauce & mix until it combines well with sauce.
4. Now add this sauce to chicken.
5. One thing remains to be done. Close pot & set timer for about 15 to 15 minutes with natural release.

6. Finally if desired, add chopped herbs over it for extra delicious taste.

Preparation Time: 25 to 30 minutes

Total Servings: 2

What's so typical or different here?

Nutritional Information:

Calories from Fat: 107

Protein: 19.8

Fat: 11.9

Saturated Fat: 3.3

Cholesterol: 71

Sugar: 3.1

Carbohydrates: 7

Fiber: 0.8

Calories: 218

65. Perfect Mixed Pepper Salad

Best combo ever... Don't you agree?

Ingredients:

- Yellow peppers 1
- Salt and pepper to taste
- Green pepper half
- Olive oil 5g
- Sliced tomatoes 1
- Fresh parsley 14g
- Red Onion 35g
- Garlic 1 clove
- Red peppers 1

Directions:

1. First of all, please make sure you've all the ingredients available. At first, wash and remove the stems & seeds from the peppers.
2. Now slice the peppers into thin strips & chop the tomatoes into small pieces.
3. This step is important. Put your instant pot cooker in sauté mode & add oil and red onions.
4. When onions begin to soften, add clove, garlic, and peppers without stirring, let one side of the pepper turn brown (approximately 5 to 10 minutes).
5. Then add the salt, tomato puree, and pepper, mix well until it mixed well.
6. One thing remains to be done. Set cooker cooking time to about 5 to 10 minutes at high pressure on natural release.
7. Finally before serving, add one raw clove, smashed garlic, freshly chopped basil & served hot.

Preparation Time: 10 to 15 minutes

Total Servings: 2

Someone is definitely ready for this.

Nutritional Information:

Calories from Fat: 87

Protein: 4g

Fat: 9.6g

Sugar: 7.7g

Saturated Fat: 1.5g

Fiber: 3.7g

Cholesterol: 0mg

Carbohydrates: 28.6g

Calories: 196

66. Pinnacle Chicken Okra Soup

Good recipe!!

Ingredients:

- Water 300g
- Cooked chicken breast 8g
- Curry sauce mix 1 portions
- Ground ginger 4g
- Broccoli paste 53g
- Frozen okra 82g
- Carrots paste 55g
- Coconut milk 125g
- Water chestnut 55g

Directions:

1. First of all, please make sure you've all the ingredients available. Then place all ingredients in instant pot cooker & select soup option.
2. Finally that it's after a few minutes your tasty soup will be ready.

Preparation Time: 20 to 25 minutes

Total Servings: 2

Lucky!!

Nutritional Information:

Calories from Fat: 39

Protein: 4.4g

Fat: 4.4g

Saturated Fat: 0.7g

Fiber: 6.5g

Cholesterol: 0mg

Carbohydrates: 32.2g

Calories: 179

Sugar: 5.1g

67. Crazy Ground Kale Soup

Yes, this is famous!!

Ingredients:

- Kale 84g

- Red pepper and salt to taste
- Almond milk 25g
- Ground garlic 5g
- Chicken stock 100ml
- Ground sausage 80g
- Chopped onion 40g
- Thyme 10g

Directions:

1. First of all, please make sure you've all the ingredients available. At first, set your instant pot cooker to sauté mode & add onion, garlic, and ground sausage.
2. Now after 2 to 5 minutes, add potatoes & seasoning (like thyme, salt, red pepper) & chicken stock, stir well.
3. Select soup option and set the timer for about 25 to 30 minutes.
4. One thing remains to be done. Open lid and add chopped kale, almond milk on sauté mode.
5. Finally before serving, top with a little parsley. It tastes great next day also.

Preparation Time: 30 to 35 minutes

Total Servings: 2

Wow, that's cute!!

Nutritional Information:

Protein: 10.6g

Calories from Fat: 155

Fat: 17g

Sugar: 3.1g

Saturated Fat: 8.1g

Fiber: 1.5g

Cholesterol: 45mg

Carbohydrates: 16.1g

Calories: 266

68. King sized Vegetable Duck

Fresh start with something new!!

Ingredients:

- Sliced cucumber half
- Salt 10g
- Sliced carrots 3
- Cooking wine 4g
- 1-inch ginger piece
- Water 255g
- Duck (small size)

Directions:

1. First of all, please make sure you've all the ingredients available. Now put all ingredients into the instant cooker pot & then press the stew option.
2. Finally within a few minutes, the delicious soup will be ready in no time.

Preparation Time: 40 to 45 minutes

Total Servings: 2

Try this my way!!

Nutritional Information:

Calories from Fat: 64

Fat: 2.9g

Protein: 19.3g

Saturated Fat: 0.9g

Sugar: 2.7g

Cholesterol: 55mg

Carbohydrates: 29.3g

Calories: 199

Fiber: 4.1g

Special Dinner Recipes

69. Pinnacle Vinegar Chicken

Simplicity is best.

Ingredients:

- White vinegar 15g
- Bay leaves about 2.5
- Fish sauce 10g
- Black peppercorns 2g
- Garlic 2 cloves
- Chicken thighs 605g

Directions:

1. First of all, please make sure you've all the ingredients available. Now select poultry option in your instant pot cooker and add chicken including your ingredients (you don't have to sauté anything).
2. Finally close the lid, and cook properly for about 15 to 20 minutes. Serve hot.

Jumpstart your taste. ?

Nutritional Information:

Carbohydrates: 26.6g

Fiber: 0.8g

Calories: 544

Calories from Fat: 272

Sugar: 22g

Protein: 38.9g

Fat: 30.2g

Cholesterol: 142mg

Saturated Fat: 6.7g

70. Perfect White Bean Stuffed Peppers

Nostalgic feeling...

Ingredients:

- 3 cups vegetable broth
- 4 red bell peppers
- About 1.5 cup goat cheese

- 1 cups white beans
- 1 cup quinoa
- About 1.5 teaspoon garlic powder

Directions:

1. First of all, please make sure you've all the ingredients available. Place the garlic powder, quinoa, vegetable broth, and beans into the pressure cooker.
2. Now place the lid on top & let these cook on the high pressure for 8 minutes.
3. This step is important. Use the quick release to remove the steam.
4. Then divide evenly in four & fill each of the peppers with the bean and quinoa mixture.
5. Clean out your pressure cooker.
6. One thing remains to be done. Place these prepared peppers back into the pressure cooker and then set it too warm for about 5 to 10 minutes.
7. Finally serve these right away.

Most fantastic recipe ever.

71. Dashing Corned Beef with Potatoes and Red Cabbage

Legend overload...

Ingredients:

- Salt and Pepper, to taste
- About 1.5 pound Red Cabbage (Chopped)
- 1/4 Onion (Diced)
- 3/4 pounds Corned Beef
- 1/2 pounds Small Potatoes

- About 1 Celery Stalk (Chopped)
- 1 3/4 cup Water
- 1/3 pounds Carrots (Sliced)

Directions:

1. First of all, please make sure you've all the ingredients available. Combine the beef & water in the IP and season with some salt and pepper.
2. Now close the lid and choose MANUAL.
3. Cook properly on HIGH for about 65 to 70 minutes.
4. Do a quick pressure release and transfer the beef to a plate.
5. Then add the remaining ingredients to the water, close the lid, and cook properly on HIGH for about 5 to 10 more minutes.
6. One thing remains to be done. Transfer the veggies to the plate with the cooked beef.
7. Finally serve & enjoy!

A little work here but will be worth it.

72. Reliable Garlic Lemon Chicken

Something is new here!!

Ingredients:

- 1/2 lemon, juiced
- 1 lbs chicken breasts
- About 1/4 cup white wine
- 1/4 tsp paprika
- 1/2 tsp sea salt
- 1/2 tsp parsley, dried
- 1/4 cup chicken broth
- 1 small onion, diced
- About 3.5 minced garlic cloves
- 1/2 tbsp butter

- 2 tsp arrowroot flour

Directions:

1. First of all, please make sure you've all the ingredients available. Set the Instant Pot to sauté. Put onion in with butter.
2. Now cook for 5 to 10 minutes until onions have softened.
3. If you want, you can let them brown.
4. This step is important. Combine remaining ingredients, minus the flour, & cover.
5. Press poultry setting. The steam valve should be closed.
6. Let it cook completely, release the valve, & then take off the lid.
7. Then you can thicken up the sauce with a slurry.
8. Mix a 1/4 cup of sauce with the flour.
9. One thing remains to be done. Mix it in with the rest of the liquid in the pot.
10. Finally stir & serve. It will also reheat well if there are any leftovers.

The best combo ever!!

73. Charming Sour-sweet chicken breast

Get ready to make it my way!!

Ingredients:

- 10 oz. chicken breast
- 1 tablespoon dried parsley
- About 1.5 teaspoon salt
- 1/2 teaspoon chili pepper
- 2 garlic cloves
- 2 tablespoon tomato paste
- About 1.5 teaspoon oregano
- 1 tablespoon butter
- 1 teaspoon brown sugar
- 1/5 cup spinach
- 1 lemon

Directions:

1. First of all, please make sure you've all the ingredients available. Slice the lemon.
2. Now beat the chicken breast gently & rub it with the lemon wedges.
3. After this, chop the lemon wedges finally.
4. Combine them with the salt, tomato paste, chili pepper, oregano, brown sugar, and butter.
5. This step is important. Chop the spinach & garlic cloves.
6. Then combine the chopped ingredients together & add dried parsley.
7. Stir it carefully.
8. Combine the chopped ingredient mixture with the lemon wedges mixture and poach it.
9. Now separate the mixture into 2 parts.
10. Make the cut across the chicken breast & spread the chicken breast fillets with the one part of the mixture.
11. Then after this, connect to 2 parts of the chicken breast together and rub it on the second part of the lemon mixture.
12. Cover the chicken breast with the foil carefully & put it in the instant pot.

13. One thing remains to be done. Close the lid and cook the dish at the poultry mode for about 30 to 35 minutes.
14. Finally when the time is over – serve the chicken breast hot.

Prep time: 10 to 15 minutes

Cooking time: 30 to 35 minutes

Servings: 2

Luxury tasty dish for you!!

Nutritional information:

Carbs 8.57

Fat 19.

Protein 31

Calories 329

Fiber 1

74. Energetic Chicken Cola Wings
Awesome, isn't it?

Ingredients:

- Garlic 2 cloves
- Green onion 1 stalk
- Vegetable oil 7g
- Sliced ginger 12g
- Coca Cola 100g
- Rice wine 7g
- Light soy sauce 16g
- Dark soy sauce 7g
- Chicken wings 300g

Directions:

1. First of all, please make sure you've all the ingredients available. At first, select sauté mode in your instant pot cooker and add oil.
2. Now when oil is hot, add garlic, ginger, onions and sauté until fragrant nicely.
3. This step is important. Add slowly chicken wings & stir approximately 2 to 5 minutes or until wings are coated all sides with gravy.
4. When edges of wings turn to golden brown & immediately add coca cola, stir using a wooden spoon & add both soy sauce (dark and light), rice wine.
5. Then mix well until it combined well & select cooker cooking timer for about 5 to 10 minutes on high pressure and wait for natural pressure release (approximately 10 to 15 minutes).
6. One thing remains to be done. If desired, add extra seasoning (it shouldn't taste like coca cola).
7. Finally serve immediately with rice or brown rice.

It is a brand new day…. Ever listened to this one!!

Nutritional Information:

Cholesterol: 78mg

Protein: 19g

Sugar: 12.8g

Fiber: 0g

Calories: 280

Calories from Fat: 115

Carbohydrates: 14.2g

Fat: 14.1g

Saturated Fat: 3.1g

75. Funny Brown Sugar and Soy Short Ribs

Simple yet fantastic!!

Ingredients:

- About 1/2 tbsp Sesame Oil
- 1 cups Water
- 2 Beef Short Ribs
- About 2.5 tsp minced Garlic
- 6 tbsp Soy Sauce
- 1/2 tsp grated Ginger
- Juice of 1/2 Orange

Directions:

1. First of all, please make sure you've all the ingredients available. Combine all of the ingredients in a bowl.
2. Then coat well & cover the bowl.
3. This step is important. Place in the fridge and let marinate for about 3 to 4 hours.
4. Transfer everything to your Instant Pot.
5. Now close the lid and set it to MANUAL.
6. One thing remains to be done. Cook properly on HIGH for about 30 to 35 minutes.

7. Finally do a natural pressure release.

Now be a legend!!

76. Scrumptious Lemongrass Chicken

This never goes out of style.

Ingredients:

- 1 tablespoon olive oil
- About 1.5 teaspoon black pepper
- 2 cloves garlic, crushed and minced
- 1 tablespoon lime juice
- 1 cup yellow onion (Sliced)
- 1 cup chicken stock
- About 1.5 tablespoon fresh lemongrass (Chopped)
- 1/2 cup soy sauce
- 1 tablespoon fresh grated ginger
- 1lb bone in chicken pieces

Directions:

1. First of all, please make sure you've all the ingredients available. Set up and prepare your electric pressure cooker according to manufacturer's instructions.
2. Now turn your pressure cooker on the "brown" or "sauté" setting.
3. This step is important. Add the olive oil, chicken and garlic to the pressure cooker and brown the meat for about 2 to 5 minutes.
4. Then add the onion, chicken stock, ginger, soy sauce, lemongrass, lime juice and black pepper.
5. One thing remains to be done. Cover & seal the pressure cooker.

6. Finally set the pressure to high and cook properly for about 15 to 20 minutes or until chicken is cooked through.

I am interested!!

77. Vintage Pot Roast

Good days!!

Ingredients:

- About 1 cup beef broth
- 1 lb rump roast or beef chuck
- About 1.5 medium onion (Chopped)
- 1/2 tbsp oil
- 1 bay leaf

Directions:

1. First of all, please make sure you've all the ingredients available. Pat your roast dry and season it well with your favorite type of seasoning.
2. Now place oil in pot & set to sauté. Once oil sizzles, brown your roast on all sides.
3. This step is important. Remove the roast and place in the bay leaf, onions, and broth.
4. Then place the roast on top of everything. Cover & seal with the lid.
5. Use the manual setting and set to about 40 to 45 minutes.
6. One thing remains to be done. Once finished, release the pressure and remove the roast.

7. Finally strain the onion & bay leaf out of the juices. You can then thicken the juices with water & flour slurry.

Can you make it? Yes, why not?

78. Lucky Spicy Shrimp and Tomato Casserole

Now that's something!!

Ingredients:

- 1/2 Jalapeno (Diced)
- About 1/2 Onion (Diced)
- 1/2 cup shredded Cheddar Cheese
- 1 tbsp Olive Oil
- 1 tbsp Lime Juice
- 3/4 pound Shrimp, peeled and deveined
- About 2.5 tbsp chopped Cilantro
- 1/4 cup Clam Juice
- 1/2 tsp minced Garlic
- 3/4 pound Tomatoes (Chopped)

Directions:

1. First of all, please make sure you've all the ingredients available. Set the IP to SAUTE.
2. Now heat the oil and saute the onions for about 2 to 5 minutes.
3. Add garlic and cook for one more minute.
4. This step is important. Add cilantro, tomatoes, and pour the clam juice over.
5. Close the lid and cook properly on HIGH for about 5 to 10 minutes.
6. Then do a quick pressure release and stir in the shrimp.
7. Cook properly for about 2 to 5 more minutes.

8. One thing remains to be done. Release the pressure quickly & top with the cheese & jalapeno.
9. Finally serve and enjoy!

Funny but definitely yummy!!

79. Vintage BBQ pork ribs

Life of a legend begins here.

Ingredients:

- 4 tablespoon tomato sauce
- About 3.5 tablespoon BBQ sauce
- 1 onion
- 1 garlic clove
- 1/2 teaspoon grapeseed oil
- 1 teaspoon salt
- 1 chili pepper
- About 1.5 teaspoon cilantro
- 1 teaspoon ground black pepper
- 2 tablespoon liquid honey
- 12 oz. pork ribs

Directions:

1. First of all, please make sure you've all the ingredients available. Peel the onion & grate it.
2. Then combine the grated onion with the tomato sauce.
3. Add salt & ground black pepper.
4. Peel the garlic clove & mince it.
5. This step is important. Add the minced garlic in the tomato sauce mixture.
6. Chop the chili pepper and combine it with the cilantro & liquid honey.
7. Now add grapeseed oil & BBQ sauce.
8. Whisk the mixture.
9. Combine the BBQ sauce & tomato sauce mixed together and poach it.
10. Then after this, rub the pork ribs with the sauce and leave them for about 10 to 15 minutes to marinate.
11. One thing remains to be done. Transfer the marinated pork ribs in the instant pot and cook the meat for about 35 to 40 minutes.
12. Finally serve the pork ribs hot.

Prep time: 20 to 25 minutes

Cooking time: 35 to 40 minutes

Servings: 2

This is epic. Take a look!!

80. Best Hot Honey Drumstick

Something is defintely different.

Ingredients:

- Rice wine 25ml
- Chopped scallions 5g
- Honey 14g
- Sesame seeds 5g
- Garlic 2 cloves
- Chicken drumsticks 4 pieces
- Fresh grated ginger 5g
- Sriracha hot sauce 3g
- Soy sauce 25ml

Directions:

1. First of all, please make sure you've all the ingredients available. Now at

first, select the sauté option in your instant pot cooker and add garlic, honey, soy sauce, ginger, rice wine, sriracha sauce and cook properly for about 2 to 5 minutes.

2. One thing remains to be done. Then add the chicken and set the cooking timer to about 20 to 25 minutes on the high pressure until the chicken is tender.

3. Finally when pressure is released naturally, add finely chopped scallions & sesame seeds over it and serve.

Dreams are good!! So dream about this one or else make it…

Nutritional Information:

Protein: 34.5g

Sugar: 18.5g

Calories: 308

Fiber: 0.5g

Calories from Fat: 161

Fat: 7.5g

Carbohydrates: 22g

Saturated Fat: 3.1g

Cholesterol: 152mg

81. Nostalgic Turkey with Cranberries and Sauerkraut

Freshness loaded!!

Ingredients:

- 1/2 cup Cranberries
- About 1.5 tsp Flour
- 3/4 cup Sauerkraut
- 1 tsp minced Garlic
- 2 Turkey Thighs
- 1/3 cup Apple Cider
- About 1 tsp Red Pepper Flakes
- 1/2 tsp Salt
- Juice of 1/2 Lemon
- 1 tbsp Raisins

Directions:

1. First of all, please make sure you've all the ingredients available. Place the sauerkraut in the IP.
2. Now top with raisins garlic, lemon juice & half of the cranberries.
3. Add the turkey on top and sprinkle with salt.
4. This step is important. Cook properly on HIGH for about 25 to 30 minutes.
5. Then transfer the meat to a plate.
6. Set the IP to saute and whisk in the flour.
7. Cook properly for about 2 to 5 minutes.
8. Stir in the remaining cranberries.
9. One thing remains to be done. Pour the mixture over the thighs.
10. Finally serve & enjoy!

Grab it!!

82. Mighty Taco Salad

Astonishing!!

Ingredients:

- 2 diced tomatoes
- 1 lb. ground beef, extra lean
- 2 cups cheese
- 1 iceberg lettuce head (Chopped)
- About 1.5 tablespoon garlic powder
- 1/4 cup water
- 2 tablespoon taco sauce
- About 1.5 tablespoon chili powder
- 2 tablespoons sour cream

Directions:

1. First of all, please make sure you've all the ingredients available. Place the taco sauce, garlic powder, water, chili powder, and beef into the pressure cooker.
2. Then turn it on to the high pressure & let it cook properly for about 15 to 20 minutes.
3. During that time, work on the salad by bringing out a bowl and combining the sour cream, cheese, tomatoes, & lettuce.
4. One thing remains to be done. Now when the time is up, release the valve on the pressure cooker & let the steam out.
5. Finally place your meat on the salad & serve with some tortilla chips or salsa.

Looking forward to healthy life.

83. King sized Beef Back Ribs

Prepare yourself for this…

Ingredients:

- About 2.5 tbsp coconut aminos
- A rack of beef back ribs
- 4 oz unsweetened applesauce
- Your choice of dry rub
- 3/4 cup water
- Kosher salt
- About 1.5 tsp fish sauce

Directions:

1. First of all, please make sure you've all the ingredients available. Pat your ribs dry & sprinkle with your seasoning of choice and the kosher salt.
2. Now wrap with foil & let it set for a couple of hours to a day.
3. Preheat your broil.
4. Cut your ribs so they will fit in your instant pot.
5. This step is important. Put ribs on a baking sheet lined with foil & a rack, and broil for a couple of minutes each side.
6. Then pour the fish sauce, aminos, applesauce, & water in the cooker. Mix well, & place your rack in.
7. Stack the ribs on top of the rack.
8. Turn to high heat, and once at high pressure, turn heat down so that the pressure is maintained at the lowest temp possible.
9. Now cook properly for about 20 to 25 minutes, and then let the pressure release.
10. Remove ribs to a wire rack.

11. Simmer the liquid until it has reduced to 2 cups, about 5 to 10 minutes.
12. One thing remains to be done. Skim the excess fat off.
13. Finally baste the ribs in the liquid & then broil for another minute.

We all are legends in some ways.

84. Crazy Mexican Rice Casserole
Royal taste…

Ingredients:

- 2 1/2 cups Water
- About 1.5 tsp Onion Powder
- 3 ounces Tomato Paste
- 1 cup Brown Rice
- About 1.5 tsp Chili Powder
- 1/2 tsp minced Garlic
- 1/2 cup Black Beans, soaked overnight and drained

Directions:

1. First of all, please make sure you've all the ingredients available. Combine everything in the Instant Pot.
2. Then close the id and set it to MANUAL.
3. Cook properly on HIGH for about 25 to 30 minutes.
4. One thing remains to be done. Now do a quick pressure release.
5. Finally serve & enjoy!

Your friends and family are waiting. Hurry!!

85. Pinnacle shredded beef

Let's dive in…

Ingredients:

- 1 tablespoon minced garlic
- 1/4 cup cream
- About 1.5 teaspoon brown sugar
- 10 oz. beef
- 4 tablespoon sour cream
- 3 cups water
- About 1.5 teaspoon olive oil
- 1 teaspoon salt
- 1/2 teaspoon ground black pepper
- 1/2 cup tomato juice

Directions:

1. First of all, please make sure you've all the ingredients available. Chop the beef, sprinkle it with the salt, & ground black pepper.
2. Then put the chopped beef in the instant pot & pour water.
3. Close the instant pot lid and cook the meat at the meat mode for about 30 to 35 minutes.
4. This step is important. Meanwhile, combine the tomato juice with the brown sugar.
5. Now add minced garlic & sour cream.
6. After this, add olive oil and cream. Whisk the mixture.
7. When the meat is soft – strain it into the bowl.
8. Shred the meat well with the help of the fork & sprinkle it with the tomato juice mixture.
9. Now churn the mass and transfer it to the instant pot again.
10. Sauté the dish for about 10 to 15 minutes more. Stir it frequently.

11. One thing remains to be done. When the shredded meat is cooked – transfer it to the serving bowls.
12. Finally serve it immediately.

Prep time: 15 to 20 minutes

Cooking time: 40 to 45 minutes

Servings: 2

Sincere efforts will be awesome.

86. Perfect Salt Roasted Chicken
Supreme level.

Ingredients:

- Dried ground ginger 5g
- Water 125ml
- Kosher salt 4g
- Optional: Ground white pepper 3g
- Five spice powder 4g
- Chicken legs 4 pieces

Directions:

1. First of all, please make sure you've all the ingredients available. At first, place the chicken legs in a large mixing bowl and season with five spice powder, dried ginger, kosher salt and mix well until the chicken legs are coated well (for better taste make a small scratch over legs)
2. Now wrap the chicken legs tightly in a large piece of parchment paper (avoid aluminum foil).
3. Put a steamer rack in the instant pot cooker & add 240ml of water.
4. Carefully place the chicken legs on the rack.
5. One thing remains to be done. Then close the lid and set the timer for about 25 to 30 minutes on high pressure with natural pressure release (natural pressure release takes approximately 20 to 25 minutes).
6. Finally when it is done, unwrap the parchment paper carefully & serve immediately.

Make it quickly.

Nutritional Information:

Protein: 19.1g

Sugar: 0g

Carbohydrates: 48.6g

Fiber: 5.2g

Calories: 483

Calories from Fat:172

Cholesterol: 55mg

Fat: 19.2g

Saturated Fat: 5.1g

87. Dashing Steamed Tilapia with Cherry Tomatoes
Silently, you were waiting for this one. Don't lie… ?

Ingredients:

- 1 cup cherry tomatoes
- 1/2 cup water
- 1/2 cup olives
- A pinch of pepper
- About 1.5 teaspoon minced garlic
- A pinch of salt
- 1/2 lb. tilapia fillet

Directions:

1. First of all, please make sure you've all the ingredients available. Cut the cherry tomatoes into halves. Set aside.
2. Then pour water into a pressure cooker then preheat the pressure cooker.
3. Place fish fillet into the pressure cooker pot then sprinkle halved cherry tomatoes, minced garlic, & olives over the fish fillet.
4. This step is important. Cover the pressure cooker with the lid and seal tightly.
5. Now select low pressure and cook properly for about 5 to 10 minutes.
6. Once it is done, naturally release the pressure cooker then open the lid.
7. One thing remains to be done. Transfer the steamed fish together with the tomatoes to a serving dish then dust with salt & pepper.
8. Finally serve and enjoy warm.

I know, this is amazing!!

88. Reliable Pasta Bolognese

I was waiting for this one.

Ingredients:

- 6 ounces Water
- About 1.5 tbsp Olive Oil
- 4 ounces dried Pasta
- 12 ounces Pasta Sauce
- About 1 tsp Italian Seasoning
- 3/4 pounds ground Beef

Directions:

1. First of all, please make sure you've all the ingredients available. Set your Instant Pot to SAUTE & heat the olive oil in it.
2. Then add the beef & cook properly until brown.
3. Add garlic and cook properly for about 2 more minutes.
4. This step is important. Stir in all of the remaining ingredients.
5. Close the lid and choose MANUAL.
6. Now cook on HIGH for about 5 to 10 minutes.
7. One thing remains to be done. Release the pressure quickly.
8. Finally serve and enjoy!

Tasty dish just one step away!!

89. Charming Chops and Cabbage

There it is.

Ingredients:

- 1/3 cup beef stock
- 2 thick pork chops
- 1 1/2 tsp oil
- About 1 tsp fennel seeds

- A small cabbage head
- 1/2 tsp salt
- 1/2 tsp pepper
- About 1.5 tsp flour

Directions:

1. First of all, please make sure you've all the ingredients available. Preheat cooker on sauté.
2. Now sprinkle the chops with fennel, pepper, and salt.
3. Slice the cabbage into 3/4 inch slices, set aside.
4. In preheated cooker, add oil & brown the chops on one side.
5. This step is important. Remove the chops & add the cabbage.
6. Place the chops browned side up on the cabbage.
7. Then pour in the stock.
8. Cover and seal with lid.
9. Cook 8 minutes on high pressure.
10. Once finished, release the pressure. Remove the meat & cabbage and tent with foil.
11. One thing remains to be done. Allow the juices to boil. Stir in the flour.
12. Finally pour the sauce over the meat & cabbage and serve.

Used to eat this one a lot.

90. Energetic Couscous lobster

Looking forward to this one!!

Ingredients:

- 4 tablespoon couscous
- About 1.5 teaspoon salt
- 4 tablespoon cream
- 2 tablespoon chicken stock
- 1 tablespoon olive oil
- 1 teaspoon onion powder
- 4 tablespoon butter
- About 1.5 teaspoon chili flake
- 1 teaspoon garlic powder
- 12 oz. lobster

Directions:

1. First of all, please make sure you've all the ingredients available. Wash the lobster carefully and make the cut in it.
2. Then remove the meat little to give the space for the filling.
3. Combine the cream, chicken stock, couscous, and onion powder together.
4. Add garlic powder, chili flakes, & salt.
5. This step is important. Stir the mixture well.
6. Now fill the lobster with the couscous mass well.
7. Then sprinkle the lobster with the olive oil and butter.
8. Place the lobster in the instant pot & close the lid.
9. One thing remains to be done. Then cook the seafood at the steam mode for about 25 to 30 minutes.
10. Finally when the time is over & the lobster is cooked – transfer it to the big serving plate.

Prep time: 10 to 15 minutes

Cooking time: 25 to 30 minutes

Servings: 2

Ironic in taste...

Nutritional information:

Carbs 21.12

Fat 37.4

Protein 33

Calories 553

Fiber 2

91. Funny Herb Turkey Thighs

Arrive in style with this recipe.

Ingredients:

- Chicken broth 125ml
- 1g each dried rosemary, sage, thyme, salt and pepper
- Red-wine vinegar 7g
- Sliced onions 72g
- Minced garlic 5g
- Portobello mushrooms 60g
- Turkey thighs 1 pieces

Directions:

1. First of all, please make sure you've all the ingredients available. At first, set your instant pot cooker on sauté mode & brown the turkey thighs.

2. Then add all your ingredients and select poultry option & set the timer for 60 minutes.

3. This step is important. When it is finished, separate the turkey pieces from gravy and cover loosely with foil.

4. Now in a small bowl, mix cornflour & water until well mixed and add this liquid to the gravy.

5. One thing remains to be done. Select keep warm option and cook gravy properly for about 15 to 20 minutes or until gravy thickened.

6. Finally before serving, add this gravy over the turkey & enjoy the delicious taste.

Classic style...

Nutritional Information:

Protein: 18.7g

Sugar: 3.6g

Fiber: 1.8g

Calories: 506

Sodium: 693mg

Carbohydrates: 9.6g

Calories from Fat: 156

Potassium: 847mg

Fat: 17.4g

Saturated Fat: 4.8g

Cholesterol: 178mg

92. Scrumptious Sage Stuffed Pork Chops

Now you're happy…?

Ingredients:

- 2 cups mushrooms (Chopped)
- 4 cups green beans, trimmed
- About 2.5 cups spinach (Chopped)
- 1 cup red onion (Diced)
- 1 cup chicken or vegetable stock
- 2 teaspoons ground sage
- 1/4 cup walnuts (Chopped)
- 1 tablespoon olive oil
- 1 teaspoon salt
- About 1.5 teaspoon black pepper
- 1 teaspoon onion powder
- 4 bone in pork chops

Directions:

1. First of all, please make sure you've all the ingredients available. Set up & prepare your electric pressure cooker according to manufacturer's instructions.
2. Now turn your pressure cooker on the "brown" or "sauté" setting.
3. In a bowl combine the mushrooms, red onion, spinach, sage and walnuts.
4. Mix well. Slice the pork chops along one side, going about two thirds of the way through the meat.
5. This step is important. Stuff the mushroom mixture into the center of each pork chop.
6. Then season the outside of each pork chop with salt, black pepper & onion powder.
7. Place the olive oil in the pressure cooker, along with the pork chops and brown the meat for about 2 to 5 minutes.
8. Add the vegetable stock.
9. Now cover and seal the pressure cooker. Set the pressure to high and cook properly for about 25 to 30 minutes.
10. Using the quick release, release the steam.
11. One thing remains to be done. Add in the green beans. Cover & bring the pressure back up to high.
12. Finally cook an additional 2 to 5 minutes, or until meat is cooked through.

Always the upper hand…

93. Tasty BBQ Beef Sandwiches

Yeah, it is a vintage recipe.

Ingredients:

- 1/2 cup barbecue sauce
- Hamburger buns
- About 1 lb beef roast

Directions:

1. First of all, please make sure you've all the ingredients available. Trim fat from meat.
2. Then place meat and sauce in the pot & lock and seal lid.
3. Cook properly for about 35 to 40 minutes.

4. One thing remains to be done. Now let pressure release.
5. Finally shred beef & serve on hamburger buns.

Magical, isn't it?

94. Titanic Stuffed sweet pepper

Now the wait is over for hungry people.

Ingredients:

- 3 tablespoon rice, cooked
- 1 teaspoon butter
- About 1.5 teaspoon minced garlic
- 2 large sweet pepper
- 1 tablespoon cream
- 1 egg, beaten
- 1 teaspoon ground black pepper
- 1/4 cup tomato juice
- About 1 teaspoon salt
- 1 teaspoon paprika
- 2 tablespoon ground chicken

Directions:

1. First of all, please make sure you've all the ingredients available. Discard the seeds from the sweet peppers very carefully.
2. Now combine the beaten egg, ground black pepper, cooked rice, paprika, ground chicken, salt, & butter together in the big bowl.
3. Stir it carefully with the help of the spoon.
4. This step is important. After this, add tomato juice & cream and churn it gently again.
5. Then when you get the steady mass – put it in the sweet peppers.
6. Transfer the stuffed peppers to the instant pot & close the lid.
7. Cook the dish properly at the pressure mode for about 20 to 25 minutes.
8. Now when the stuffed peppers are cooked – chill them well.
9. One thing remains to be done. Transfer them carefully to the serving plates.
10. Finally enjoy the dish!

Prep time: 10 to 15 minutes

Cooking time: 20 to 25 minutes

Servings: 2

Awesomeness fully loaded…

Nutritional information:

Carbs 14.8

Fat 13.3

Fiber 4

Calories 211

Protein 13

95. Rich Barbeque Pork

Mystery with this recipe or rather a chemistry with it.

Ingredients:

- Garlic powder 2g
- Barbecue sauce 45g
- Salt and Pepper to taste
- Pork butt roast 300g

Directions:

1. First of all, please make sure you've all the ingredients available. At first, season the pork with salt, pepper and garlic powder.
2. Then place this seasoned pork into instant pot cooker & fill enough water until pork covers.
3. Close the pot & set the timer for about 60 to 65 minutes with the natural pressure release.
4. One thing remains to be done. Now after a natural pressure release, separate juices from the meat.
5. Finally shred the pork & mix with barbecue sauce, add reserved juice if needed to reach your desired consistency.

Speed defines it...

Nutritional Information:

Calories: 353

Fiber: 0.3

Calories from Fat: 192

Fat: 21.3

Sugar: 11

Protein: 23.1

Saturated Fat: 7.8

Cholesterol: 89

Carbohydrates: 15.4

96. Elegant Beef Cheese Sandwich

Jaw dropping!!

Ingredients:

- 1/2 teaspoon salt
- 2 buns
- About 1.5 teaspoon black pepper
- 1/2 cup mozzarella cheese
- 3 teaspoons Worcestershire sauce
- 1/2 cup beef broth
- About 1.5 teaspoon minced garlic
- 1 teaspoon garlic powder
- 1 lb. roast beef

Directions:

1. First of all, please make sure you've all the ingredients available. Cut the roast beef into small chunks then place in a pressure cooker pot.
2. Now season with salt, minced garlic, black pepper, Worcestershire sauce, & garlic powder then pour the beef broth in.
3. Cover and seal the pressure cooker properly then cook properly for about 15 to 20 minutes on high pressure.
4. This step is important. Use the quick release to remove the steam then open the lid. Stir the beef then remove from the pressure cooker.

5. Then cut the buns horizontally then place cooked beef inside & add mozzarella cheese on top.

6. One thing remains to be done. Toast the bread in the oven for about 2 to 5 minutes—just until the mozzarella cheese melts.

7. Finally serve & enjoy.

Ready in about 30 to 35 minutes

Servings 2

Legends are born in…

97. Wonderful Bell Kabadiya Sausage
Sizzle your taste buds…

Ingredients:

- Chicken breasts and thighs 155g
- Andouille sausage 95g (pre-cooked and sliced)
- Prawns 50g
- Red onions 56g
- Worcestershire sauce 7g
- Bell peppers 50g (mixed colors)
- Garlic 14g
- Ginger 16g
- Creole seasoning 7g
- Chicken stock 200g
- Tomatoes 70g
- Olive oil 28g

Directions:

1. First of all, please make sure you've all the ingredients available. At first, set your instant pot cooker on sauté mode.

2. Now add chicken with creole seasoning & brown until all sides coated with golden color and keep aside.

3. Add onions, garlic, peppers & sauté until translucent. Add rice, and sauce and mix for about 2 to 5 minutes.

4. Then add tomato puree, chicken, Worcestershire & close the lid and press rice option.

5. One thing remains to be done. When the rice is cooked, release steam & add sausage and prawns.

6. Finally place lid back on the pressure cooker and set timer again for about 2 to 5 minutes.

Preparation Time: 20 to 25 minutes

Total Servings: 2

Don't forget this one…

Nutritional Information:

Calories from Fat: 124

Protein: 22.1g

Fat: 13.8g

Sugar: 1.4g

Saturated Fat: 4.5g

Fiber: 2.2g

Cholesterol: 72mg

Calories: 348

Carbohydrates: 32.3g

98. Quick Chile Posole Beer

Amazing cooking starts here...

Ingredients:

- Lean boneless pork 400g
- Fresh ground pepper
- Chopped onion 55g
- Garlic 3g
- Sea salt 2g
- Cumin 1g
- Chicken broth/stock 2 cups
- Bay leaves 1
- Ground chile 15g
- Beer 1/2 bottle
- Frozen posole 455g
- Mexican oregano 7g

Garnish:

- Cilantro, lime, queso fresco, avocado

Directions:

1. First of all, please make sure you've all the ingredients available. At first, add the posole to the instant pot cooker & fill water to the maximum line.
2. Now select beans mode and wait for natural release (approximately 5 to 10 minutes).
3. Drain posole, and set aside (tender but firm).
4. This step is important. Set your cooker in browning mode and brown your pork cubes, including chopped onions, garlic, cumin.
5. Then in a separate bowl, add chicken broth, red chili powder, beer, salt, oregano, bay leaf, pepper & mix well and add the mixture to the pot.
6. Select stew option. While the pork is cooking, try to prepare for garnishes.
7. One thing remains to be done. When the timer beeps, add the posole into the pot with the tender pork.
8. Finally stir once and pour into the serving bowl, & top with preferred garnishes.

Preparation Time: 25 to 30 minutes

Total Servings: 2

Being rich is a plus point ?

Nutritional Information:

Calories from Fat: 92

Protein: 15.4g

Fat: 10.6g

Saturated Fat: 2.7g

Sugar: 5.7g

Carbohydrates: 31.8g

Fiber: 5.5g

Calories: 321

99. Awesome Vegan Chickpea Curry

When you're fantastic, this is best!!

Ingredients:

- Cumin seeds 5g
- Water 100ml
- Onion 35g
- Crushed garlic 5g
- Salt and pepper to taste
- Ground coriander 5g
- Garam masala 2g
- Ground turmeric 2g
- Potatoes 25g
- Cooked chickpeas 125g
- Olive oil 10ml
- Diced tomatoes 100g

Garnish:

- Cilantro, parsley

Directions:

1. First of all, please make sure you've all the ingredients available. At first, add oil to your instant pot cooker on sauté mode, add cumin seeds.
2. Now when it starts to crackle, add the sliced onion and cook properly for about 5 to 10 minutes, when onions turns to golden color, add garlic & all remaining ingredients (except garnish).
3. One thing remains to be done. Close the lid and set timer for about 15 to 20 minutes, when it releases pressure naturally, open & add cilantro and parsley.
4. Finally serve with basmati rice, naan or pappadums for better taste.

Preparation Time: 25 to 30 minutes

Total Servings: 2

Being a legend.

Nutritional Information:

Calories from Fat: 74

Protein: 11.6g

Fat: 8.3g

Sugar: 6g

Saturated Fat: 1.1g

Fiber: 12g

Carbohydrates: 68.9g

Calories: 384.2

100.   Legendary Green Chicken Thighs

Being super is a matter of recipe... ?

Ingredients:

- Fresh cilantro 14g
- Worcestershire sauce 3g
- Minced garlic 4g
- Minced ginger 3g
- Balsamic Vinegar 15g
- Salt 2g
- Pepper 2g
- Olive oil 14g
- Minced green onion 12g
- Garlic powder 2g
- Chicken thighs 223g

Directions:

1. First of all, please make sure you've all the ingredients available. At first, take one plastic bag and add salt, garlic, pepper, minced onions, Worcestershire sauce and balsamic vinegar.
2. Now add chicken to the mixture, make sure that chicken nicely covered in sauce & set aside.
3. This step is important. Select sauté and add olive oil, minced garlic & stirring frequently.
4. Select poultry mode in your instant pot cooker & add chicken sauce bag mixture in olive oil & garlic mixture.
5. Then wait for natural release.
6. One thing remains to be done. While serving, sprinkle chopped cilantro for extra taste.
7. Finally you can also serve with your favorite vegetable mix.

Preparation Time: 30 to 35 minutes

Total Servings: 2

Feast for you!!

Nutritional Information:

Calories from Fat: 110

Protein: 20.6g

Fat: 12.2g

Sugar: 4g

Saturated Fat: 3.4g

Fiber: 2.6g

Cholesterol: 72mg

Carbohydrates: 10.8g

Calories: 238

Beef & Pork

101.   Mighty Beef & Broccoli
The hit list recipe.

Ingredients:

- 3 cloves garlic
- About 1.5 tbsp cornstarch
- 1.5 pounds thinly sliced steak
- Fresh or frozen Broccoli
- 3 tbsp sesame oil
- About 3.5 tbsp olive oil
- 1/3 cup brown sugar
- 1/3 cup soy sauce
- 3/4 cup beef broth
- 1 small onion

Directions:

1. First of all, please make sure you've all the ingredients available. Place oil and meat on SAUTE in your Instant Pot. Until meat is brown.
2. Then add in onions and garlic continue to sauté until onions are tender.
3. This step is important. Add in beef broth & soy sauce. Stir in brown sugar & stir until dissolved.
4. Place on 10 minutes high pressure & do a natural release (10 to 15 minutes).
5. Now mix 2 tablespoons water with 1 tablespoon cornstarch & add to your mixture.

6. One thing remains to be done. Meanwhile, steam your broccoli & cook properly your rice according to directions (in this book).
7. Finally stir in the broccoli & serve over rice.

Some things never fail you.

Prep + Cooking Time: 50 to 55 minutes

Servings: 2

102. King sized Beef Ribs in Spices

Mushroom fries bring back a lot of memories.

Ingredients:

- 2 teaspoons Chinese five spice powder
- About 2.5 tablespoons brown sugar or plain raw sugar
- Kosher salt
- 2 tablespoons canola oil
- 2 tablespoons soy sauce
- 3 large garlic cloves (Grated)
- 1/2 cup beef broth
- About 3.5 tablespoons fresh ginger, grated
- 3 tablespoons rice wine vinegar
- 2 medium boneless beef rib portions, fat trimmed

Directions:

1. First of all, please make sure you've all the ingredients available. Heat oven and keep at Broil.

2. Now rub salt & spices on ribs. Place on a flat baking sheet.
3. Broil for about 2 to 5 minutes on each side.
4. Select Sauté and preheat your Instant Pot. Pour oil.
5. This step is important. Add ginger, garlic & fry until light brown.
6. Then pour vinegar and boil for about 30 to 35 seconds.
7. Cancel cooking, pour broth, ribs, sugar, soy sauce, stir well & secure the lid.
8. Now select Manual and cook on high for about 45 to 50 minutes.
9. When done, release the pressure manually.
10. One thing remains to be done. Remove the ribs and bake on baking sheet for about 2 to 5 minutes until crispy on the surface.
11. Finally meanwhile, reduce cooking liquid with Sauté option & use the sauce to rub onto broiled ribs. Serve.

Preparation Time: 15 to 20 minutes

Pressure Time: 40 to 45 minutes

Servings: 2

My sister makes it every now & then.

103. Crazy Russian Beef

For a eternal experience.

Ingredients:

- About 1.5 tbsp vegetable oil

- 3 green onions, sliced into 1-inch pieces
- 4 cloves garlic, minced or pressed
- 1/2 cup soy sauce
- 3 tbsp water
- 1/2 cup water
- About 2.5 tbsp cornstarch
- 2/3 cup dark brown sugar
- 1/2 tsp minced fresh ginger
- 2 pounds flank steak, cut into 1/4" strips

Directions:

1. First of all, please make sure you've all the ingredients available. Season beef with salt & pepper. Put oil in the cooking pot and select SAUTE.
2. Now when oil begins to sizzle, brown meat in batches until all meat is browned - do not crowd. Transfer meat to a plate when browned.
3. This step is important. Add the garlic & Sauté 2 minutes.
4. Add soy sauce, brown sugar, 1/2 cup water, and ginger. Stir to combine.
5. Then add browned beef & any accumulated juices.
6. Select High Pressure. Set timer for about 10 to 15 minutes.
7. When beep sounds turn pressure cooker off & use a quick pressure release.
8. Now when valve drops carefully remove the lid.
9. Combine the cornstarch & 3 tablespoons water, whisking until smooth.
10. One thing remains to be done. Add cornstarch mixture to the sauce in the pot stirring constantly.

11. Finally select SAUTE & bring to a boil, stirring constantly until sauce thickens. Stir in green onions.

Prep + Cooking Time: 40 to 45 minutes

Servings: 2

Like never before…

104.   Pinnacle Hawaii Themed Pork Dish

Worth it…

Ingredients:

- 1 large onion, cut into quarters
- About 1.5 bunch cilantro, freshly chopped
- 5 large garlic cloves, sliced thin
- About 1.5 tablespoon Hawaiian coarse salt
- 2 cups water
- Black pepper powder
- 1.5 lb pork roast, with bone

Directions:

1. First of all, please make sure you've all the ingredients available. Divide the roast into 4 equal portions & arrange at the bottom of Pot.
2. Now top with salt, pepper powder, onion, garlic and water and secure the lid.
3. Use Manual and cook properly on high for about 1.5 hours.

4. One thing remains to be done. Then cancel cooking, & release pressure.
5. Finally shred with forks. Let cool, sprinkle chopped cilantro & serve.

Preparation Time: 5 to 10 minutes

Pressure Time: 90 to 95 minutes

Servings: 2

Simple recipe for you...

105. Perfect Beef Maple Smoked Brisket

Delightful...

Ingredients:

- 2 tsp smoked sea salt
- About 1.5 tbsp liquid smoke
- 2 tbsp date sugar, maple sugar, or coconut sugar
- 1 tsp each: onion powder mustard powder black pepper
- 3 fresh thyme sprigs
- 2 cups bone broth or your choice of stock
- About 1 tsp smoked paprika
- 1 1/2 pound beef brisket

Directions:

1. First of all, please make sure you've all the ingredients available. Take the beef from the refrigerator approximately 30 to 35 minutes before cooking so that it will be at room temperature.
2. Now use two paper towels to pat it dry, & set it aside.

3. Combine the spices by mixing the pepper, smoked sea salt, maple sugar, onion powder, smoked paprika, & mustard powder.
4. This step is important. Rub the mix each side of the brisket.
5. Then set the Instant Pot on the SAUTE setting for about 2 to 5 minutes.
6. Lightly grease the bottom of the cooker with some oil & place the brisket into the pot.
7. Now continue to sauté until all sides are browned.
8. Turn the brisket with the fatty side up. Add the thyme, liquid smoke, & broth.
9. Then scrape the bottom for the browned pieces.
10. Change the setting manually for about 50 to 55 minutes, allowing the pot to release on its own. (The quick release may leave the meat dry.)
11. One thing remains to be done. Remove it from the pot & cover it with some aluminum foil to rest.
12. Finally turn on the SAUTE function for about 10 to 15 minutes so the sauce can thicken.

Prep + Cooking Time: 25 to 30 minutes

Servings: 2

For those who're ultra fantastic.

106. Dashing One Pot IP Roast

Simple yet tasty recipe.

Ingredients:

- 1 medium beef chuck roast, 2 pounds
- 2 large parsnips, cut into 1 inch cubes
- Kosher salt
- About 1 teaspoon black pepper powder
- 1 medium onion, sliced thin
- 2 large carrots, cubed into 1/2 inch pieces
- 3 large garlic cloves (Chopped)
- 2 cups baby potatoes, cut into 1 inch cubes
- 6 thyme sprigs
- About 2.5 bay leaves
- 2 cups beef broth
- 3 tablespoons canola oil

Directions:

1. First of all, please make sure you've all the ingredients available. Select Saute and preheat your Instant Pot.
2. Then pour oil. Rub salt & pepper onto the chuck roast and place into the pot & brown evenly on all sides.
3. Transfer to a plate.
4. This step is important. Sauté onions until golden brown.
5. Now add bay leaves, garlic, thyme & broth and stir well to scrape the bottom.
6. Place chuck roast back in the pot & secure the lid.
7. Select Manual and cook properly on HIGH for about 70 to 75 minutes.
8. Then once done, release pressure & add the vegetables.
9. One thing remains to be done. Secure the lid & cook again on High at Manual for about 15 to 20 minutes.
10. Finally when done, let the pressure release naturally. Serve.

Preparation Time: 20 to 25 minutes

Pressure Time: 75 to 80 minutes

Servings: 2

Wizard of all recipes.

107.   Reliable Marinated Steak
Another fantastic recipe for you guys…

Ingredients:

- 2 tbsp onion soup mix
- 1/4 cup apple cider vinegar
- 1/2 cup olive oil
- 1 tbsp worcestershire sauce
- 2 pounds flank steak

Directions:

1. First of all, please make sure you've all the ingredients available. Set the Instant Pot to the SAUTE function. Pour in the olive oil & add the steak.
2. Now sauté each side of the steak until browned.
3. This step is important. Pour in the vinegar, Worcestershire sauce, and soup mix.
4. Lock down the lid & seal the steam nozzle.
5. One thing remains to be done. Then place the Instant Pot on the MEAT/ STEW setting or set it manually for about 35 to 40 minutes.
6. Finally naturally release the pressure for about 5 to 10 minutes,

& quick release the remainder of the pressure.

Prep + Cooking Time: 60 to 65 minutes

Servings: 2

Magical taste.

108.   Charming Barbecued Brisket

Vintage overload…

Ingredients:

- 2 pounds of beef brisket (Quartered)
- About 2.5 tablespoons apple cider vinegar
- Kosher salt
- 1 teaspoon chili powder
- 3/4 teaspoon black pepper powder
- 1 large tablespoon Worcestershire sauce
- 2 medium onions, sliced thin
- 3 large garlic cloves (Chopped)
- About 2.5 tablespoons brown sugar
- 1 cup tomato sauce
- 1 cup of water
- 2 tablespoons canola oil

Directions:

1.   First of all, please make sure you've all the ingredients available. Select Saute and preheat your instant pot.

2.   Then pour oil. Rub salt & pepper onto the brisket and place into the pot and brown evenly on all sides.

3.   Transfer to a plate.

4.   Add garlic and onions & sauté for about 5 to 10 minutes.

5.   This step is important. Pour water, brown sugar, tomato sauce, Worcestershire sauce, chili powder, mustard & paprika and mix well.

6.   Now place brisket back in the pot and secure the lid.

7.   Select Manual and cook properly on HIGH for about 60 to 65 minutes.

8.   Once done, release pressure.

9.   Select Sauté. Open the cover & let the juices evaporate.

10.   Then add vinegar & stir well.

11.   One thing remains to be done. Slice brisket into thin slices.

12.   Finally place them into the thickened sauce & mix well. Serve.

Preparation Time: 15 to 20 minutes

Pressure Time: 60 to 65 minutes

Servings: 2

What do you think?

Desserts

109.   Energetic Chocolate Cake

Best combo ever… Don't you agree?

Ingredients:

- About 1 tsp lemon juice
- 3/4 cup flour
- 1/4 cup milk
- 1/4 cup water
- 3/4 tsp baking soda
- 1 egg
- 1/2 cup sugar
- About 3.5 tbsp cocoa powder
- 1/4 tsp salt
- 3 tbsp butter (Softened)
- 1/2 tsp vanilla

Directions:

1. First of all, please make sure you've all the ingredients available. Combine the flour, baking soda, and salt together.
2. Now in separate bowl, combine sugar & butter and just combined. Mix in the egg until fluffy.
3. This step is important. Whisk in the cocoa and water & mix until incorporated.
4. Mix in lemon juice and vanilla. Mix in milk.
5. Then slowly fold in the flour mixture. Don't over mix.
6. Grease 6 inch cake pan, & pour in batter.
7. Heat cooker with a plate or tray on bottom, close lid. No water, no gasket.
8. One thing remains to be done. Once it has heated for about 2 to 5 minutes, gently place cake pan in the cooker with a pot holder.
9. Finally close lid, & keep heat low.

Someone is definitely ready for this.

110.   Funny Strawberry sweet toast cake

Good recipe!!

Ingredients:

- 1/4 cup brown sugar
- About 1.5 teaspoon caramel
- 1/2 cup strawberries
- 2 tablespoon coconut flour
- 1 tablespoon butter
- 1/2 cup cream
- About 1 teaspoon cinnamon
- 10 oz. white French bread
- 1/2 teaspoon ground cardamom
- 2 eggs (Beaten)

Directions:

1. First of all, please make sure you've all the ingredients available. Whisk the eggs in the bowl.
2. Then add brown sugar & butter.
3. After this, add cream & ground cardamom.
4. Sprinkle the mixture with the coconut flour & caramel.
5. This step is important. Whisk the mass well.
6. Now after this, chop French bread into the small cubes.

7. Put the bread cubes in the instant pot.
8. Blend the strawberries and sprinkle the bread with it to make the layer.
9. Then the pour the whisked egg mixture and close the lid.
10. Cook the dish at the pressure mode for about 10 to 15 minutes.
11. One thing remains to be done. Then chill it little the toasts are warm.
12. Finally cut it into 2 parts & sprinkle with the 1/2 teaspoon of the cinnamon.

Prep time: 10 to 15 minutes

Cooking time: 10 to 15 minutes

Servings: 2

Lucky!!

Nutritional, information:

Carbs 44.97

Fat 29.3

Protein 14

Calories 490

Fiber 3

111. Scrumptious Chocolate and Orange Pudding

Yes, this is famous!!

Ingredients:

- 1/2 tbsp Orange Juice
- Pinch of Salt
- About 1 tsp Orange Zest

- 1/4 tsp Caramelized Ginger
- 3 tbsp Sugar
- 1 large Egg, white and yolk separated
- 1/2 cup Milk
- 2 tbsp Cornstarch
- About 1.5 tbsp Butter (Softened)
- 1 ounce Chocolate (Chopped)

Directions:

1. First of all, please make sure you've all the ingredients available. In a bowl, combine the butter, salt, cornstarch, juice, zest, sugar, and salt.
2. Now whisk in the milk, ginger, and yolk, until well combined.
3. Beat the white until stiff form peaks.
4. Gently fold the beaten white to the yolk mixture,
5. This step is important. Divide the mixture between 2 custard cups.
6. Then cover them with aluminum foil.
7. Pour 1 1/2 cups of water into the IP & lower the rack.
8. Place the cups on the rack & close the lid.
9. Now cook on MANUAL for about 10 to 15 minutes.
10. Do a quick pressure release.
11. One thing remains to be done. Stir in the chocolate.
12. Finally serve & enjoy!

Total Time: 20 to 25 Minutes

Serves: 2

Wow, that's cute!!

112. Astonishing Fresh Berry Compote

Fresh start with something new!!

Ingredients:

- 1 pound Fresh Blueberries washed
- About 2.5 tsp Orange juice or 2 tsp Lemon juice
- 1/4 cup sugar
- About 1.5 pound Fresh Strawberries washed, trimmed and cut in half

Directions:

1. First of all, please make sure you've all the ingredients available. Add fruit to Pressure Cooker cooking pot.
2. Now sprinkle with sugar and let sit 20 to 25 minutes.
3. This step is important. Add a little squeeze of orange juice.
4. Lock on lid and Close Pressure Valve.
5. Then cook at HIGH Pressure for about 2 minutes.
6. One thing remains to be done. When Beep sounds, allow a 15 to 20 minutes Natural Pressure Release.
7. Finally compote will thicken as it cools.

Prep + Cooking Time: 35 to 40 minutes

Servings: 2

Try this my way!!

113. Excellent Mixed Berry Pudding
Baking does the trick!!

Ingredients:

- 1/4 cup raspberries
- Milk or cream to serve
- 1/4 cup strawberries (Chopped)
- About 1/2 cup plums, pitted, chopped
- 1/4 cup red wine
- 1/2 cups water
- About 1.5 tablespoon corn starch
- 1/4 cup red currants (Halved)

Directions:

1. First of all, please make sure you've all the ingredients available. Setting aside about 2 tablespoons of the berries, add the rest to the instant pot. Add sugar & stir.
2. Now close the lid. Press 'Slow cook' button & set timer for about 45 to 50 minutes.
3. Cook the berries until are still in shape. Add more sugar if necessary.
4. This step is important. Mix together in a bowl, cornstarch, & water and pour into the pot.
5. Then press 'Sauté' button. Press 'Adjust' button twice. Stir constantly until it thickens. Press 'Cancel' button.
6. Add the red wine & mix well.
7. One thing remains to be done. Blend the berries that were set aside & add to the thickened berries.
8. Finally can be served either hot or cold. Serve with milk or cream.

I don't know about you, but I include this one everytime I get a chance.

114.   Legendary Brown Bread Pudding

I repeat… Try it if you want to. No regrets. Right!!

Ingredients:

- 1/2 cup palm sugar
- 1/4 cup chopped pecans
- 3 cups almond milk
- 1/2 cup raisins
- 3 eggs
- About 1.5 teaspoon vanilla extract
- 8 slices bread
- 1/2 teaspoon cinnamon
- About 1/2 teaspoon salt
- 1/4 cup butter

Directions:

1. First of all, please make sure you've all the ingredients available. Prepare a pressure cooker proof dish then cover with aluminum foil.
2. Now pour water into the pressure cooker then place a trivet inside.
3. Preheat a saucepan then melt the butter.
4. This step is important. Once it is melted, pour the butter into a bowl then combine with palm sugar, eggs, almond milk, vanilla extract, salt, & cinnamon. Whisk until incorporated.
5. Then cut the bread into cubes then add into the butter mixture together with raisins.
6. Let it sit for about 20 to 25 minutes until the milk mixture is completely absorbed by the bread.
7. Now pour the mixture into the prepared dish then sprinkle chopped pecans over the bread.
8. Place the dish on the trivet then seal the pressure cooker properly.
9. Then select high-pressure from the menu & set the time to about 20 to 25 minutes.
10. Once it is done, naturally release the pressure cooker open the lid.
11. One thing remains to be done. Remove the bread pudding from the pressure cooker then let it cool for a few minutes.
12. Finally serve & enjoy.

Why not??

115.   Awesome Cherry Bowls

Legends are born in…

Ingredients:

- 1 cup water+ 1 tablespoon
- About 1 teaspoon almond extract
- 1/2 cup steel cut oats
- 2 tablespoons maple syrup
- About 1.5 tablespoon cocoa powder
- 1 cup milk
- 1 cup cherries, pitted + 3 tablespoons

Directions:

1. First of all, please make sure you've all the ingredients available. Now put the milk in your instant pot, add 1 cup water, 3 tablespoons cherries, oats,

cocoa powder, maple syrup and half of the almond extract, stir, cover and cook properly on High for about 10 to 15 minutes.

2. One thing remains to be done. Then meanwhile, in a pot, mix 1 tablespoon water with 3 tablespoons cherries & the rest of the almond extract, stir & simmer for a few minutes over medium high heat.

3. Finally divide cherries mix into 2 bowls, drizzle the sauce all over and serve.

Preparation time: 10 to 15 minutes

Cooking time: 10 to 15 minutes

Servings: 2

Jaw dropping!!

Nutritional information:

Fiber 2

Calories 120

Carbs 4

Fat 1

Protein 4

116.   Awesome Rice Pudding
Leave a mark!!

Ingredients:

- About 1/2 tsp vanilla
- 1/3 cup Arborio rice
- 1/4 cup half and half
- 1 egg
- About 1/4 tsp salt

- 1 1/4 cup milk
- 1/3 cup sugar
- 1/4 cup raisins

Directions:

1. First of all, please make sure you've all the ingredients available. In pot mix milk, salt, rice, and sugar.

2. Now set to sauté and let boil, stir constantly until sugar dissolves.

3. When boiling cover & seal lid.

4. This step is important. Choose low pressure & set to about 15 to 20 minutes.

5. Then while cooking, whisk half & half, eggs, and vanilla together.

6. When rice is done, turn off cooker & let it set for about 10 to 15 minutes then use quick release. Fluff the rice.

7. Now mix in the eggs. Set to sauté and bring to boil.

8. One thing remains to be done. Turn off cooker & stir raisins in.

9. Finally you can serve at this time or store in an air tight container. Pudding thickens as is cools.

Spice up!!

117.   Quick Blood Orange and Ginger Compote
What do you think? ?

Ingredients:

- 1 tbsp Crystalized Ginger (Chopped)
- Pinch of Nutmeg
- About 1.5 tsp Triple Sec
- 1/4 tsp Cinnamon Powder

- 1 cup Water
- About 1.5 tbsp Maple Syrup
- 1 Blood Oranges

Directions:

1. First of all, please make sure you've all the ingredients available. Squeeze the juice from 1 orange.
2. Now chop the other blood orange finely.
3. Place them in the IP.
4. This step is important. Pour the water over & stir in the nutmeg, cinnamon, and ginger.
5. Then close the lid and cook properly on STEAM for about 2 to 5 minutes.
6. Do a natural pressure release.
7. One thing remains to be done. Stir in the maple syrup & triple sec.
8. Finally serve and enjoy!

What makes this the best? Check it out for yourself!!

118. Wonderful Nutella mini cake

Just got better!!

Ingredients:

- 4 tablespoon flour
- About 1 teaspoon vanilla extract
- 1/4 teaspoon baking soda
- 1 tablespoon almond flour
- 3 tablespoon milk
- 2 tablespoon Nutella
- About 1.5 teaspoons sugar

- 1 tablespoon lemon juice
- 1 egg

Directions:

1. First of all, please make sure you've all the ingredients available. Beat the egg in the mixer bowl.
2. Now add flour, baking soda, lemon juice, almond flour, sugar, and milk.
3. In the end, add the vanilla extract.
4. This step is important. Knead the dough with the help of the mixer.
5. Then when you get smooth & plastic dough – transfer it to the instant pot.
6. Close the lid and cook the mini cake properly for about 25 to 30 minutes in the pressure mode.
7. One thing remains to be done. Now when the cake is cooked – chill it well.
8. Finally spread the cooked cake with the Nutella & cut it into 2 parts.

Prep time: 10 to 15 minutes

Cooking time: 25 to 30 minutes

Servings: 2

Got the idea!!

Nutritional information:

Fat 17

Protein 9

Fibre 3

Calories 349

Carbs 38.52

119.   Great Sweet Blueberry Butter

Ingredients:

- 1/2 teaspoons cinnamon powder
- About 1/2 teaspoon ginger (Ground)
- Zest from 1/3 lemon (Grated)
- A pinch of nutmeg (Ground)
- About 2.5 tablespoons sugar
- 1 cup blueberries puree

Directions:

1. First of all, please make sure you've all the ingredients available. Now in your instant pot, mix blueberries with cinnamon, sugar, lemon zest, nutmeg and ginger, stir, cover & cook properly on High for about 10 to 15 minutes.
2. Finally divide into jars & serve cold.

Preparation time: 10 to 15 minutes

Cooking time: 5 to 10 minutes

Servings: 2

Speed defines it...

Nutritional information:

Fat 1

Fiber 2

Calories 133

Carbs 4

120.   Elegant Fresh Currant Bread Pudding

Relax and enjoy this recipe!!

Ingredients:

- 4 1/2 cups sweet stale bread, cubed
- 1 1/2 cups heavy cream
- About 1 tbsp candied lemon peel
- 1/3 cup dried currants
- 4 eggs, beaten
- 2 1/2 tbsp butter
- 1/2 tsp vanilla essence
- 2 1/4 cups milk
- A pinch of kosher salt
- About 1 tsp cinnamon powder
- 1/3 cup caster sugar

Directions:

1. First of all, please make sure you've all the ingredients available. Prepare your cooker by adding 3 cups of water.
2. Now add the steam rack, too.
3. Take a casserole dish that will fit in the inner pot.
4. Butter the casserole dish. Add bread cubes to the dish.
5. This step is important. Combine the remaining ingredients in a mixing bowl; whisk vigorously until everything is well combined.
6. Then pour the mixture over the bread cubes.

7. Cover with two layers of foil.
8. Select the STEAM function and cook properly for about 10 to 15 minutes or until the pudding is set.
9. One thing remains to be done. Now remove the casserole dish from the cooker.
10. Finally serve & enjoy!

Prep + Cooking Time: 15 to 20 minutes

Servings: 2

Try this one if you're hungry!!

121. Rich Coconut and Peanut Butter Quinoa Pudding

Make me remember the good old days!!

Ingredients:

- 1/4 cup Maple Syrup
- Pinch of Nutmeg
- 2/3 cup unsweetened Coconut Milk
- About 1 tsp Vanilla Extract
- 2 tbsp Coconut Flakes
- Pinch of Cinnamon
- 1/4 cup Peanut Butter
- 2/3 cup Water
- 2/3 cup Quinoa

Directions:

1. First of all, please make sure you've all the ingredients available. Combine the milk, quinoa, maple, nutmeg, cinnamon, water, and vanilla, in the Instant Pot.
2. Now close the lid & set the pot to RICE.
3. This step is important. Cook properly for about 5 to 10 minutes.
4. Do a quick pressure release.
5. Then stir in the peanut butter.

6. Divide between 2 serving cups.
7. One thing remains to be done. Top with coconut flakes.
8. Finally enjoy!

Luxury in its own class!!

122. Titanic Raspberry Curd

Healthy is a new trend these days!! ?
Always I guess…

Ingredients:

- 24 ounces raspberries
- 2 cups sugar
- About 4.5 tablespoons lemon juice
- 4 tablespoon butter
- 4 egg yolks

Directions:

1. First of all, please make sure you've all the ingredients available. Add raspberries, sugar and lemon juice into the instant pot. Stir.
2. Now close the lid. Press 'Manual' button & set timer for about 2 minutes.
3. When the timer goes off, let the pressure release naturally for about 5 to 10 minutes.
4. This step is important. Strain the contents through a fine wire mesh strainer.
5. Then discard the seeds.
6. Whisk the yolks. Add the strained raspberry pulp into the yolks a little at a timer & whisk each time.
7. Pour into the instant pot.
8. One thing remains to be done. Now press 'Sauté' button. Stir constantly

for a few minutes. Switch off the pot and add butter.

9.   Finally stir and pour into a serving bowl. Chill & serve.

Stunner!!

123.   Tasty New York Cheesecake

Super awesome plus unique!!

Ingredients:

Crust:

- About 1.5 tablespoon granulated sugar
- 3/4 cup graham crackers
- 2 tablespoons unsalted butter

Filling:

- 1/2 cup granulated sugar
- 4 tablespoons whipping cream
- About 1 tablespoon multi-purpose flour
- 1 egg yolk
- 1/2 teaspoon vanilla extract
- 1/2 teaspoon lemon zest
- About 1 teaspoon orange zest
- 1 cup cream cheese

Topping:

- About 1 tablespoon granulated sugar
- 1/2 cup plain yogurt

Directions:

1.   First of all, please make sure you've all the ingredients available. Make the crust first. Prepare a cheesecake pan then grease with cooking spray.
2.   Now place graham crackers & sugar in a food processor then process until becoming small crumbs.
3.   Place butter in a saucepan then melt over very low heat.
4.   Add melted butter into the crackers mixture then mix well.
5.   This step is important. Place the crust into the prepared cheesecake pan then press completely.
6.   Then freeze the crust for approximately 15 to 20 minutes.
7.   Make the filling. Place cream cheese in a mixing bowl then beat until smooth and creamy.
8.   Place the egg yolk, vanilla extract, lemon zest, orange zest, flour, sugar and whipping cream in the cream cheese mixture.
9.   Continue mixing until well combined.
10.   Now pour the mixture into the crust & spread evenly.
11.   Pour one cup water into a pressure cooker then put a trivet inside.
12.   Place the cheesecake on the trivet.
13.   Then close the pressure cooker with its lid then seal properly.
14.   Select the menu to high pressure and set the time to about 35 to 40 minutes.
15.   Once it is done, naturally release the pressure cooker & let the pressure cooker comes down.

16. Now open the lid then remove the cheesecake from the pressure cooker. Make the topping.
17. Combine yogurt and sugar in a bowl then stir until incorporated.
18. One thing remains to be done. Spread over the top of the Cheesecake & let them cool.
19. Finally keep in the refrigerator for at least 3 to 4 hours or overnight. Serve & enjoy cool.

Ready in about 60 to 65 minutes

Servings 2

Iconic recipe of my list!!

124.   King sized Quinoa Dessert

Ingredients:

- 1/2 cup red quinoa
- 3 cups water
- 1/4 cup steel cut oats
- 1/4 cup hazelnuts, toasted and chopped
- About 1.5 tablespoon sugar
- 1/2 cup apricots, dried and chopped
- 1/4 teaspoon vanilla bean paste

Directions:

1. First of all, please make sure you've all the ingredients available. Now in your instant pot, mix quinoa with apricots, vanilla paste, oats, sugar, hazelnuts & water, stir, cover and cook properly on High for about 20 to 25 minutes.
2. Finally divide into 2 bowls & serve.

Preparation time: 10 to 15 minutes

Cooking time: 20 to 25 minutes

Servings: 2

Now the wait is over for hungry people.

Nutritional information:

Fat 3

Fiber 5

Calories 151

Carbs 6

Protein 5

125.   Yummy Key Lime Pie
Well it is a Grandma's recipe!!

Ingredients:

- About 1.5 tsp Sugar
- 3 tbsp Sugar
- 1/4 cup Sour Cream
- 1 Egg Yolk
- 2 tbsp Lime Juice
- 1 tbsp Butter
- About 1 tsp Lime Zest
- 1/4 tsp Vanilla Extract
- 7 ounces canned Sweetened Condensed Milk
- 1/2 cup Graham Cracker Crumbs

Directions:

1. First of all, please make sure you've all the ingredients available. Pour about 1 1/2 cups of water into the IP.
2. Now grease a small round baking pan with cooking spray.
3. In a bowl, combine the butter, cracker crumbs, & 2 tsp sugar.
4. Press this mixture into the prepared pan.
5. This step is important. In another bowl, whisk together the remaining ingredients.
6. Then pour the filling over the crust.
7. Wrap the pan with foil & place it onto the lowered trivet.
8. Close the lid and cook properly on MANUAL for about 15 to 20 minutes.
9. Now do a quick pressure release.
10. One thing remains to be done. Wait to cool down before serving.
11. Finally enjoy!

Total Time: 30 to 35 Minutes

Serves: 2

Happiness has finally arrived!!

126. Legendary Baked Plums

Yeah, it is a vintage recipe.

Ingredients:

- 1 cup sugar
- About 1 tablespoon cornstarch
- About 1 teaspoon cinnamon powder
- 3 tablespoons water
- 6 plums, stones removed and halved

Directions:

1. First of all, please make sure you've all the ingredients available. Now in your instant pot, mix plums with sugar, water and cornstarch, cinnamon, stir, cover & cook properly on High for about 5 to 10 minutes.
2. Finally divide into 2 bowls & serve cold.

Preparation time: 10 to 15 minutes

Cooking time: 5 to 10 minutes

Servings: 2

Now you're happy...?

Nutritional information:

Fat 2

Fiber 1

Calories 140

Carbs 3

Protein 4

127. Unique Tapioca Pudding
Whenever you want a great recipe!!

Ingredients:

- 1/4 cup water
- 3 tbsp tapioca pearls
- 3/4 cup whole milk
- 1/4 cup sugar

Directions:

1. First of all, please make sure you've all the ingredients available. Add a cup of water and steamer basket to cooker.
2. Now rinse tapioca.
3. In a heat proof bowl, mix milk, tapioca, lemon zest, sugar, and milk until sugar dissolves.
4. This step is important. Ease the bowl into the cooker and seal lid.
5. On high pressure, cook properly for about 5 to 10 minutes.
6. Then when finished, turn off cooker and let pressure release on its own.
7. After pressure is released allow it to set another 5 to 10 minutes.
8. One thing remains to be done. Carefully remove bowl & stir with fork pouring into bowls.
9. Finally cover and refrigerate 2 to 3 hours.

How is it? Only one way to find out…

128. Ultimate Vanilla crème brule

I can eat them all day!!

Ingredients:

- 1 cup heavy cream
- About 1/2 teaspoon salt
- About 4.5 tablespoon brown sugar
- 1/2 teaspoon vanilla extract
- 4 egg yolks

Directions:

1. First of all, please make sure you've all the ingredients available. Whisk the egg yolks with the brown sugar & vanilla extract.
2. Now add salt and whisk the mixture for about 2 to 5 minutes more.
3. This step is important. After this, add the heavy cream & mix the mixture up with the help of the hand mixer.
4. When you get the fluffy mass – pour it into 2 ramekins.
5. Then put the ramekins in the instant pot & cook the dish properly for about 10 to 15 minutes.
6. One thing remains to be done. When the crème Brule is cooked – stir it gently with the help of the spoon.
7. Finally serve it & enjoy!

Prep time: 5 to 10 minutes

Cooking time: 10 to 15 minutes

Servings: 2

Different take on this one…

Nutritional information:

Carbs 22.65

Fat 31.2

Calories 396

Protein 7

Fiber 0

129.   Iconic Mango Cake
Grandfather of Recipes!!

Ingredients:

- 3/4 cup milk
- About 1/2 tsp salt
- 1/2 cup sugar
- 1/4 tsp baking soda
- 1/4 cup coconut oil
- About 1.5 tsp baking powder
- 1 tbsp lemon juice
- 1 tsp mango syrup
- 1 1/4 cups flour

Directions:

1. First of all, please make sure you've all the ingredients available. Grease a baking pan that will fit in your Instant Pot.
2. Now mix the sugar, oil, & milk in a bowl until the sugar has melted.
3. Pour in mango syrup and mix again. Pour all the dry ingredients through a sieve into the wet.
4. This step is important. Add lemon juice & mix well.
5. Then pour into the baking pan. Pour 1 cup of water into the Instant Pot & lower in a trivet.
6. Lower the baking pan into the cooker & close the lid.
7. Select MANUAL, and cook properly on HIGH pressure for about 35 to 40 minutes.
8. One thing remains to be done. Now when time is up, hit CANCEL & wait for the pressure to come down naturally.
9. Finally check the cake for doneness before cooling for about 10 to 15 minutes. Serve.

Prep + Cooking Time: 45 to 50 minutes

Servings: 2

I am actually popular among my friends for eating this one a lot.

130.   Awesome Pear Crunch
So, what's your opinion?

Ingredients:

- 1/3 cup Sugar
- About 1/2 tsp Nutmeg
- 1 1/4 cups Oats
- 1 tbsp Orange Juice
- 2 tbsp melted Butter
- 1/3 tsp Cinnamon
- About 1 tsp Vanilla
- 1 1/2 cups Water
- 2 Pears (Sliced)

Directions:

1. First of all, please make sure you've all the ingredients available. Grease a baking dish with cooking spray.
2. Now in a bowl, combine the oats, nutmeg, juice, cinnamon, sugar, and vanilla.
3. Press 1/4 of the mixture into the bottom of the greased pear.
4. Top with 1/4 of the pear slices.

5. This step is important. Repeat the process 3 more times.
6. Then drizzle with melted butter.
7. Pour the water into the IP & lower the trivet.
8. Wrap the dish with foil & place onto the trivet.
9. Then close the lid and cook properly for about 15 to 20 minutes on RICE.
10. One thing remains to be done. Do a quick pressure release.
11. Finally serve & enjoy!

Yeah, you can make it in your free time…

131. Super Cranberry Stuffed Apples

Supremacy defined!!

Ingredients:

- 1 tablespoons walnuts (Chopped)
- Whipped cream to serve (Optional)
- About 3.5 tablespoons packed brown sugar
- 1/4 teaspoon ground cinnamon
- 1/4 cup fresh or frozen cranberries, thawed, chopped
- About 1/4 teaspoon ground nutmeg
- 2 medium apples

Directions:

1. First of all, please make sure you've all the ingredients available. Leave the bottom part of the apples intact & core the apples.
2. Now slowly scoop out some more pulp from inside the apple.

3. Mix together rest of the ingredients & stuff inside the apple.
4. Place the apples in the instant pot.
5. One thing remains to be done. Then close the lid. Press 'Slow cook' button and set timer for about 2.5 hours.
6. Finally serve with whipped cream if desired.

Time for an iconic recipe.

132. Delightful Baked Apples with Cinnamon

What do you think?

Ingredients:

- About 2.5 tablespoons raisins
- 1/2 teaspoon cinnamon
- 1/2 cup red wine
- About 4.5 tablespoons granulated sugar
- 2 apples

Directions:

1. First of all, please make sure you've all the ingredients available. Core the apples then place on the bottom of a pressure cooker.
2. Then add granulated sugar & raisins into the pot then pour red wine over the apples.
3. This step is important. Dust cinnamon on top then seal the pressure cooker properly.
4. Now select the menu to high pressure & select the time to about 10 to 15 minutes.

5. One thing remains to be done. Once the timer beeps, naturally release the pressure cooker then open the lid.

6. Finally remove the apples and the liquid from the pressure cooker then place in a serving dish. Serve & enjoy.

Ready in about 25 to 30 minutes

Servings 2

Vintage overload…

133. Fantastic Oreo Cheesecake
Magical taste.

Ingredients:

Crust:

- About 2.5 tbsp butter (Melted)
- 12 Oreos (Crushed)

Cake:

- 2 tsp vanilla
- 16 oz cream cheese
- 1/4 cup heavy cream
- About 1.5 tbsp All Purpose flour
- 1/2 cup sugar
- 2 large eggs
- 8 Oreos (Chopped)

Topping:

- 8 Oreos (Chopped)
- 1 cup whipped cream

Directions:

1. First of all, please make sure you've all the ingredients available. Cover the bottom of 7 inch springform pan with foil.

2. Now spray the pan with nonstick cooking spray.

3. Mix the butter & crushed cookies. Press them into the pan.

4. Freeze for about 15 to 20 minutes.

5. With a stand mixer or hand mixer, mix the cream cheese until it is smooth.

6. This step is important. Beat in the sugar, then the eggs until completely incorporated.

7. Then scrape sides down periodically. Next, mix in vanilla, flour, and cream until smooth. Fold in the 8 Oreos, pour into pan.

8. Cover with foil.

9. Place 1 1/2 cup water & trivet in the cooker.

10. Now make a sling of foil around the pan to easily remove it from the cooker.

11. Put sling around pan and ease into the cooker. Cover & seal lid.

12. Then set for 40 minutes on high pressure.

13. When done, turn off and let pressure release for about 10 to 15 minutes then use quick release.

14. One thing remains to be done. Carefully take out the pan using the sling and put on a cooling rack. Once cool, refrigerate 7 to 8 hours.

15. Finally top with whipped cream and cookies.

Another fantastic recipe for you guys…

134. Great Tapioca pudding

Wizard of all recipes.

Ingredients:

- 4 tablespoon almond milk
- 1/4 teaspoon ground nutmeg
- About 1.5 teaspoon coconut
- 1/2 cup almond milk
- About 1 teaspoon vanilla extract
- 1 tablespoon brown sugar
- 1 tablespoon tapioca

Directions:

1. First of all, please make sure you've all the ingredients available. Combine the almond milk & coconut milk together.
2. Then add coconut and brown sugar.
3. After this, sprinkle the mixture with the vanilla extract & ground nutmeg.
4. This step is important. Stir the mixture gently and pour it in the instant pot.
5. Now preheat the liquid at the sauté mode for about 10 to 15 minutes.
6. After this, add the tapioca & stir it gently.
7. One thing remains to be done. Cook the pudding at the sauté mode till it is getting thick.
8. Finally chill it well & serve the dish warm.

Prep time: 5 to 10 minutes

Cooking time: 10 to 15 minutes

Servings: 2

Simple yet tasty recipe.

Nutritional information:

Protein 1

Fiber 1

Calories 67

Fat 1.2

Carbs 13.03

135. Happy Hot Chocolate Fondue

For those who're ultra fantastic.

Ingredients:

- Pinch of Cinnamon
- About 1.5 tsp Coconut Liqueur
- Pinch of Nutmeg
- 5 ounces Milk Chocolate
- Pinch of Salt
- 4 ounces Heavy Cream

Directions:

1. First of all, please make sure you've all the ingredients available. Pour 1/2 lukewarm water into the IP.
2. Now lower the metal trivet.
3. Melt the chocolate in a heatproof bowl in the microwave.
4. Add the remaining ingredients, except the liqueur, to the bowl.
5. This step is important. Stir well to combine.
6. Then place the bowl on the trivet & close the lid.
7. Choose STEAM and cook properly for about 2 to 5 minutes.
8. Do a quick pressure release.
9. One thing remains to be done. Stir in the liqueur.
10. Finally serve with fruits & enjoy!

Total Time: 15 to 20 Minutes

Serves: 2

Delightful…

136. Lucky Vegan Pumpkin Cake (VEG)

Simple recipe for you…

Ingredients:

- 1 cup applesauce
- About 1 tsp pumpkin pie spice
- 1 1/4 cups sugar
- A pinch of salt
- 2 cups flour
- 1 1/2 tsp baking soda
- About 1.5 tsp ginger, grated
- 1/2 tsp vanilla extract
- 1 1/4 cups pumpkin puree

Directions:

1. First of all, please make sure you've all the ingredients available. In a mixing bowl, combine the vanilla extract, flour, baking soda, pumpkin pie spice, and the salt.
2. Now in a separate bowl, combine the applesauce and the sugar.
3. Stir in the ginger & the pumpkins puree & mix well to combine.
4. This step is important. Add the applesauce mixture to the dry flour mixture.
5. Then spoon batter into a cake pan oiled with cooking spray. Cover with a foil.
6. Pour 2 cups of water into the cooker. Lay a metal rack on the bottom of your cooker.
7. Now lay prepared cake pan on the metal rack. Cook properly for about 20 to 25 minutes at HIGH pressure.
8. One thing remains to be done. Transfer the pan to a wire rack before serving.
9. Finally dust your cake with icing sugar or decorate with vegan frosting.

Prep + Cooking Time: 35 to 40 minutes

Servings: 2

Worth it…

137. Vintage Apricot Crisp

Like never before…

Ingredients:

- 3 tablespoons packed light brown sugar

- About 1.5 tablespoons butter, unsalted, divided
- About 3.5 tablespoons ground crackers
- 8 ounces canned apricots, drained, sliced

Directions:

1. First of all, please make sure you've all the ingredients available. Grease the inside of the instant pot with cooking spray.
2. Now layer with half the apricot slices followed by half the cracker crumbs followed by brown sugar & finally half the butter.
3. Repeat the above layer.
4. One thing remains to be done. Then close the lid. Select 'Slow cook' button & set timer for about 2.5 hours.
5. Finally serve warm.

For a eternal experience.

138. Best Almond Rice Pudding

My sister makes it every now & then.

Ingredients:

- 21/2 cups almond milk
- 1/2 cup roasted almond
- 1/2 cup water
- About 1 teaspoon cinnamon
- 2 tablespoons honey
- About 1.5 teaspoon orange zest
- 1 cup condensed milk
- 1/2 cup Arborio rice

Directions:

1. First of all, please make sure you've all the ingredients available. Place Arborio rice in a pressure cooker pot then pour almond milk & water in it.
2. Then add cinnamon and orange zest into the Arborio rice and stir well.
3. This step is important. Cover the pressure cooker and seal properly then cook on high-pressure for about 15 to 20 minutes.
4. Once it is done, naturally release the pressure cooker & open the lid.
5. Now pour condensed milk over the rice then mix until combined.
6. One thing remains to be done. Transfer the cooked Arborio rice to a serving dish & let it cool for a few minutes.
7. Finally drizzle honey over the rice then sprinkle roasted almonds on top. Serve and enjoy.

Ready in about 20 to 25 minutes

Servings 2

Mushroom fries bring back a lot of memories.

139. Nostalgic Salted Caramel Cheesecake

Some things never fail you.

Ingredients:

Crust:

- 1 1/2 cup crushed ritz
- About 2.5 tbsp sugar

- 4 tbsp butter (Melted)

Cake:

- 1 1/2 tsp vanilla
- 16 oz cream cheese
- About 1 tsp kosher salt
- 1 tbsp flour
- 1/2 cup brown sugar
- 1/4 cup sour cream
- 2 eggs

Top:

- About 1.5 tsp sea salt
- 1/2 cup caramel sauce

Directions:

1. First of all, please make sure you've all the ingredients available. Spray 7-inch springform with nonstick spray.
2. Now line the bottom with parchment and spray again.
3. Combine sugar, butter, and ritz. Press into pan.
4. With a mixer, beat sugar & cream cheese until smooth.
5. This step is important. Add sour cream and beat, & then beat in salt, vanilla, and flour.
6. Then scrap sides when needed. Lastly beat in eggs.
7. Pour into prepared pan.
8. Put 2 cups water in pot and place in trivet.
9. Wrap the bottom of pan with foil, & make a foil sling and place around pan. Place in the cooker.
10. Now cover and seal with lid. Set to high for about 35 to 40 minutes.

11. One thing remains to be done. Once finished, release pressure naturally, & remove cake from pot and place on wire rack.
12. Finally cool then refrigerate 3 to 4 hours. Once ready to serve, top with caramel and sea salt.

The hit list recipe.

140. Mighty sweet Cardamom applesauce

Right on track.

Ingredients:

- 1 teaspoon ground cardamom
- About 1/2 teaspoon vanilla extract
- 1 tablespoon brown sugar
- 3 tablespoon water
- About 1/2 teaspoon salt
- 4 red apples

Directions:

1. First of all, please make sure you've all the ingredients available. Wash the apples carefully & peel them.
2. Now after this, cut the apples into the halves & remove the seeds.

3. Sprinkle the apples with the ground cardamom & brown sugar.
4. This step is important. Put the apples in the instant pot and add water.
5. Then close the lid and cook the dish for about 10 to 15 minutes at the pressure mode.
6. When the time is over – transfer the cooked apples to the blender.
7. Now add vanilla extract & salt.
8. Blend the mixture well till it is smooth.
9. One thing remains to be done. When the applesauce is cooked – chill it very well.
10. Finally serve the applesauce immediately or keep it in the fridge, not more than 5 days.

Prep time: 10 to 15 minutes

Cooking time: 10 to 15 minutes

Servings: 2

Magical…

Nutritional information:

Fat 0.9

Protein 1

Fiber 10

Carbs 65.27

Calories 274

141.   King sized Lemon Crème Brulée

As the name suggests….

Ingredients:

- 6 tablespoons granulated sugar
- About 1.5 teaspoon lemon juice
- 1 cup heavy cream
- 4 egg yolks

Directions:

1. First of all, please make sure you've all the ingredients available. Pour water into the pressure cooker then place a trivet in it.
2. Then place egg yolks, 3 tablespoons granulated sugar, heavy cream, & lemon juice in a bowl. Whisk until incorporated.
3. This step is important. Strain the mixture then divide into 3 custard cups.
4. Now cover the cup with aluminum foil then arrange on the trivet.
5. Close and seal the pressure cooker then cook properly on high pressure for about 5 to 10 minutes.
6. Then naturally, release the pressure cooker then open the lid.
7. One thing remains to be done. Remove the cups into a serving tray.
8. Finally sprinkle the remaining sugar on the top then serve & enjoy.

Ready in about 25 to 30 minutes

Servings 2

Light taste.

142.   Crazy Sweet Caramel Flan

Legendary taste.

Ingredients:

Caramel:

- 4 tablespoons granulated sugar
- 1 tablespoon water

Custard:

- 1 egg yolk
- 3 teaspoons maple syrup
- About 2.5 tablespoons granulated sugar
- 3/4 cup fresh milk
- 1/2 teaspoon vanilla extract
- About 3.5 tablespoons whipped cream
- 1 egg

Directions:

1. First of all, please make sure you've all the ingredients available. Pour water into a pressure cooker then place a trivet inside. Set aside.
2. Then place the caramel ingredients in a saucepan over very low heat. Bring to boil.
3. Swirl the saucepan gently then once the sugar is caramelized, pour into 2 custard cups. Set aside.
4. This step is important. Combine egg and egg yolk in a bowl then add 2 tablespoons granulated sugar.
5. Now whisk until smooth & fluffy. Pour fresh milk into a pan then bring to boil.
6. Once it is boiled, pour the hot milk into the egg mixture then whisk slowly until incorporated.
7. Stir in vanilla extract, whipped cream, & maple syrup. Stir well and strain the mixture.
8. Then pour the mixture into the custard cups with caramel then cover each cup with aluminum foil.
9. Arrange the cups on the trivet then close the pressure cooker with its lid and seal properly.
10. Now select the menu to high pressure & set time to about 5 to 10 minutes.
11. Once it is done, naturally release the pressure cooker then remove the lid.
12. Then take the cups out from the pressure cooker then let them cool.
13. One thing remains to be done. Chill the cups for at least 4 hours or overnight. Run a sharp knife around the cups & flip the flan on a serving dish.
14. Finally garnish with whipped cream then serve.

Ready in about 25 to 30 minutes

Serving 2

Oh yeah. This is the recipe I was waiting for.

Grains

143. Excellent Gluten Free Mixed-Grain Blend

Show time!!

Ingredients:

- 1/2 cup Mekong Flower or Brown Volcano Rice
- About 2.5 tablespoons teff or amaranth
- 1/4 Cup Red or Pink Rice
- 2 Cups Water or Veggie Stock
- 1/3 Cup Millet

Directions:

1. First of all, please make sure you've all the ingredients available. Mix up all the grains in your Instant Pot.
2. Then stir in the water/stock.
3. Secure the lid. Select 'Manual' & cook properly for about 10 to 15 minutes on high pressure.
4. One thing remains to be done. Now once cooked, let the pressure release naturally.
5. Finally remove the lid & stir the mixture. Season as you like.

Preparation Time: 5 to 10 minutes

Pressure Time: 15 to 20 minutes

Servings: 2

Wow, just wow!!

144. Astonishing Farro Salad with Arugula

Be amazed ?

Ingredients:

- 3 garlic cloves (Minced)
- Salt and freshly ground black pepper, to taste
- About 2.5 tablespoons chopped sun-dried tomatoes, finely chopped
- 3/4 cup arugula (Chopped)
- 1/2 tablespoon Italian Seasoning
- 1 cup chopped tomatoes (ripe)
- 3/4 cup whole farro (not pearled), soaked overnight and drained
- 1 cup vegetable stock
- 1 1/2 tablespoons vinegar
- About 2.5 tablespoons freshly chopped parsley
- 1 medium onion (Chopped)

Directions:

1. First of all, please make sure you've all the ingredients available. Set your IP to Sauté. Add the chopped onion and half the minced garlic.
2. Now sauté for about 2 to 5 minutes or until fragrant.
3. Add the chopped sundried tomatoes, Italian seasoning, farro, and the veggie stock.
4. This step is important. Secure the lid. Select Manual and cook properly for

about 15 to 20 minutes on High pressure.

5. Then let the pressure release naturally.
6. Remove the lid and transfer the content to a large bowl.
7. Add the remaining garlic & vinegar and stir gently.
8. Allow to cool.
9. Now once cooled, add the tomatoes, freshly chopped parsley, & arugula.
10. One thing remains to be done. Season with salt & pepper.
11. Finally serve the salad on top of a bed of arugula.

Preparation Time: 5 to 10 minutes

Pressure Time: 15 to 20 minutes

Servings: 2

For those who are not ordinary, try this one

145. Delightful Pancetta with Tomato Lentil Combo

Uber fantastic!!

Ingredients:

- 1/2 cup pancetta, chopped into small pieces
- About 1.5 medium onion (Chopped)
- 2 cups tap water or chicken broth
- 1 medium carrot (Chopped)
- 2 celery stalks, thinly sliced
- 1/2 cup dried green lentils
- 1 teaspoon Kosher salt
- About 1 teaspoons freshly ground black pepper
- 2 medium tomatoes (Chopped)
- 2 tablespoons extra virgin olive oil

Directions:

1. First of all, please make sure you've all the ingredients available. Select Sauté and preheat the Instant Pot.
2. Now once hot, pour oil, add pancetta & coat in oil.
3. Add onion and stir.
4. This step is important. Season with pepper and salt.
5. Toss in tomatoes, water (or broth), lentils, mix & secure the lid.
6. Then set to 'Manual' and cook properly on HIGH for about 15 to 20 minutes.
7. Let pressure release naturally (5 to 10 minutes).
8. One thing remains to be done. Drain beans, discard bay leaves, check seasonings & serve hot.
9. Finally if lentils are not cooked, then cook properly for about 5 to 10 more minutes and serve hot.

Preparation Time: 15 to 20 minutes

Pressure Time: 15 to 20 minutes

Servings: 2

Cooking level infinite….

146. Fantastic Ginger Barley Salad

Long way to go...

Ingredients:

- 1/2 cup broccoli florets (Sliced)
- About 1.5 tablespoons sesame seeds (Toasted)
- 2 cups vegetable stock or water
- 1/2 cup sliced scallions
- 3/4 cups whole (or hulled) barley, soaked overnight and drained
- 1 1/2 tablespoons tamari or soy sauce
- 1/2 cup English cucumber (unpeeled), diced
- 1/2 tablespoon or balsamic vinegar
- 1/2 cup carrot, finely diced
- About 1.5 teaspoon toasted sesame oil
- 1/2 tablespoon freshly grated ginger
- 2 large garlic cloves (Minced)
- 3/4 cup mixed green and yellow beans, cut into 1-inch pieces

Directions:

1. First of all, please make sure you've all the ingredients available. Mix the beans & broccoli in your IP. Pour 1/3 cup water/stock.
2. Now secure the lid. Select Manual and cook properly for about 2 minutes under high pressure.
3. Quick release the pressure & remove the lid.
4. Transfer the cooked veggies to a large bowl. Set aside.
5. This step is important. Drain the liquid from your Instant Pot.
6. Then add the barley & remaining cups of water/stock. Secure the lid.
7. Select Manual and cook properly for about 15 to 20 minutes on High Pressure.
8. Meanwhile, combine the soy/tamari sauce, sesame oil, vinegar, garlic, & ginger in a small mixing bowl.
9. Now mix well & set aside.
10. Once the IP is done cooking, let the pressure release naturally.
11. Then remove the lid and allow to cool for about 5 to 10 minutes.
12. One thing remains to be done. Transfer the barley to the bowl with the cooked beans & broccoli.
13. Finally add the carrot, cucumber, chopped scallions & the dressing. Stir well to combine. Serve.

Preparation Time: 5 to 10 minutes

Pressure Time: 1 minute + 15 to 20 minutes

Servings: 2

Deserved!!

International

147. Great Korean Beef

Be super

Ingredients:

- About 1.5 Small Apple, Chopped And Peeled
- 1 Lb Bottom Roast, Cubed
- 1/4 Cup Beef Broth
- Salt
- 1/2 Tsp Grated Ginger
- Pepper
- About 1.5 Tsp Olive Oil
- 2 Garlic Cloves (Minced)
- 3 Tbsp Soy Sauce
- 1 Small Orange, Juiced

Directions:

1. First of all, please make sure you've all the ingredients available. Season roast with pepper and salt.
2. Then heat pot to sauté. Coat with oil & brown meat in batches.
3. Deglaze pot with broth, scrap up browned bits.
4. This step is important. Mix in soy sauce. Return meat to pot & add ginger, apple, and garlic and stir.
5. Now mix in orange juice.
6. Cover and seal lid.
7. Then set to normal pressure for about 45 to 50 minutes.
8. One thing remains to be done. When finished, release pressure & shred meat.
9. Finally serve with rice.

The speed matters…

148.   Happy Pork Carnitas

Mystery is unveiled!!

Ingredients:

- 1 Bay Leaf
- 1/2 Pound Pork Shoulder
- 1 Chipotle Pepper
- Salt
- 1/4 Cup Chicken Broth
- Pepper
- About 1/4 Tsp Oregano
- 1/4 Tsp Sazon
- 1 Sliced Garlic Clove
- 1/8 Tsp Dry Adobo
- About 1/2 Tsp Cumin
- 1/4 Tsp Garlic Powder

Directions:

1. First of all, please make sure you've all the ingredients available. Sprinkle salt and pepper over pork.
2. Now set instant pot to sauté & brown pork. Remove from pot and cool.
3. Cut pockets in pork to insert slices of garlic.
4. This step is important. Season with garlic powder, oregano, cumin, adobo, and sazon.
5. Then put broth, chipotle, & bay leaf in pot and mix.
6. Place pork in pot, cover and seal. Set to high pressure for about 50 to 55 minutes.
7. One thing remains to be done. Once done and pressure has released, shred with fork.

8. Finally remove bay leaf, & mix meat back in juices. Adjust seasonings as needed.

Being lucky is definitely better.

149. Lucky Chicken Marsala

If you're a legend, then make this one.

Ingredients:

- 3/4 Cup Chicken Stock
- 2 8-Oz Chicken Breasts
- 1/3 Cup Marsala
- About 1 Tsp Salt
- 1.5 Tbsp All Purpose Flour
- 1 Tsp Minced Garlic
- 6 Oz Mushrooms – Button Or Shiitake, Clean, Sliced, And Stemmed
- About 1/4 Tsp Pepper
- Sprig Thyme
- 1/2 Cup Sliced Onion
- Cooked Pasta
- 2 Tbsp Butter

Directions:

1. First of all, please make sure you've all the ingredients available. Coat chicken with pepper and salt.
2. Now set to sauté and add 1 1/2 tsp butter.
3. Brown chicken in melted butter, 5 to 10 minutes each side. Set chicken aside.
4. This step is important. Add remaining butter. Once heated add thyme & onion. Cook until soft.
5. Then add the mushrooms; cook properly for about 5 to 10 minutes until well browned.
6. Mix in garlic, pepper and salt. Mix in flour; cook 2 to 5 minutes.
7. Pour in marsala & simmer 2 to 5 minutes. Pour in chicken stock. Place the chicken back in the pot.
8. Now lock and seal lid. Cook properly on low for about 2 to 5 minutes.
9. Boil a pot of water and cook the pasta properly according to the directions.
10. One thing remains to be done. Release the pressure from the pot. Place chicken on a plate. Remove thyme.
11. Finally set to sauté & let the sauce reduce. Pour over the chicken and pasta.

Something is special!!

150. Vintage Moroccan Chicken

Be unique, be extraordinary…

Ingredients:

- 2 tsp molasses
- 1 lb chicken drumsticks
- 1/4 cup honey
- 1/2 cup broth
- About 1 tsp pepper
- 1 tsp paprika
- 1 tsp salt
- 1/4 tsp saffron threads
- 1/4 tsp ground coriander
- 1 tsp cumin
- About 1.5 tsp garlic powder
- 1/2 tsp cinnamon

- 1 medium lemon, juice & zest
- 1/2 tsp ginger

Directions:

1. First of all, please make sure you've all the ingredients available. Mix the dry seasonings and rub into chicken.
2. Then set cooker to sauté. Once hot, grease with butter.
3. Brown the chicken on all sides.
4. Pour in broth. Turn off pot, cover & seal, then set to high for about 10 to 15 minutes.
5. This step is important. When finished, turn off & quick release pressure.
6. Now don't use natural, it will dry the chicken out.
7. Remove chicken, & tent with foil. Turn pot to sauté.
8. Then mix lemon zest, molasses, juice, & honey together and pour in the pot.
9. One thing remains to be done. Bring to boil, stirring occasionally until liquid has reduced.
10. Finally coat chicken with sauce, & enjoy.

Stupidly simple…

151. Best Salsa Verde Chicken
Oh yeah!!

Ingredients:

- About 1 tsp salt
- 1 lb boneless chicken breast
- About 1 tsp paprika
- 1/2 tsp cumin
- 8 oz salsa verde

Directions:

1. First of all, please make sure you've all the ingredients available. Put everything in cooker.
2. Then set to high for about 25 to 30 minutes.
3. Finally once finished, quick release pressure & shred chicken.

Good luck!!

Meat

152. Mighty Creamy Chicken and Mushroom Potpie
Baking does the trick!!

Ingredients:

- 2 carrots, peeled, cut into 1 inch pieces
- About 1.5 tablespoon cream
- 3/4 pound chicken thighs, skinless, boneless
- 1 small onion (Chopped)
- 3 tablespoons all-purpose flour
- Pepper powder to taste
- 1 sheet puff pastry, thawed
- 1/2 cup frozen green beans
- 1/2 cups frozen green peas

- Salt to taste
- 1 bay leaves
- About 1/2 teaspoon dried thyme
- 4 ounces cremini mushrooms, stems trimmed, halved if the mushrooms are large
- 1/4 cup water

Directions:

1. First of all, please make sure you've all the ingredients available. Add onions, onion, mushrooms, carrots, all-purpose flour, thyme, bay leaves & water to the instant pot. Stir well.
2. Then lay the chicken thighs over the vegetable mixture.
3. Sprinkle salt and pepper over the chicken as well as over the vegetables.
4. Close the lid. Press 'Slow cook' & timer for 3 1/2 hours.
5. This step is important. When done, switch off the instant pot & keep it covered.
6. Now meanwhile, cut the pastry sheet into 2 circles.
7. Place the circles on a baking sheet and bake in a preheated oven at 410 to 420 degree F for about 5 to 10 minutes.
8. Just before serving, add green beans, peas, cream & salt to the instant pot.
9. Then cover and heat the contents thoroughly.
10. One thing remains to be done. Divide & serve chicken along with vegetables in 2 serving bowls.
11. Finally place a baked pastry round over each bowl & serve.

I don't know about you, but I include this one everytime I get a chance.

153.   Nostalgic Creamy Butter Chicken

I repeat… Try it if you want to. No regrets. Right!!

Ingredients:

- 1 medium onion (Chopped)
- About 4.5 tablespoons lemon juice
- 3 garlic cloves (Grated)
- One inch fresh ginger, finely chopped
- 1 1/2 teaspoons cumin powder
- Ground black pepper
- 1 teaspoon paprika
- 1/2 teaspoon of ground turmeric
- About 1/2 teaspoon cayenne
- Kosher salt
- 1 heaped tablespoon sugar
- One can (14 1/2 oz.) chopped tomatoes with juice
- 4 large chicken breasts, skinless
- 2 tablespoons butter
- 3/4 cup chicken broth

Directions:

1. First of all, please make sure you've all the ingredients available. Select Saute and preheat the pot. Add butter.
2. Now once hot, add in ginger, onions, garlic and cook until fragrant.

3. Hit Cancel and add cumin, cayenne, turmeric and paprika.
4. Mix well. Add tomatoes along with the juice, sugar, broth and chicken.
5. This step is important. Stir well. Secure the lid.
6. Then select Manual and cook properly on HIGH for about 5 to 10 minutes.
7. Once done, release the pressure.
8. Remove the chicken and shred with forks. Set aside.
9. Select Sauté and let simmer for about 5 to 10 minutes & cook properly until water is reduced.
10. One thing remains to be done. Keep simmering, pour cream & then add shredded chicken.
11. Finally check seasonings & serve hot.

Preparation Time: 15 to 20 minutes

Pressure Time: 10 to 15 minutes

Servings: 2

Why not??

154. Best Steaks with Garlic Cream Sauce

Leave a mark!!

Ingredients:

- 2 steaks, room temperature
- 3/4 cup heavy cream
- Salt and pepper, to taste
- 1/4 cup dry white wine
- 4 garlic cloves, finely chopped
- About 1 tsp fresh oregano, finely chopped
- Olive oil

Directions:

1. First of all, please make sure you've all the ingredients available. Press the SAUTE button on your Instant Pot & adjust the temperature to HIGH, drizzle some olive oil into the pot.
2. Now once the oil is very hot, carefully place the steaks into the pot & cook according to your preference (medium, rare, well done), turn the steak & cook properly the other side.
3. Remove the steaks from the pot & leave on a board to rest, and sprinkle the steaks with salt & pepper at this stage.
4. This step is important. Don't wash the Instant Pot before you make the sauce, the leftover steak juices will add lovely flavor to the sauce.
5. Then keep the Instant Pot on the SAUTE function, but adjust the temperature to NORMAL.
6. Add the garlic, herbs, & wine to the pot, sauté until the wine has reduced & the smell of alcohol has disappeared.
7. Now add the salt, cream, and pepper to the pot & stir to combine.
8. One thing remains to be done. Simmer the sauce for about 5 to 10 minutes until thick & creamy.

9. Finally serve the steak with a generous helping of creamy garlic sauce spooned over the top.

Spice up!!

155. Vintage Lamb Skewers with Pita Bread and Eggplant Dip

What do you think? ?

Ingredients:

- 2 lamb steaks, cut into cubes
- 2 pita breads (store bought is fine)
- Salt and pepper
- About 1 tsp ground cumin
- 1/2 tsp chili powder
- 1/2 cup plain Greek yogurt
- 3 garlic cloves, finely chopped
- About 1.5 large eggplant, cut into chunks
- Olive oil

Directions:

1. First of all, please make sure you've all the ingredients available. Press the SAUTE button on your Instant Pot & adjust the temperature to HIGH, drizzle some olive oil into the pot.
2. Now coat the lamb with salt, cumin, pepper, and chili powder.
3. This step is important. Once the oil is very hot, add the lamb cubes & sauté for about 5 to 10 minutes, turning a few times so the lamb cubes are golden & brown on all sides.
4. Take the lamb cubes out of the pot & leave aside, don't wash the pot (the lamb juices & leftover spices will flavor the eggplant!).
5. Then keep the Instant Pot on the sauté function, adjust the temperature to NORMAL.
6. Drizzle some more olive oil into the Instant Pot and add the garlic, cook properly for about 20 to 30 seconds until the garlic is soft.
7. Now add the eggplant and keep stirring as the eggplant sautés and becomes soft and mushy.
8. One thing remains to be done. Remove the eggplant and place into a small bowl, add the salt, yogurt, and pepper, stir to combine.
9. Finally toast the pita breads & fill with eggplant filling, lamb cubes, & any other fillings you desire (baby spinach is a great match!).

What makes this the best? Check it out for yourself!!

156. Lucky Caesar Chicken

Just got better!!

Ingredients:

- 1/4 cup parmesan cheese (Shredded)
- About 2.5 chicken breasts, boneless, skinless
- 5 ounces Caesar dressing

Directions:

1. First of all, please make sure you've all the ingredients available. Add chicken into the instant pot.
2. Now close the lid. Press 'Slow cook' button & set timer for 2 to 3 hours or until done.
3. Drain the liquid in the pot.
4. Then pour dressing on top of the chicken.
5. One thing remains to be done. Sprinkle cheese over it.
6. Finally cover and cook properly for about 30 to 35 minutes more.

Got the idea!!

157. Happy Instant Pot Chicken Pie

Relax and enjoy this recipe!!

Ingredients:

- About 2.5 tablespoons extra virgin olive oil
- Black pepper powder
- 1 medium onion (Chopped)
- 1 medium carrot chopped, skin peeled
- 3/4 cup frozen peas
- 3 small celery stalks/ 2 medium stalks, sliced thin
- 1 large potato/ 3 small potatoes, peeled and cubed
- 4 small chicken breasts with bone and skin
- 3/4 cup milk
- 2 cups chicken broth
- About 1.5 teaspoons Kosher salt
- 3 tablespoons all-purpose flour
- 3 tablespoons butter
- 1 puff pastry frozen sheet

Directions:

1. First of all, please make sure you've all the ingredients available. Preheat oven to about 390 to 400F. Meanwhile, let the pastry sheet thaw.
2. Now sauté onions in the Instant pot with a little oil for about 2 to 5 minutes.
3. Then add chopped celery, chicken, carrots, potatoes, salt and broth.
4. Secure the lid.
5. This step is important. Set to 'Manual' and cook properly on High for about 5 to 10 minutes.
6. Then once pastry sheet is pliable, lay out on a flat surface & cut into 4 rectangles and bake for about 10 to 15 minutes.
7. Release pressure quickly once chicken is done.
8. Take out chicken, & debone once you can handle with your hands.
9. Now shred chicken into smaller pieces.
10. Put pot on Sauté. Mix butter and flour to form a paste.
11. Pourto the simmering pot of chicken broth.
12. Then pour milk and peas also & mix well.
13. One thing remains to be done. Stir slowly until the paste is mixed well & broth thickens.
14. Finally check seasonings & serve in individual bowls. Serve with baked pastry.

Preparation Time: 20 to 25 minutes

Pressure Time: 5 to 10 minutes

Servings: 2

Try this one if you're hungry!!

158.   Great Mini Pork Roast

Make me remember the good old days!!

Ingredients:

- 1 cup (8fl oz) stock (veggie or chicken)
- Olive oil
- About 1.5 apple, cut into 5 pieces
- Small pork loin (approximately 1 lb), sprinkled with salt and pepper
- 1/2 cup (4fl oz) apple juice

Directions:

1. First of all, please make sure you've all the ingredients available. Pour the apple juice & stock into the Instant Pot.
2. Now place the apple chunks & pork loin into the pot (it will sit in the liquid).
3. Secure the lid onto the pot and press the MEAT/STEW button, adjust the time to about 20 to 25 minutes.
4. This step is important. Once the pot beeps, quick-release the pressure & remove the lid.

5. Then place the pork loin onto a board to rest as you heat a skillet or fry pan with a drizzle of oil.
6. Once the fry pan is very hot, place the cooked pork loin into the pan & fry on all sides for a minute or so, or until crispy & golden.
7. Now you can utilize the leftover liquid in the Instant Pot by pressing the SAUTE button & simmering the liquid until reduced (on NORMAL heat).
8. One thing remains to be done. Serve with your favorite vegetables & a drizzle of reduced liquid.
9. Finally any leftover meat will make an amazing sandwich!

Time: approximately 40 to 45 minutes

Luxury in its own class!!

159.   Fantastic Lamb Steaks with Feta and Potatoes

Healthy is a new trend these days!! ?
Always I guess...

Ingredients:

- Salt and pepper, to taste
- 5 oz feta cheese, crumbled
- Olive oil
- About 2.5 lamb steaks
- 3 garlic cloves (Sliced)
- About 1 tsp dried mixed herbs

- 2 medium-large potatoes, skin on, cut into cubes

Directions:

1. First of all, please make sure you've all the ingredients available. Pour 2 cups of water into the Instant Pot & place the steaming basket into the pot.
2. Then place the potato cubes into the steaming basket & sprinkle with salt.
3. Secure the lid onto the pot & press the STEAM button, adjust the time to about 2 to 5 minutes.
4. This step is important. Once the pot beeps, quick-release the pressure & remove the lid.
5. Take the basket of potatoes out of the pot & set aside, discard any leftover water from the pot.
6. Now drizzle some olive oil into the Instant Pot & press the SAUTE button, adjust the temperature to HIGH.
7. Sprinkle the lamb with pepper, salt, and herbs, and once the oil is hot, add the steaks to the pot & cook properly for about 2 minutes each side, (or more if you prefer more well-done meat).
8. Then remove the lamb steaks from the pot & place on a board to rest. Don't wash the pot, just leave it as it is.
9. Place the garlic into the pot & adjust the temperature to NORMAL (the pot should still be on the SAUTE function), sauté the garlic for about 30 to 40 seconds.
10. One thing remains to be done. Add the steamed potatoes to the pot and stir to coat in oil and garlic, sauté for about 5 to 10 minutes until crispy & golden, don't worry if they get a bit mushy, that's part of the charm!
11. Finally before serving, stir the feta cheese into the potatoes.

Stunner!!

160.   Delightful Thai Lime Chicken

Super awesome plus unique!!

Ingredients:

- 1/4 cup fish sauce
- Fresh mint and cilantro (Chopped)
- 1/2 cup lime juice
- About 1.5 tablespoon coconut nectar
- 2 tablespoons olive oil
- About 1 teaspoon ginger (Grated)
- 1 pound chicken thigh, skinless, boneless

Directions:

1. First of all, please make sure you've all the ingredients available. Now add all the ingredients to the instant pot & stir until well combined.
2. One thing remains to be done. Then close the lid. Press 'Poultry' button & set timer for about 10 to 15 minutes.
3. Finally when the timer goes off, let the pressure release naturally.

Iconic recipe of my list!!

161. Super Mushrooms with Duck and Sweet Onions

Well it is a Grandma's recipe!!

Ingredients:

- 4 small duck legs
- 1 cups chicken broth
- Kosher salt
- About 1 teaspoon black pepper powder
- 1/2 cup dry red wine
- 1 cup pearl onions (Chopped)
- About 2.5 tablespoons canola oil
- 2 cups assorted mushrooms (Sliced)

Directions:

1. First of all, please make sure you've all the ingredients available. Select Saute & preheat your Instant Pot.
2. Now pour oil. Rub salt & pepper onto the duck legs.
3. Transfer to the pot with skin facing down.
4. Saute until crispy brown.
5. This step is important. Cancel the heat. Remove the sautéed duck.
6. Then remove the extra oil into a bowl reserving about 3 tablespoons of the fat in the pot.
7. Toss in onions and sauté until soft & lightly caramelized.
8. Add garlic & mushrooms. Pour wine.
9. Now stir gently while scrapping the bits from the bottom of the pot.
10. Remove the sautéed mushrooms.
11. Replace the sautéed duck. Add broth and secure the lid.
12. One thing remains to be done. Select Manual and cook properly on HIGH for about 25 to 30 minutes.
13. Finally once done, release pressure quickly. Serve with the mushrooms & gravy.

Preparation Time: 15 to 20 minutes

Pressure Time: 20 to 25 minutes

Servings: 2

Happiness has finally arrived!!

162. Awesome Cold Beef Noodle Salad

Whenever you want a great recipe!!

Ingredients:

- Olive oil
- About 2.5 tsp fish sauce (if you have it, you can use soy sauce as a substitute)
- 1 large sirloin steak (about 1 lb)
- Salt and pepper, to taste
- 1 tsp sesame oil (if you have it)
- 1 scallion, finely chopped
- Handful of fresh coriander, finely chopped
- About 1.5 tsp brown sugar
- 1 fresh red chili, finely chopped (seeds removed if you don't want too much spice)
- 1 fresh lime

- 10 oz dried rice noodles (flat or vermicelli, any kind works)

Directions:

1. First of all, please make sure you've all the ingredients available. Bring a pot of water to the boil and add the rice noodles, cook properly until soft (or follow the packet instructions if they need alternate cooking methods, some are pre-cooked and just need to be soaked in hot water), run cold water over the noodles until they are cold, then leave aside.
2. Then press the SAUTE button on your Instant Pot & adjust the temperature to HIGH, drizzle some olive oil into the pot.
3. This step is important. Once the oil is hot, add the steak to the pot & cook properly for about 2 to 5 minutes on both sides, or longer if you want your steak well done.
4. Now remove the steak from the pot & place on a board to rest, sprinkle with salt and pepper.
5. In a large salad bowl, add the scallions, chili, coriander, juice of one lime, sesame oil, brown sugar, and fish or soy sauce, stir to combine.
6. One thing remains to be done. Add the cooked noodles & toss to coat in the dressing.
7. Finally slice the steak into thin strips & scatter over the noodle salad before serving.

Time: approximately 20 to 25 minutes

How is it? Only one way to find out…

163.   Iconic Bow Tie Pasta

I can eat them all day!!

Ingredients:

- 1 3/4 cups water
- About 1/2 teaspoon pepper or to taste
- 1/2 pounds lean ground chicken sausage
- 1/4 teaspoon salt or to taste
- 1 1/2 teaspoons olive oil
- 1 clove garlic (Crushed)
- About 1 teaspoons dried basil
- 1 small onion (Chopped)
- 14 ounces canned crushed tomatoes
- 1/8 teaspoon red pepper flakes
- 8 ounces bow tie pasta

Directions:

1. First of all, please make sure you've all the ingredients available. Press 'Sauté' button. Press 'Adjust' button once.
2. Then add oil and heat. Add meat, onion & garlic and cook properly until brown.
3. Add rest of the ingredients and stir. Press 'Cancel' button.
4. Now close the lid. Press 'Manual' button & set timer for about 5 to 10 minutes.
5. One thing remains to be done. Season with salt & pepper.
6. Finally stir & serve.

Different take on this one…

164. Ultimate Crispy Wings

Grandfather of Recipes!!

Ingredients:

- 1 1/4 cups of water
- Cooking oil (for frying)
- Kosher salt
- 2 cups any sauce for wings
- About 1.5 pound chicken wings

Directions:

1. First of all, please make sure you've all the ingredients available. Preheat Pot. Coat the wings with salt & place on the pot.
2. Now add water and secure the lid.
3. This step is important. Cook properly on Manual for about 10 to 15 minutes on HIGH pressure.
4. Once done, let the pressure release naturally. Set aside.
5. Select broil the on oven & preheat.
6. Then dip each wing in the sauce of your preference.
7. One thing remains to be done. Arrange them neatly on a greased baking sheet & broil in oven for about 5 to 10 minutes on each side until crispy on the outside.
8. Finally (Alternatively, you can heat oil in a pot, & once hot, fry wings in batches and then toss in sauce and serve.)

Preparation Time: 10 to 15 minutes

Pressure Time: 15 to 20 minutes

Servings: 2

I am actually popular among my friends for eating this one a lot.

One pot grains

165. Unique Gluten Free Mixed-Grain Blend

So, what's your opinion?

Ingredients:

- 1/2 cup Mekong Flower or Brown Volcano Rice
- About 2.5 tablespoons teff or amaranth
- 1/4 Cup Red or Pink Rice
- 2 Cups Water or Veggie Stock
- About 1/4 Cup Millet

Directions:

1. First of all, please make sure you've all the ingredients available. Mix up all the grains in your Instant Pot. Stir in the water/stock.
2. Then secure the lid. Select 'Manual' & cook properly for about 15 to 20 minutes on high pressure.
3. Once cooked, let the pressure release naturally.
4. One thing remains to be done. Now remove the lid & stir the mixture.

5.   Finally season as you like.

Preparation Time: 5 to 10 minutes

Pressure Time: 10 to 15 minutes

Servings: 2

Yeah, you can make it in your free time…

166.   Yummy Minty Kamut Salad

Deserved!!

Ingredients:

- About 1 teaspoon salt
- 1 cup Kamut, soaked overnight and drained
- 7 oz. (200 gm) cherry tomatoes, halved
- 2 cups veggie stock
- 2 pitted dates, soaked in 1/4 cup hot water
- 1/2 cup freshly chopped mint
- 1 cup summer squash, sliced into 1/4 inch pieces
- 1/4 cup freshly chopped cilantro
- 1 jalapeño chili, de-stemmed
- 1 hot chili (cayenne / serrano), de-stemmed
- About 1.5 tablespoon garlic (Minced)
- 4 tablespoons lemon juice
- 2 scallions (Chopped)
- 1 bay leaf
- 1/2 tablespoon grated lemon zest
- 1 tablespoon garlic (Chopped)

Directions:

1.   First of all, please make sure you've all the ingredients available. Set your IP to 'Saute'. Add 1/2 tablespoon of chopped garlic, and dry saute for about 20 to 25 seconds or until soft (not browned).

2.   Then add the Kamut, veggie stock, and a bay leaf.

3.   Secure the lid. Select Manual and cook properly for about 15 to 20 minutes on high pressure.

4.   This step is important. Once cooked, let the pressure release naturally.

5.   Remove the lid and transfer the cooked grains to a bowl.

6.   Now remove the bay leaf. Set aside and allow to cool.

7.   To prep the dressing, combine 1/2 tablespoon of chopped garlic, pitted dates (along with the water), freshly chopped mint and cilantro, scallions, chilies, lemon juice and zest, and salt in a blender & blend until smooth.

8.   Then add the summer squash slices & halved cherry tomatoes into the Kamut mixture.

9.   One thing remains to be done. Pour in the dressing and mix gently without smashing the tomatoes.

10.   Finally taste & adjust the seasonings.

Preparation Time: 5 to 10 minutes

Pressure Time: 15 to 20 minutes

Servings: 2

Long way to go...

167. Tasty Farro Salad with Arugula

Cooking level infinite....

Ingredients:

- 3 garlic cloves (Minced)
- Salt and freshly ground black pepper, to taste
- About 2.5 tablespoons chopped sun-dried tomatoes, finely chopped
- 1/2 tablespoon Italian Seasoning
- 3/4 cup arugula (Chopped)
- 3/4 cup whole farro (not pearled), soaked overnight and drained
- 1 cup vegetable stock
- 1 cup chopped tomatoes (ripe)
- About 1.5 tablespoons vinegar
- 2 tablespoons freshly chopped parsley
- 1 medium onion (Chopped)

Directions:

1. First of all, please make sure you've all the ingredients available. Set your IP to Sauté. Add the chopped onion & half the minced garlic.
2. Now sauté for about 2 to 5 minutes or until fragrant.
3. Add the chopped sundried tomatoes, Italian seasoning, farro, & the veggie stock.
4. This step is important. Secure the lid. Select Manual & cook properly for about 15 to 20 minutes on High pressure.
5. Then let the pressure release naturally.
6. Remove the lid and transfer the content to a large bowl.
7. Add the remaining garlic and vinegar & stir gently. Allow to cool.
8. Now once cooled, add the freshly tomatoes, chopped parsley, and arugula.
9. One thing remains to be done. Season with salt and pepper.
10. Finally serve the salad on top of a bed of arugula.

Preparation Time: 5 to 10 minutes

Pressure Time: 10 to 15 minutes

Servings: 2

Uber fantastic!!

168. Titanic Barley, Wheat Berry, and Almond Salad

For those who are not ordinary, try this one.

Ingredients:

- 1/4 cup wheat berries
- 2 large garlic cloves (Minced)
- 13/4 cups water
- About 2.5 tablespoons lemon juice
- 4 tablespoons chopped toasted almonds or toasted hazelnuts
- 2 tablespoons olive oil
- 1/3 cup parsley, freshly chopped
- Salt and black pepper, to taste
- 2 celery stalks, finely chopped
- 3/4 cup pearled barley (not quick barley)
- About 1.5 medium carrot, finely chopped

Directions:

1. First of all, please make sure you've all the ingredients available. Mix the pearl barley, wheat berries and water in your IP.
2. Now secure the lid. Select Manual and cook properly for about 25 to 30 minutes on High Pressure.
3. Once done, let the pressure release naturally.
4. This step is important. Remove the lid and transfer the content to a large bowl.
5. Then allow to cool for about 10 to 15 minutes.
6. Meanwhile, combine the lemon juice, olive oil, salt and pepper in a medium mixing bowl.
7. Now mix well and set aside.
8. One thing remains to be done. Once the grains cool, add the dressing, parsley, carrot, almonds (or hazelnuts), celery & garlic.

9. Finally adjust the seasonings & serve.

Preparation Time: 5 to 10 minutes

Pressure Time: 20 to 25 minutes

Servings: 2

Be amazed ?

169.   Rich Ginger Barley Salad

Wow, just wow!!

Ingredients:

- 1/2 cup broccoli florets (Sliced)
- About 1.5 tablespoon sesame seeds, toasted
- 2 cups vegetable stock or water
- 3/4 cups whole (or hulled) barley, soaked overnight and drained
- 11/2 tablespoons tamari or soy sauce
- 1/2 cup sliced scallions
- 1/2 tablespoon or balsamic vinegar
- About 1.5 teaspoon toasted sesame oil
- 1/2 cup English cucumber (unpeeled), diced
- 1/2 tablespoon freshly grated ginger
- 2 large garlic cloves (Minced)
- 3/4 cup mixed green and yellow beans, cut into 1-inch pieces
- 1/2 cup carrot, finely diced

Directions:

1. First of all, please make sure you've all the ingredients available. Mix the beans and broccoli in your IP. Pour 1/3 cup water/stock.
2. Then secure the lid. Select Manual & cook properly for about 2 minutes under high pressure.
3. Quick release the pressure & remove the lid.
4. This step is important. Transfer the cooked veggies to a large bowl. Set aside.
5. Drain the liquid from your Instant Pot. Add the barley & remaining cups of water/stock. Secure the lid.
6. Now select Manual and cook properly for about 15 to 20 minutes on High Pressure.
7. Meanwhile, combine the vinegar, soy/tamari sauce, sesame oil, garlic, and ginger in a small mixing bowl.
8. Mix well and set aside.
9. Once the IP is done cooking, let the pressure release naturally.
10. Then remove the lid and allow to cool for about 5 to 10 minutes.
11. One thing remains to be done. Next, transfer the barley to the bowl with the cooked beans and broccoli.
12. Finally add the cucumber, carrot, chopped scallions & the dressing. Stir well to combine. Serve.

Preparation Time: 5 to 10 minutes

Pressure Time: 1 minute + 10 to 15 minutes

Servings: 2

Show time!!

170.   Elegant Veggie Quinoa Salad

Feast for you!!

Ingredients:

- 2 garlic cloves (Minced)
- Salt and black pepper powder, to taste
- About 2.5 tablespoons lime juice
- 3/4 cup quinoa, rinsed and drained
- 3/4 cup tomatoes, freshly diced
- 1 medium capsicum, cored, deseeded, & diced
- 3 tablespoons freshly chopped coriander
- 1 cup water/veggie stock
- About 2.5 scallions (Chopped)
- 8 oz. / 225 gm tomatillos (Mexican Husk Tomatoes), husks removed and rinsed

Directions:

1. First of all, please make sure you've all the ingredients available. Cut about half of the tomatillos into bite-sized pieces. Set aside.

2. Now combine the remaining tomatillos with garlic & lime juice and blend in a blender until smooth. Set aside.
3. Set your Instant Pot to Sauté.
4. This step is important. Add the quinoa and sauté for about 2 to 5 minutes.
5. Throw in the capsicum and dry sauté for a minute.
6. Then pour in the water/stock.
7. Secure the lid. Select Manual and cook properly for about 5 to 10 minutes on High Pressure.
8. Once cooked, let the pressure release naturally.
9. Remove the lid and check if the quinoa is thoroughly cooked.
10. Now fully cooked quinoa are translucent puffed up.
11. Transfer the quinoa to a large mixing bowl.
12. Mix in the bite-sized tomatillos, coriander, freshly cut scallions, & tomatoes.
13. One thing remains to be done. Top with the blended tomatillo mixture & mix well to combine.
14. Finally season with the desired amount of salt & pepper. Serve.

Preparation Time: 5 to 10 minutes

Pressure Time: 5 to 10 minutes

Servings: 2

Being super is a matter of recipe... ?

171.   Wonderful Quinoa Stuffed Squash

Being a legend.

Ingredients:

- 3 tablespoons raw sunflower seeds
- 4 small winter squash halves, cooked
- About 1 teaspoon cinnamon powder
- 2 tablespoons freshly chopped cilantro
- Dash of cardamom, coriander, and black pepper powder
- About 1.5 medium onion (Diced)
- Salt, to taste
- 1/4 cup dried cranberries
- 1 cup veggie stock
- 3/4 cup quinoa, rinsed and drained

Directions:

1. First of all, please make sure you've all the ingredients available. Set your Instant Pot to Sauté.
2. Then add the quinoa, & dry sauté for a minute.
3. Mix in the sunflower seeds, powdered spices & diced onion. Dry sauté for about 2 to 5 minutes.
4. This step is important. Next, add the cranberries and veggie stock.
5. Secure the lid. Select Manual and cook properly for about 5 to 10 minutes on High Pressure.
6. Now once cooked, let the pressure release naturally.

7. Remove the lid and allow to cool for about 2 to 5 minutes.
8. Transfer the contents to a medium mixing bowl.
9. Then season with salt and garnish with freshly chopped cilantro.
10. One thing remains to be done. Spoon this stuffing into the centers of the cooked squash halves.
11. Finally transfer to a baking sheet & bake at 340 to 350 F (180 C) for about 15 to 20 minutes, or until light crisp.

Preparation Time: 5 to 10 minutes

Pressure Time: 5 to 10 minutes

Servings: 2

When you're fantastic, this is best!!

172. Quick Tomato Freekeh with Brinjal

Being rich is a plus point ?

Ingredients:

- 2 large garlic cloves (Minced)
- About 3.5 tablespoons fresh parsley (Chopped)
- 1 medium capsicum (Chopped)
- 3/4 cup cracked freekeh
- Salt and pepper, to taste
- 1 small-medium brinjal (Diced)
- 1 cup veggie stock
- 1/2 cup tomatoes, freshly diced
- About 1.5 medium red onion (Diced)

Directions:

1. First of all, please make sure you've all the ingredients available. Select Saute and heat your Instant Pot.
2. Then add the chopped onion & dry sauté for about 2 to 5 minutes until fragrant.
3. Add garlic and capsicum and cook properly for about 2 more minutes.
4. This step is important. Next, add the freekeh, and brinjal. Pour in the veggie stock.
5. Now secure the lid, select Manual & cook properly for about 5 to 10 minutes on High Pressure.
6. Allow the pressure release naturally.
7. Then once done, remove the lid & throw in the diced tomatoes.
8. Cover the lid and allow to sit for a couple of minutes.
9. One thing remains to be done. Once done, remove the lid, season with salt & pepper.
10. Finally add the freshly chopped parsley & stir. Serve.

Preparation Time: 5 to 10 minutes

Pressure Time: 10 to 15 minutes

Servings: 2

Amazing cooking starts here…

Porridge, Rice & Potato

173. Awesome Oatmeal (VEG, S&F)

Don't forget this one...

Ingredients:

- 4 cups water
- 2 cups of steel cut oats
- Salt and butter to taste

Directions:

1. First of all, please make sure you've all the ingredients available. Add 2 cups of steel cut oats & 4 cups of water
2. Then cook properly on HIGH pressure for about 2 to 5 minutes
3. Then let it naturally release
4. One thing remains to be done. Now add salt & butter to taste.
5. Finally serve.

Sizzle your taste buds...

174. Legendary Steel-Cut Oats (VEG, S&F)

Legends are born in...

Ingredients:

- About 1.5 cup steel-cut oats
- Sugar
- Pinch of salt
- Milk
- 2 cups of water

Directions:

1. First of all, please make sure you've all the ingredients available. Pour 1 cup of water into the Instant Pot & lower in the trivet.
2. Now in a heatproof bowl, mix 2 cups of water, oats, and salt.
3. This step is important. Set on top of the trivet & lock the pressure cooker lid.
4. Select the MANUAL setting and cook properly on HIGH pressure for at least 5 to 10 minutes, but no more than 7.
5. Then heat a cup or so of milk (depending on how much you want) in the microwave.
6. One thing remains to be done. When the oats are done, scoop into individual serving bowls.
7. Finally pour milk on top & add sugar before serving.

Jaw dropping!!

175. Excellent Peach and Oats Crumble (VEG, S&F)

Speed defines it...

Ingredients:

- 1/2 cup peach juice
- About 2.5 tbsp butter (Melted)
- 1/4 cup bilberries

- 1 cup sour cream
- 1 peach (Sliced)
- 1 cup milk
- 1 pinch salt
- 1/4 cup brown sugar
- About 4.5 tbsp maple syrup
- 2 cups oats

Directions:

1. First of all, please make sure you've all the ingredients available. Combine oats, milk, peach juice, brown sugar, blueberries, maple syrup, sour cream, and salt in a bowl.
2. Now brush the pot of pressure cooker with butter.
3. Transfer oats mixture to the Instant Pot & cover with lid.
4. Cook properly on SLOW cook mode for about 35 to 40 minutes.
5. Then transfer to serving dish & place peach slices.
6. One thing remains to be done. Drizzle some maple syrup on top.
7. Finally serve & enjoy.

Mystery with this recipe or rather a chemistry with it.

176. Astonishing Cranberry with Oatmeal (VEG, S&F)

Awesomeness fully loaded…

Ingredients:

- 2 cups milk
- About 2.5 tbsp olive oil
- 1 egg, whisked
- 4 tbsp butter (Melted)

- 1 cup cranberry sauce
- 1/2 cup brown sugar
- 1 pinch salt
- About 2.5 tbsp honey
- 1/2 tsp ginger powder
- 2 cups oats

Directions:

1. First of all, please make sure you've all the ingredients available. Grease Instant Pot with olive oil.
2. Now combine oats, egg, honey, butter, cranberry sauce, brown sugar, milk, ginger powder, & salt in a bowl.
3. Transfer to greased Instant Pot & cover with lid.
4. One thing remains to be done. Then leave to cook properly on slow cook mode for about 40 to 45 minutes.
5. Finally serve & enjoy.

Now the wait is over for hungry people.

Poultry

177. Great Turkey Verde & Rice

Magical, isn't it?

Ingredients:

- 11/4 cups long grain brown rice
- About 1 tsp salt
- 1 small yellow onion (Sliced)
- 1/2 cup salsa Verde
- 11/2 lb. Jennie-O turkey tenderloins
- 2/3 cup chicken broth

Directions:

1. First of all, please make sure you've all the ingredients available. Add the chicken broth and rice into the Instant Pot.
2. Now top with the sliced onions, turkey & salsa verde.
3. Sprinkle with salt and close the lid.
4. Close the vent to pressure cooker mode & set on HIGH for about 15 to 20 minutes.
5. Then when the timer beeps, and the cooking is complete, do NOT open the lid.
6. One thing remains to be done. Let the pot sit for about 5 to 10 additional minutes.
7. Finally after 5 to 10 minutes turn off the Instant Pot, open the lid & the turkey and rice are ready to serve.

Yeah, it is a vintage recipe.

178. Happy White Wine Chicken Breasts on Creamy Polenta

Always the upper hand…

Ingredients:

- 2 chicken breasts, skinless
- 1 knob of butter
- 1 cup (8fl oz) chicken stock (for the chicken breasts)
- 1/2 cup (4fl oz) dry white wine
- 1 cup (8fl oz) heavy cream
- 1 cup instant polenta
- About 1.5 sprig fresh rosemary
- 1 cup (8fl oz) chicken stock (for the polenta)

- 4 garlic cloves, finely chopped
- Salt and pepper, to taste
- About 1.5 cup (8fl oz) milk
- Olive oil

Directions:

1. First of all, please make sure you've all the ingredients available. Drizzle some olive oil into the Instant Pot & press the SAUTE button, adjust the temperature to HIGH.
2. Now once the oil is hot, add the chicken breasts to the pot and sauté for about 2 to 5 minutes on each side until golden and crispy.
3. Add the stock, garlic, cream, wine, rosemary, salt, and pepper to the pot and stir to combine.
4. This step is important. Secure the lid onto the pot & press the POULTRY button, keep the time at the default 15 to 20 minutes.
5. Once the pot beeps, quick-release the pressure & remove the lid.
6. Then for the polenta: you can either remove the chicken & sauce from the Instant Pot & use it to cook the polenta on the SAUTE button if you wish, or you could simply use a pot on the stove to cook the polenta properly while the chicken cooks.
7. Simply pour the milk and stock into a pot & bring to a simmer.
8. Now pour the polenta into the pot as you whisk continuously.
9. Keep whisking the polenta until it becomes thick and creamy.
10. One thing remains to be done. Add the salt, butter, & pepper and stir to combine.

11. Finally place a good dollop of polenta onto a plate & place a chicken breast on top, pour over a generous amount of white wine sauce before serving!

Now you're happy...?

179. Lucky Honey-Glazed Cashew Chicken Drumsticks

Classic style...

Ingredients:

- 4 garlic cloves, crushed
- 1/3 cup roasted, salted cashew nuts, roughly chopped
- About 3.5 tbsp honey
- 3 tbsp soy sauce
- 1 cup (8fl oz) chicken stock
- 8 chicken drumsticks (2 each for dinner, then 2 each for lunch the next day)

Directions:

1. First of all, please make sure you've all the ingredients available. Place the drumsticks, soy sauce, garlic, honey, and chicken stock into the Instant Pot, stir to combine & coat the drumsticks.
2. Now secure the lid onto the pot and press the POULTRY button, keep

the time at the default 15 to 20 minutes.
3. One thing remains to be done. Then once the pot beeps, quick-release the pressure & remove the lid.
4. Serve the drumsticks with a drizzle of honey/soy liquid & a sprinkling of crushed cashew nuts.

Arrive in style with this recipe.

180. Vintage Honey Sesame Chicken

Ironic in taste...

Ingredients:

- About 1.5 tbsp vegetable oil
- Salt and pepper to taste
- 1/2 cup diced onion
- Sesame seeds, toasted
- 2 cloves garlic (Minced)
- 1/2 cup soy sauce
- 2 green onions (Chopped)
- 1/4 cup ketchup
- About 2.5 tsp sesame oil
- 3 tbsp water
- 1/2 cup honey
- 1/4 tsp red pepper flakes
- 2 tbsp cornstarch
- 4 large boneless skinless chicken breasts, diced (about 2 lbs.)

Directions:

1. First of all, please make sure you've all the ingredients available. Salt and pepper chicken. Preheat pressure cooking pot using the SAUTE setting.

2. Now add oil, garlic, onion, and chicken to the pot and sauté occasionally stirring until onion is softened, about 2 to 5 minutes.
3. Add ketchup, soy sauce, and red pepper flakes to the pressure cooking pot and stir to combine.
4. This step is important. Pressure cook properly on high for about 2 to 5 minutes.
5. Then when timer beeps, turn pressure cooker off & do a quick pressure release.
6. Add sesame oil and honey to the pot & stir to combine.
7. Now in a small bowl, dissolve cornstarch in water & add to the pot.
8. One thing remains to be done. Select SAUTE & simmer until sauce thickens. Stir in green onions.
9. Finally serve over rice sprinkled with sesame seeds.

Looking forward to this one!!

181.   Best The Greek Chicken
Used to eat this one a lot.

Ingredients:

*   1/4 cup extra virgin olive oil, divided and more for garnish
*   Fresh black pepper powder
*   4 large garlic cloves cut small
*   2 rosemary sprig torn into bits
*   Kosher salt
*   About 1 tbsp oregano dried

*   1/2 tsp red pepper flakes
*   1/4 cup olives
*   1 large potato peeled, washed and pricked
*   2 cups chicken broth
*   1/2 cup frozen peas
*   4 small chicken breasts with skin and bone in
*   About 1.5 medium lemon

Directions:

1. First of all, please make sure you've all the ingredients available. Rub pepper and salt on chicken & smear 2 tablespoon oil on top.
2. Then sprinkle rosemary, red pepper flakes, oregano and marinate for about 35 to 40 minutes.
3. Select SAUTE & preheat the pot.
4. This step is important. Pour 1 tablespoon oil, add chicken, & cook without stirring.
5. The skin side should touch the pan. Cook until crispy.
6. Now once done, remove the chicken & transfer to a plate.
7. Pour broth in Pot and add potatoes, place fried chicken on top and rest of marinade Cook properly on HIGH on Manual option for about 10 to 15 minutes.
8. One thing remains to be done. Release pressure naturally, removes the chicken, add peas & stir until cooked in the heat.
9. Finally serve chicken topped with peas & potatoes and drizzle oil if you like.

There it is.

182. Nostalgic Roast Chicken for Dinner and Leftovers

Tasty dish just one step away!!

Ingredients:

- 1 onion, skin on, cut into quarters
- Salt, to taste
- About 1.5 lemon, cut in half
- 1 tsp dried mixed herbs
- 2 cups (16fl oz) chicken stock
- About 1.5 tbsp butter
- 1 whole chicken
- 4 garlic cloves, skin on, crushed with the back of a knife

Directions:

1. First of all, please make sure you've all the ingredients available. Place the crushed garlic cloves, onion quarters & lemon halves into the Instant Pot, pour the chicken stock over top.
2. Now place the chicken on top of the lemon & onions.
3. Rub the top of the chicken with the butter, then sprinkle with the dried herbs & salt.
4. This step is important. Secure the lid onto the pot and press the POULTRY button, adjust the time to about 30 to 35 minutes.
5. Then once the pot beeps, allow the pot to release naturally before you remove the lid.
6. OPTIONAL STEP: heat a frying pan before you remove the chicken from the pot.
7. Place the chicken into the hot pot & fry on all sides for a couple of minutes until the skin is golden and crispy.
8. Now you can use any leftover liquid in the pot to make gravy by removing the lemon & onion, adding about 2 teaspoons of plain flour and stirring until a thick sauce forms.
9. Use the leftover chicken carcass to make homemade stock by boiling the carcass in a large pot with enough water to cover the carcass.
10. One thing remains to be done. Add onions, carrots, & celery to flavor the stock, (boil for as long as you can, at least 3 to 4 hours).
11. Finally drain through a sieve before using or storing.

I was waiting for this one.

183. Mighty Chicken and Mushroom Pies

I know, this is amazing!!

Ingredients:

- About 1.5 onion, finely chopped
- Store-bought puff pastry (you don't need much at all, just 2 circles to cover the pies)

- 3 garlic cloves, finely chopped
- 2 large Portobello mushrooms
- 1/2 cup (4fl oz) dry white wine
- Small amount of butter
- 1/2 cup (4fl oz) heavy cream
- About 1 tsp dried mixed herbs
- Salt and pepper, to taste
- 14 oz chicken thighs, boneless and skinless, cut into small pieces

Directions:

1. First of all, please make sure you've all the ingredients available. Place the chicken, mushrooms, onion, garlic, salt, wine, cream, herbs, and pepper into the Instant Pot, stir to combine.
2. Now secure the lid onto the pot and press the MEAT/STEW button, adjust the time to about 20 to 25 minutes.
3. Once the pot beeps, quick-release the pressure & remove the lid, stir the mixture.
4. This step is important. Preheat the oven to about 360 to 370 degrees Fahrenheit and grease 2 pie tins with butter.
5. Then place the tins face-down onto a sheet of pastry and cut around the edge of the tin to create a circle to fit neatly on top of the pie.
6. Divide the chicken mixture into the 2 tins & then place the pastry rounds on top.
7. Now cut 4 little slits into the pastry & place the pies into the oven.
8. One thing remains to be done. Bake for about 25 to 30 minutes or until

the pastry is golden and the mixture is bubbling underneath.

9. Finally serve with fresh greens!

Silently, you were waiting for this one. Don't lie… ?

184. King sized Instant Pot Chicken

Make it quickly.

Ingredients:

- 3 tbsp tamari
- 2 pounds boneless chicken thighs
- About 1 tsp finely ground black pepper
- 1/4 cup ghee
- 3 tbsp ketchup
- About 2.5 tsp garlic powder
- 1/4 cup honey
- 1 1/2 tsp sea salt

Directions:

1. First of all, please make sure you've all the ingredients available. Place the ingredients in the Instant Pot & stir to mix and then close the lid ensuring the valve is in the seal position.
2. Then press MANUAL & set 15 to 20 minutes for fresh chicken or 40 minutes for frozen chicken.
3. After the set cooking time elapses, do a quick release.
4. Now remove & shred the chicken.
5. One thing remains to be done. Press CANCEL & then press the SAUTE function and let the sauce cook properly for about 5 to 10 minutes.

6. Finally serve with vegetables & rice.

Supreme level.

185. Crazy Chicken and Pesto Spaghetti

Sincere efforts will be awesome.

Ingredients:

- About 3.5 chicken thighs, boneless and skinless, cut into small pieces
- Parmesan cheese
- 7 oz dried spaghetti
- About 3.5 garlic cloves, finely chopped
- 2 tbsp store-bought basil pesto
- 2 cups (8fl oz) chicken stock
- Olive oil

Directions:

1. First of all, please make sure you've all the ingredients available. Drizzle some olive oil into the Instant Pot & press the SAUTE button, keep the temperature at NORMAL.
2. Now add the chicken to the hot pot & sauté for a couple of minutes to brown and pre-cook slightly.
3. This step is important. Add the spaghetti, stock, garlic, & 1 cup of water to the pot.
4. Secure the lid onto the pot & press the POULTRY button, adjust the time to about 10 to 15 minutes.

5. Then once the pot beeps, quick-release the pressure & remove the lid.
6. One thing remains to be done. Stir the pesto through the pasta & add a pinch of salt and pepper.
7. Finally serve immediately, with a sprinkling of grated Parmesan cheese!

Let's dive in...

Seafood Recipes

186. Pinnacle Fish with Orange & Ginger Sauce

Your friends and family are waiting. Hurry!!

Ingredients:

- Juice and zest from 1 orange
- 1 cup of fish stock or white wine
- Thumb size piece of ginger (Chopped)
- 3 to 4 spring onions
- Salt and pepper to taste
- About 1.5 tbsp olive oil
- 4 white fish fillets

Directions:

1. First of all, please make sure you've all the ingredients available. Take your fish fillets & dry them with a paper towel.
2. Now rub olive oil onto them & season lightly.

3. Add fish stock or white wine, ginger, spring onions, orange zest and juice into your pressure cooker.
4. One thing remains to be done. Place fish into the steamer basket, pop the lid on, bring up to HIGH pressure and cook properly for about 5 to 10 minutes.
5. Finally serve on top of an undressed garden salad, the sauce will dress it beautifully.

Royal taste…

187. Perfect Lemon Pepper Tilapia with Asparagus

We all are legends in some ways.

Ingredients:

- 1/4 bundle asparagus (Chopped)
- 1/4 cup lemon juice
- About 1 teaspoon lemon pepper seasoning or to taste
- 1 tablespoon butter
- About 2.5 tilapia fillets, thawed if frozen

Directions:

1. First of all, please make sure you've all the ingredients available. Take 2 foils. Lay the fillets in the middle of the foil.
2. Now sprinkle lemon pepper seasoning over it.
3. This step is important. Place 1/2 tablespoon of butter on each of the fillets.
4. Place asparagus over the fish.
5. Then wrap foil all around the fish. Seal it well.

6. One thing remains to be done. Place the packets in the instant pot. .
7. Finally close the lid. Press 'Slow cook' button & set timer for about 2.5 hours if thawed & for 3 hours if frozen.

Prepare yourself for this…

188. Dashing White Fish Curry for Two, with Banana and Coconut Side Dish

Looking forward to healthy life.

Ingredients:

- 12 oz fresh white fish (use any kind you can find as long as it's fresh), cut into chunks
- 1 lemon
- 12 oz coconut milk
- About 2.5 tbsp desiccated or shredded coconut
- 8 oz fish stock
- 1 lime
- Salt and pepper, to taste
- 1 large banana, peeled and sliced
- Fresh coriander, roughly chopped
- About 4.5 tbsp store-bought curry paste (it's not cheating if it's a high-quality paste!)

Directions:

1. First of all, please make sure you've all the ingredients available. Press the SAUTE button on your Instant Pot & adjust the temperature to HIGH.
2. Now add the curry paste to the hot pot and heat until fragrant.
3. Add the fish, coconut milk, stock, salt, juice of 1 lime, and pepper to the pot and stir to combine.
4. This step is important. Secure the lid onto the pot & press the SOUP button, adjust the time to about 20 to 25 minutes.
5. Then while the curry cooks, prepare the banana coconut side dish: place the coconut, sliced bananas, & juice of one lemon into a small bowl, stir to combine.
6. One thing remains to be done. Once the Instant Pot beeps, quick-release the pressure & remove the lid.
7. Finally serve the curry on its own, or with rice and/or naan, with freshly chopped coriander, & of course, the banana & coconut side dish.

Time: approximately 30 to 35 minutes

Astonishing!!

189.　　Reliable Smoked Fish Pots

Grab it!!

Ingredients:

- 14 oz smoked fish (smoked trout is lovely, but any fish works)
- A few slices of lemon wedges
- 3 eggs, lightly beaten
- 4fl oz milk
- About 1 tsp baking powder
- 2 slices of thick bread (sure, this is optional…but buttered toast goes so well with these smoky pots!)
- Handful of fresh parsley, finely chopped
- Salt and pepper, to taste
- About 1.5 tbsp butter (Melted)

Directions:

1. First of all, please make sure you've all the ingredients available. Grease your ramekins or individual pie dishes with butter.
2. Now flake the smoked fish with a fork & place the fish into a bowl.
3. Add the eggs, milk, salt, baking powder, parsley, and pepper to the fish bowls.
4. This step is important. Pour 2 cups of water into your Instant Pot & place a trivet or rack into the pot.
5. Then place the filled smoked fish pots onto the trivet or rack (above the water), secure the lid onto the pot, press the STEAM button, and adjust the time to about 10 to 15 minutes.
6. Once the pot beeps, quick-release the pressure & remove the lid.
7. One thing remains to be done. The fish pots will be very hot so be careful when removing them from the Instant Pot.

8. Finally serve with hot, buttered toast & a wedge of lemon.

Freshness loaded!!

190. Charming Mediterranean Tuna Pasta

Dreams are good!! So dream about this one or else make it...

Ingredients:

- 1/2 cup chopped red onion
- Fresh chopped parsley
- 1 cup egg pasta (uncooked)
- 2 cup diced tomatoes
- 1 tbsp basil
- Crumbled feta cheese
- About 1.5 tbsp garlic
- 1 tsp oregano
- 7 oz marinated artichoke
- 1 1/2 cup water
- Salt and pepper to taste
- About 1.5 tbsp olive oil
- 7 oz tuna fish

Directions:

1. First of all, please make sure you've all the ingredients available. SAUTE the red onion for about 2 minutes.
2. Then add the dry noodles, salt, tomatoes, water, and pepper then set your Instant Pot to SOUP for about 10 to 15 minutes.
3. One thing remains to be done. Now turn off the warm setting & add tuna, artichokes and your reserved liquid from the artichokes & sauté on normal while stirring for about 2 to 5 more minutes till hot.

4. Finally top with a little feta cheese & parsley for your taste.

Prep + Cook Time: 30 to 35 minutes

Servings: 2

Something is defintely different.

191. Energetic with Asparagus, Broccoli and Spinach

This is epic. Take a look!!

Ingredients:

- Seasoning of your choice
- About 2.5 tablespoons water
- 1 teaspoon olive oil
- 1/3 pound spinach (Chopped)
- 1 1/2 teaspoon lemon juice
- 1 asparagus, chopped into 1 inch pieces
- About 1.5 small head broccoli, chopped into florets
- 2 mahi mahi fish

Directions:

1. First of all, please make sure you've all the ingredients available. Mix together in a bowl, lemon juice, seasoning, and oil.
2. Then rub over the fish.
3. One thing remains to be done. Add all the ingredients into the instant pot & stir.
4. Finally close the lid. Press 'Slow cook' button & set timer for about 1 to 2 hours.

Life of a legend begins here.

192. Funny Orange-Glazed Steamed Salmon

Funny but definitely yummy!!

Ingredients:

- 1 tbsp honey
- 2 salmon filets, skin on, bones removed, seasoned with a pinch of salt and pepper
- About 1.5 tbsp soy sauce
- 2 fresh oranges

Directions:

1. First of all, please make sure you've all the ingredients available. Squeeze the juice of both oranges into a pot and add the honey & soy sauce, (you could use your Instant Pot on the SAUTE function, but honestly, I find it easier to just use a small pot on the stove for this glaze).
2. Now place the pot over a low heat & bring the mixture to a simmer, leave to gently simmer for about 5 to 10 minutes as you prepare the salmon.
3. The glaze will thicken slightly & will become sticky.
4. This step is important. Pour 2 cups of water into the Instant Pot & place the steaming basket into the pot.
5. Then place the salmon filets into the basket & secure the lid onto the pot.
6. Press the STEAM button and adjust the time to about 2 to 5 minutes (this will result in a lightly-cooked salmon).
7. Now once the pot beeps, quick-release the steam & remove the lid.
8. Take the salmon filets out of the basket & place them into the pot of hot orange glaze, spoon the glaze over the salmon so it's completed coated.
9. One thing remains to be done. Serve the salmon with an extra drizzle of orange glaze over top.
10. Finally some serving ideas: mashed potatoes, fresh green beans, long-stemmed broccoli, or a simple fresh salad.

Now that's something!!

193. Scrumptious Fish Balls with Garlic Aioli Dip

Can you make it? Yes, why not?

Ingredients:

- 1 garlic clove
- Olive oil
- 1 lemon
- Salt and pepper, to taste
- About 1.5 tsp chili powder
- 13 oz cooked or smoked fish of your choice
- 1 egg, lightly beaten1
- 1 tsp paprika

- 1 cup bread crumbs
- About 1.5 tbsp tomato puree
- 1/2 cup plain aioli (or mayo if you don't have aioli)
- Handful of fresh cilantro finely chopped

Directions:

1. First of all, please make sure you've all the ingredients available. Prepare the garlic aioli by mixing the aioli or mayo with the crushed garlic clove, pepper, salt, & a squeeze of lemon in a small bowl.
2. Now have a taste & add more garlic if it's not garlicky enough, or a dash more aioli if it's a bit too garlicky for your taste.
3. This step is important. Flake the cooked or smoked fish into a bowl, add the egg, chili powder, tomato puree, paprika, bread crumbs, fresh cilantro, salt, & pepper, stir to combine.
4. Then drizzle plenty of olive oil into your Instant Pot & press the SAUTE button, adjust the temperature to HIGH.
5. Roll the fish mixture into golf ball-sized balls & add them to the hot pot.
6. One thing remains to be done. Sauté the fish balls for about 10 to 15 minutes, turning every couple of minutes until they are golden & crispy all round.
7. Finally serve with some toothpicks for easy eating, lemon wedges, & your garlic aioli.

Good days!!

194.   Elegant Steamed Fish Fillet
I am interested!!

Ingredients:

- 1/2 kg cherry tomatoes (Sliced)
- Salt and pepper to taste
- 1 cup olives
- About 1.5 tbsp olive oil
- 1 clove of garlic, crushed
- a large pinch of fresh thyme
- 4 white fish fillets

Directions:

1. First of all, please make sure you've all the ingredients available. Heat the Instant Pot and add a cup of water.
2. Now put the fish fillets in a single layer in the steaming basket fitted for the pressure cooker.
3. Place the sliced cherry tomatoes & olives on top of the fillets.
4. This step is important. Add the crushed garlic, a few sprigs of fresh thyme, a dash of olive oil, and a little salt.
5. Then put the steaming basket inside the pressure cooker.
6. Seal the lid of the cooker properly.
7. Once it reaches pressure, reduce heat.
8. Now cook the fillets for 5 to 10 minutes on low pressure (or 2 to 5 minutes on high pressure).
9. One thing remains to be done. When finished, release pressure through the normal release method.

10. Finally serve the fillets in separate bowls, sprinkled with the pepper, remaining thyme, & little amount of olive oil.

This never goes out of style.

195. Rich Spicy Lemon Salmon

Now be a legend!!

Ingredients:

- About 1.5 tablespoon nanami togarashi
- Pepper to taste
- Juice of 1/2 lemon
- Salt to taste
- About 2.5 thin lemon slices
- 2 salmon fillets

Directions:

1. First of all, please make sure you've all the ingredients available. Pour 1 cup water into the instant pot.
2. Then place the steamer basket in it.
3. Mix together all the ingredients & place over the basket.
4. One thing remains to be done. Now close the dish. Press 'Manual' button & set timer for about 5 to 10 minutes.
5. Finally when the timer goes off, quick release excess pressure.

Simple yet fantastic!!

196. Titanic Salmon Al Cartoccio

It is a brand new day…. Ever listened to this one!!

Ingredients:

- 3 tomatoes (Sliced)
- Salt and pepper to taste
- About 1.5 lemon (Sliced)
- 1 white onion (Shaved)
- Olive oil
- 4 sprigs of parsley
- 4 salmon fillets, fresh or frozen
- About 4.5 sprigs of thyme

Directions:

1. First of all, please make sure you've all the ingredients available. Lay the ingredients on the parchment paper in this order: a swirl of oil, salt, a layer of potatoes, pepper and oil, fish fillets, salt, pepper and oil, lemon slices, herbs, onion rings, salt, and oil.
2. Now fold the packet. Wrap the packet snugly in tinfoil.
3. Pour two cups of water in the pressure cooker.
4. This step is important. Place the steamer basket in position & lay the packet on the steamer.
5. Then cook 2 fillets at a time.
6. Close the pressure cooker top. Turn to HIGH heat, & let it reach pressure.
7. Turn down the heat to the lowest setting.

8. Now cooking time should be between 10 to 15 minutes, after which you can release the vapor but do NOT open the top just yet.
9. One thing remains to be done. Let the packets of fish sit inside the locked pan for another 5 to 10 minutes.
10. Finally open the top and take out the packets. Take off the tinfoil & serve.

Awesome, isn't it?

197.   Tasty Calamari Linguine

Luxury tasty dish for you!!

Ingredients:

- 10 oz cleaned calamari (frozen is fine)
- A few fresh oregano leaves, finely chopped
- 7 oz dried linguine
- Small bunch of fresh parsley, finely chopped
- 32fl oz chicken stock (you could use fish stock but I find chicken stock is nicer)
- Small sprig of thyme, stalks removed, leaves finely chopped
- About 1 tsp chili flakes (you can leave this out, but I can't help putting chili in everything!)
- 1 lemon
- Salt and pepper, to taste
- About 2.5 oz butter
- Olive oil

Directions:

1. First of all, please make sure you've all the ingredients available. Drizzle some olive oil into the Instant Pot & press the SAUTE button, adjust the temperature to HIGH.
2. Then place the calamari into the hot pot & sauté for about 5 to 10 minutes, stirring as they cook.
3. Place the linguini, salt, chicken stock, chili, and pepper into the pot & make sure all of the linguine is covered in stock.
4. This step is important. Secure the lid onto the pot and press the MANUAL button, adjust the pressure to HIGH, & adjust the time to about 5 to 10 minutes.
5. Now once the pot beeps, quick-release the pressure and remove the lid, give the pasta a stir.
6. One thing remains to be done. Place the butter, juice of one lemon, salt, fresh herbs, & pepper into the pot & leave for a couple of minutes to allow the butter to melt.
7. Finally serve immediately.

Get ready to make it my way!!

198.   Yummy Crawfish Tails
The best combo ever!!

Ingredients:

- 2/3 pound crawfish tails, peeled
- Salt to taste
- 8 ounces canned diced tomatoes with green chilies
- About 1.5 teaspoon Cajun seasoning

- 2 cups chicken broth
- 1 small onion (Chopped)
- 3 tablespoons butter
- 2 green onions (Chopped)
- 1 small green bell pepper (Chopped)
- 1 cup rice, rinsed
- About 1.5 tablespoon dried parsley

Directions:

1. First of all, please make sure you've all the ingredients available. Then add all the ingredients to the instant pot & stir.
2. One thing remains to be done. Now close the lid. Press 'Rice' option.
3. Finally when done, fluff with a fork & serve.

Something is new here!!

Side Dishes

199. Unique Deluxe Potatoes

A little work here but will be worth it.

Ingredients:

- About 1.5 teaspoon garlic powder
- 4 medium potatoes
- 1 cup broccoli florets
- About 2.5 tablespoons butter (Melted)
- 1 cup cheese (Cheddar)
- 1 teaspoon pepper

Directions:

1. First of all, please make sure you've all the ingredients available. Take the potatoes and poke them with a fork.
2. Now after melting the butter, dip them in the butter & then wrap each of them in some tin foil.
3. Place the potatoes in the pressure cooker & place the lid on top.
4. Cook this at a high setting for twenty minutes.
5. This step is important. When this is done, take the potatoes out of the pressure cooker & allow them a minute to cool down. Then slice up the potatoes in half.
6. Then stuff these with the broccoli & cheddar cheese and then sprinkle with some garlic and pepper.
7. Wrap these back up in the tin foil.
8. Now place the potatoes into the pressure cooker again & turn it on low.
9. One thing remains to be done. Let these warm up for a few minutes so that the cheese can begin to melt again.
10. Finally serve these with a fish or meat dish of your choice or make this a full meal.

Try it...

200. Ultimate Cheesy Mushroom Potatoes

This is different, isn't it?

Ingredients:

- 1 tablespoon olive oil
- About 1 teaspoon pepper powder
- 1 cup white mushrooms, sliced
- 2 tablespoons garlic salt or to taste
- 1/4 cup milk
- 2 tablespoons onions (Minced)
- About 1.5 tablespoon butter
- 2 cups cheddar cheese (Shredded)
- 2 large Yukon gold potatoes, quartered, sliced

Directions:

1. First of all, please make sure you've all the ingredients available. Press 'Sauté' button. Add oil & a tablespoon of butter.
2. Now when butter melts, add mushrooms & sauté until tender.
3. Add rest of the ingredients and stir.
4. Then press 'Cancel' button.
5. One thing remains to be done. Close the lid. Press 'Slow cook' button & set timer for about 2 1/2 hours or until done.
6. Finally serve hot.

Yeah, this is a new variation.

201.   Iconic Red Cabbage with Bacon

Classic, isn't it?

Ingredients:

- 2 Bacon Slices
- Pinch of Pepper
- 1 cup Beef Broth
- 1/4 tsp Salt

- About 1.5 tbsp Butter
- 1/4 pounds Red Cabbage (Chopped)

Directions:

1. First of all, please make sure you've all the ingredients available. Set the IP to saute & cook the bacon properly until crispy. Set aside.
2. Now add the cabbage, salt, butter, and pepper.
3. Stir to combine and lock the lid.
4. Cook properly on HIGH for about 5 to 10 minutes.
5. Then do a natural pressure release.
6. One thing remains to be done. Serve the braised cabbage with crumbled cooked bacon.
7. Finally enjoy!

Different yet fantastic in many ways.

202.   Awesome Baked Potatoes

Yeah, direct from the heaven; yeah?

Ingredients:

- Potatoes, as many as you want, whole, peeled, or chopped

Directions:

1. First of all, please make sure you've all the ingredients available. Place the rack in the pot.
2. Then pour in a cup of water.
3. Place the potatoes on the rack.
4. Now cover & seal lid.
5. One thing remains to be done. Press manual & set time to about 10 to 15 minutes.

6. Finally after finished, let the pressure release naturally.

What's so typical or different here?

203. Super Spiced roasted vegetables

Best combo ever… Don't you agree?

Ingredients:

- 1 red onion
- 1 garlic clove
- About 1.5 potato
- 2 tablespoon butter
- 1/2 carrot
- 3 oz. cauliflower
- 1 teaspoon ground black pepper
- About 1.5 tablespoon olive oil
- 1 teaspoon oregano
- 1/2 teaspoon turmeric
- 1/2 teaspoon cilantro
- 1 teaspoon paprika
- 1 bell pepper

Directions:

1. First of all, please make sure you've all the ingredients available. Cut the bell pepper into the big strips.
2. Now peel the onion and chop it roughly.
3. Peel the potato & carrot.
4. Wash the cauliflower carefully & chop it roughly.
5. Chop the carrot and the potato.
6. This step is important. Mix all the ingredients together in the big bowl.
7. Then combine the olive oil, paprika, oregano, cilantro, turmeric, & ground black pepper.
8. Mince the garlic clove & add it to the spice mixture.
9. Add butter and churn the mass.
10. Then add the spice mixture to the vegetable bowl & stir it carefully with the help of the fingertips.
11. Toss the vegetables in the instant pot.
12. Close the lid and cook the dish at the sauté mode for about 20 to 25 minutes.
13. One thing remains to be done. When the vegetables are cooked but not soft – they are done.
14. Finally serve the vegetables immediately.

Prep time: 10 to 15 minutes

Cooking time: 20 to 25 minutes

Servings: 2

Someone is definitely ready for this.

Nutritional information:

Fat 18.9

Protein 6.69

Fiber 8

Carbs 47.18

Calories 370

204.   Delightful Butter Beets

Good recipe!!

Ingredients:

- 2 tbsp Butter (Melted)
- About 1/2 tsp Salt
- 1/2 pound Beets
- 1 tsp mixed Herbs
- About 1/2 tsp Garlic Powder
- 1 cup Chicken Broth
- 1 tbsp Olive Oil

Directions:

1. First of all, please make sure you've all the ingredients available. Pour the broth into the IP and place the beets inside.
2. Then let cook properly for about 15 to 20 minutes on HIGH.
3. Drain the liquid.
4. Stir in the olive oil, herbs, garlic powder, and salt.
5. One thing remains to be done. Now cook properly on SAUTE with the lid off for about 5 to 10 minutes.
6. Finally serve the beets drizzled with butter.

Lucky!!

205.   Fantastic Cranberry Applesauce

Yes, this is famous!!

Ingredients:

- 1/2 cup apple cider
- 12 oz. cranberries
- About 1.5 apple (Chopped)
- 1 orange, juiced and zested
- 1/2 cup maple syrup

Directions:

1. First of all, please make sure you've all the ingredients available. Place all the ingredients into the pressure cooker and stir.
2. Then add the lid on and cook properly at high pressure for about 5 to 10 minutes.
3. One thing remains to be done. Now when this is done, use the natural release to let go of the pressure for about 5 to 10 minutes.
4. Finally simmer the ingredients for a few minutes to thicken the sauce.

Wow, that's cute!!

206.   Great Garlic Potatoes

Fresh start with something new!!

Ingredients:

- 3/4 pound potatoes, chopped like fries
- About 1.5 teaspoons oil
- 1/2 teaspoon chili powder
- About 1 teaspoon salt
- 4 cloves garlic, unpeeled, slightly crushed

Directions:

1. First of all, please make sure you've all the ingredients available. Press 'Sauté' button. Add oil and heat.
2. Then add garlic & sauté until brown.
3. Add rest of the ingredients & 2 tablespoons water.
4. One thing remains to be done. Now close the lid. Press 'Manual' button & timer for about 10 to 15 minutes.
5. Finally when the timer goes off, quick release excess pressure.

Try this my way!!

207. Happy Refried Beans
Baking does the trick!!

Ingredients:

- 1/4 cup salsa
- 1 cup dried pinto beans, rinsed
- About 1/2 tsp black pepper
- 2 cloves chopped garlic
- 1 medium onion (Quartered)
- 1/2 tsp cumin
- About 1 tsp paprika
- 1 seeded jalapeno
- 1/2 tsp chili powder
- 1/2 tsp salt
- 1 1/2 cup water

Directions:

1. First of all, please make sure you've all the ingredients available. Mix all ingredients in the instant pot.

2. Now close & seal the lid.
3. Press manual and set time to about 25 to 30 minutes.
4. This step is important. Once finish, allow to set 10 to 15 minutes before releasing the pressure.
5. Then open, and stir.
6. Blend to the consistency that you would like with a blender, potato masher, or immersion blender.
7. One thing remains to be done. Be careful because the beans will be hot.
8. Finally if you want them to be thicker you can drain off some of the water as well.

I don't know about you, but I include this one everytime I get a chance.

208. Lucky Potato Side with Peas
I repeat... Try it if you want to. No regrets. Right!!

Ingredients:

- 1/2 tsp Cumin
- Salt and Pepper, to taste
- About 1.5 tbsp Tomato Paste
- 1 cup Water
- 1/2 cup Peas
- 1 Large Sweet Potato (Chopped)
- 1/2 tsp Garlic Powder
- 1 cup Spinach
- About 1.5 tbsp Olive Oil
- 1/2 Onion (Chopped)

Directions:

1. First of all, please make sure you've all the ingredients available. Set

your Instant Pot to SAUTE and heat the oil in it.

2. Now add onions and garlic & cook properly for about 2 to 5 minutes.
3. Whisk the spices along with the tomato ingredients.
4. This step is important. Pour the water into the pot & stir in the potatoes.
5. Close the lid and cook properly for about 15 to 20 minutes on MANUAL.
6. Then do a quick pressure release.
7. Stir in the peas & spinach.
8. One thing remains to be done. Let sit covered with the heat off for about 2 to 5 minutes.
9. Finally serve & enjoy!

Why not??

209.   Vintage Caramelized asparagus

Leave a mark!!

Ingredients:

- 4 tablespoon brown sugar
- 1/2 teaspoon paprika
- About 2.5 tablespoon water
- 1/2 teaspoon cinnamon
- 1 cup chicken stock
- About 1/2 teaspoon salt
- 12 oz. asparagus
- 2 tablespoon butter

Directions:

1. First of all, please make sure you've all the ingredients available. Wash the asparagus carefully & cut the vegetables into 2 parts.
2. Now combine the water & brown sugar together.
3. Pour the sweet mixture in the instant pot & melt it at the sauté mode.
4. Add cinnamon, butter, salt, & paprika.
5. This step is important. When the mixture starts to boil – pour it into the bowl and chill little.
6. Then put the asparagus pieces in the instant pot.
7. Add the chicken stock & cook the vegetables properly at the pressure mode for about 2 to 5 minutes.
8. After this, discard the asparagus from the liquid & put them back in the empty instant pot.
9. Now sprinkle the asparagus with the caramel mixture & close the lid.
10. One thing remains to be done. Sauté the dish for about 2 to 5minutes more.
11. Finally when the time is over – & the asparagus is cooked – remove it from the instant pot immediately.

Prep time: 5 to 10 minutes

Cooking time: 10 to 15 minutes

Servings: 2

Spice up!!

Nutritional information:

Fat 13.3

Protein 7

Fiber 4

Carbs 11.69

Calories 182

210.   Best Original Baked Potatoes

What do you think? ?

Ingredients:

- 3 teaspoons butter
- 1/2 teaspoon black pepper
- About 1/2 teaspoon salt
- 4 medium potatoes

Directions:

1. First of all, please make sure you've all the ingredients available. Wash the potatoes properly then prick using a fork.
2. Now pour a cup of water in a pressure cooker then place a trivet in it.
3. Arrange the potatoes on the trivet then close the pressure cooker properly.
4. This step is important. Select the high-pressure button then select time for about 10 to 15 minutes.
5. Now when the beep sounds, press cancel then naturally release the pressure cooker.
6. Meanwhile, preheat the oven to about 390 to 400 °F & line a baking pan with aluminum foil.
7. Then transfer the potatoes to the baking pan then bake for about 10 to 15 minutes.
8. One thing remains to be done. Once it is done, remove from the oven then arrange the baked potatoes on a serving dish.
9. Finally brush with butter then sprinkle salt & black pepper on top.

What makes this the best? Check it out for yourself!!

211.   Nostalgic Veggie Casserole with Sour Cream

Just got better!!

Ingredients:

- About 2.5 tbsp chopped Onion
- 1/2 cup Sour Cream
- 1/3 cup chopped Carrots
- 1 tbsp Olive Oil
- 1/4 cup Panko Breadcrumbs
- About 1.5 tbsp Butter, melted
- 1 Bell Pepper (Chopped)
- 1/4 cup shredded Cheddar Cheese
- 2 Potatoes (Chopped)

Directions:

1. First of all, please make sure you've all the ingredients available. Heat the oil in your IP on SAUTE.
2. Then add onions and cook properly for a few minutes,
3. Add the other veggies & cook properly for additional 2 to 5 minutes.
4. Pour enough water to cover the veggies and close the lid.
5. This step is important. Cook properly on MANUAL for about 5 to 10 minutes.
6. Do a quick pressure release & transfer the veggies to a baking dish.
7. Now lower the rack & leave the cooking liquid in the IP.
8. Place all of the other ingredients in the baking dish.
9. Stir to combine.
10. Then place the baking dish on the rack and close the lid.
11. One thing remains to be done. Cook properly on HIGH for about 5 to 10 minutes.
12. Finally serve & enjoy!

Got the idea!!

212. Mighty Old fashioned Baked Beans

Relax and enjoy this recipe!!

Ingredients:

- 1/2 cup onions (Chopped)
- 2 cups water
- 1.5 ounces tomato paste
- 1 cloves garlic (Minced)
- 1/2 chili paste

- About 1.5 tablespoon canola oil
- 1 1/2 tablespoons brown sugar
- Salt to taste
- 1/2 teaspoon prepared mustard
- About 1.5 tablespoon molasses
- 1 cup dry navy beans, soaked in water overnight, drained
- 1/4 teaspoon ground cumin

Directions:

1. First of all, please make sure you've all the ingredients available. Add all the ingredients to instant pot.
2. Then stir and close the lid.
3. One thing remains to be done. Now press 'Manual' button & timer for about 20 to 25 minutes.
4. Finally when the timer goes off, let the pressure release naturally.

Try this one if you're hungry!!

213. King sized Beans and Rice

Make me remember the good old days!!

Ingredients:

Beans:

- About 1.5 tsp kosher salt
- 1/4 lb red kidney beans, rinsed
- 1 pint water

Seasoning:

- Pepper
- 1 1/4 cup water
- 1 small onion (Minced)
- About 1/2 tsp kosher salt
- 1 bay leaf

- 1 tsp oil
- 1/4 tsp fresh thyme
- 1/4 lb smoked sausage, cut 1/4 in wedges
- 1/2 stalk celery (Minced)
- About 1.5 clove sliced garlic
- Salt
- 1/4 bell pepper (Minced)

Serving:

- Minced green onions
- Cooked long grain rice
- Minced parsley
- Hot sauce

Directions:

1. First of all, please make sure you've all the ingredients available. Allow beans to soak overnight.
2. Then sort through the beans & remove stones, dirt, & broken beans. Rinse & place in a large bowl with salt.
3. Cover completely with water.
4. Set cooker to sauté & heat the oil until simmering.
5. This step is important. Add sausage, pepper, garlic, celery, onion, thyme, and 1/4 tsp salt.
6. Now cook until sausage & onions are brown.
7. Drain beans and rinse. Place beans in the cooker with a bay leaf & another 1/2 tsp salt, and stir in water.
8. Seal lid and cook properly on high pressure 15 to 20 minutes.
9. Then allow pressure to release naturally. Open carefully.
10. Take out the bay leaf. Remove 1/2 cup of the beans and liquid and puree.
11. Pour into the pot and stir.
12. One thing remains to be done. Now allow to simmer for about 15 to 20 minutes, uncovered.
13. Finally check the seasoning before serving.

Luxury in its own class!!

214.   Crazy Lentil Salad with Peas and Scallions

Healthy is a new trend these days!! ? Always I guess…

Ingredients:

- 1/2 cups canned Peas, drained
- About 1.5 tbsp Olive Oil
- 1/3 cup chopped Scalluions
- 1/4 tsp Garlic Powder
- 1/3 cup chopped Tomatoes
- About 2.5 tbsp Tamari
- 2 tbsp Champagne Vinegar
- 1/2 cup dry Lentils

Directions:

1. First of all, please make sure you've all the ingredients available. Place the lentils in the IP & add enough water to cover them.
2. Now close the lid and cook properly on HIGH for about 10 to 15 minutes.
3. Do a quick pressure release & transfer the coked lentils to a bowl.
4. Stir in the scallions, peas, and tomatoes.

5. Then in a bowl, whisk together the tamari, oil, vinegar, and garlic powder.

6. One thing remains to be done. Pour the mixture over the salad.

7. Finally serve & enjoy!

Stunner!!

215.   Pinnacle Potato salad

Super awesome plus unique!!

Ingredients:

- 1/2 cup chicken stock
- About 1.5 teaspoon minced garlic
- 1 potato
- 1 tablespoon chives
- 1 carrot
- 5 oz. Parmesan cheese
- 1/3 cup cream
- About 1.5 teaspoon salt
- 5 tablespoon pasta
- 1/2 teaspoon ground black pepper

Directions:

1. First of all, please make sure you've all the ingredients available. Peel the potato and cut it into the cubes.

2. Now sprinkle the potato cubes with the salt & ground black pepper.

3. Add minced garlic and stir the mixture.

4. Peel the carrot & cut chop it.

5. This step is important. Pour the chicken stock in the instant pot.

6. Then toss the vegetables in the instant pot & start to sauté the vegetables for about 10 to 15 minutes.

7. After this, open the instant pot lid & add pasta and chives.

8. Stir the vegetable-pasta mixture gently with the help of the spatula and close the lid.

9. Now cook the dish at the pressure mode for about 5 to 10 minutes.

10. Meanwhile, grate Parmesan cheese.

11. When the time is over – strain the instant mixture into the big bowl.

12. Then sprinkle it with the grated cheese & cream.

13. One thing remains to be done. Stir it carefully and wait till the cheese starts to melt.

14. Finally stir the cooked salad again & serve it immediately.

Prep time: 10 to 15 minutes

Cooking time: 15 to 20 minutes

Servings: 2

Iconic recipe of my list!!

Nutritional information:

Protein 26

Fat 27.8

Fiber 6

Calories 564

Carbs 54.17

216. Perfect Tomato Mushroom Risotto

Well it is a Grandma's recipe!!

Ingredients:

- 1/4 cup chopped onion
- A pinch of salt
- 1 cup Arborio rice
- About 2.5 tablespoons white wine
- 11/2 teaspoons tomato paste
- 1/2 cup chopped mushroom
- About 1.5 teaspoons olive oil
- 2 cups vegetable broth

Directions:

1. First of all, please make sure you've all the ingredients available. Choose the sauté from the menu in the pressure cooker then place onion with olive oil in the pot.
2. Now stirring occasionally until brown.
3. Toss in Arborio rice & a splash of wine then stir until the rice completely absorbs the wine.
4. This step is important. Pour vegetable broth into the pot then add the remaining ingredients into the pot.
5. Then place the lid on the pressure cooker then close properly.

6. Select the menu to high & set the time to about 5 to 10 minutes.
7. Now when the beep sounds, turn it off then naturally release the pressure cooker.
8. One thing remains to be done. Carefully open the lid then stirs the cooked rice.
9. Finally transfer the cooked rice to a serving dish & enjoy warm.

Happiness has finally arrived!!

217. Dashing Sweet Squash Spaghetti with Ginger

Whenever you want a great recipe!!

Ingredients:

- 1/3 cup Honey
- About 2.5 tbsp Brown Sugar
- 1 cup Water
- 1 tbsp Coconut Oil
- 1/4 tsp Salt
- About 1.5 tsp grated Ginger
- 1 pound Spaghetti Squash

Directions:

1. First of all, please make sure you've all the ingredients available. Pour the water into the IP.
2. Then place the squash in the basket and lower it.
3. Close the lid and cook properly on MANUAL for about 20 to 25 minutes.
4. This step is important. Allow a couple of minutes to cool down.
5. With a fork, scrape the flash of the squash & place in a bowl.

6. Now in another bowl, whisk together the remaining ingredients.
7. Pour over the spaghetti.
8. One thing remains to be done. Serve with fish or meat.
9. Finally enjoy!

How is it? Only one way to find out

218. Reliable Asian Sesame Carrots
I can eat them all day!!

Ingredients:

- 1 teaspoons grated ginger
- Pepper to taste
- About 2.5 teaspoons toasted sesame seeds
- Salt to taste
- 1 scallions (Chopped)
- 1 1/2 teaspoons rice vinegar
- About 2.5 teaspoons sesame oil
- 1 1/2 teaspoons soy sauce
- 1 large carrots, chopped into chunks

Directions:

1. First of all, please make sure you've all the ingredients available. Add all the ingredients except sesame into the instant pot.
2. Then close the lid. Press 'Steam' button & set timer for about 10 to 15 minutes.
3. If there is liquid in it, simmer until dry.
4. One thing remains to be done. Now add sesame seeds & stir.
5. Finally serve hot.

Different take on this one…

219. Charming Mac and Cheese
A little work here but will be worth it.

Ingredients:

- 8-oz shredded sharp cheddar cheese
- About 1.5 tsp mustard
- 2 cup water
- 1/2 lb macaroni
- 1 1/2 tsp salt
- About 1.5 tbsp butter
- 6-oz evaporated milk
- 1/2 tsp hot suace
- 3-oz shredded parmigiano

Directions:

1. First of all, please make sure you've all the ingredients available. Mix together salt, water, butter, hot sauce, mustard, and macaroni in pot.
2. Now lock lid and cook properly on high, 2 to 5 minutes.
3. Set to sauté.
4. One thing remains to be done. Then stir in evaporated milk.
5. Finally mix in cheese a handful at a time. Serve.

Something is new here!!

220. Energetic SautEed white onion

The best combo ever!!

Ingredients:

- 1/4 teaspoon baking soda
- About 1.5 teaspoon dill
- 1/4 cup chicken stock
- 1 tablespoon brown sugar
- 3 tablespoon butter
- About 1.5 teaspoon salt
- 1 teaspoon apple cider vinegar
- 4 big white onion

Directions:

1. First of all, please make sure you've all the ingredients available. Peel the white onions & cut them into the medium petals.
2. Now toss the onion petals in the big bowl.
3. Add salt, brown sugar, & apple cider vinegar.
4. Stir the mixture little.
5. This step is important. Sprinkle it with the dill.
6. Then toss the butter in the instant pot & melt it.
7. Sprinkle the melted butter with the baking soda.
8. Add the onion petals & sauté them for about 10 to 15 minutes.

9. Then turn the onions into another side once.
10. One thing remains to be done. When the onion petals start to be gentle – close the instant pot lid & cook the dish properly at the pressure mode for about 2 minutes more.
11. Finally serve the dish immediately.

Prep time: 5 to 10 minutes

Cooking time: 10 to 15 minutes

Servings: 2

Get ready to make it my way!!

Nutritional information:

Fat 18

Protein 4

Fiber 4

Calories 256

Carbs 22.49

221.   Funny Pumpkin Risotto

Luxury tasty dish for you!!

Ingredients:

- About 1.5 teaspoon sage
- 2 tablespoons white wine
- About 1.5 tablespoon olive oil
- 11/2 cup pumpkin (Diced)

- 1 yellow onion (Diced)
- 1/2 cup cream cheese (optional)
- 1 cup risotto rice
- 2 cups chicken broth
- 2 garlic cloves

- 1/4 cup diced, cooked bacon
- 2 lbs acorn squash
- About 1.5 tbsp maple syrup
- 1 tbsp butter
- About 1 tsp salt

Directions:

1. First of all, please make sure you've all the ingredients available. Add the olive oil along with the garlic & onion to the pressure cooker.
2. Now cook these for two minutes & add in the pumpkin and cook another minute.
3. Add in the spices & white wine before adding in the chicken broth and the risotto.
4. Then place the lid on top and cook this properly at a high pressure for about 5 to 10 minutes.
5. One thing remains to be done. Lower the pressure & cook properly for an additional three minutes.
6. Finally use the natural release method & then take the lid off. Stir in the cream cheese and enjoy.

Awesome, isn't it?

Directions:

1. First of all, please make sure you've all the ingredients available. Pour a cup of water in the pot, and add the trivet.
2. Now place squash on trivet.
3. Lock and seal the lid. Cook properly 5 to 10 minutes.
4. Release pressure and let cool.
5. This step is important. Carefully take out the squash.
6. Then cut open & take out seeds.
7. Put the squash in pot. Lock & seal lid.
8. Cook properly for about 5 to 10 more minutes.
9. Then quick release pressure & let cook.
10. One thing remains to be done. Take out squash. Scrape out flesh & mash with the maple syrup and butter.
11. Finally mix in salt & bacon.

Simple yet fantastic!!

222.   Scrumptious Maple Bacon Squash

It is a brand new day…. Ever listened to this one!!

Ingredients:

223.   Awesome Baby carrot with the dill

Now be a legend!!

Ingredients:

- 1/2 teaspoon salt
- 1/4 teaspoon paprika
- About 1.5 teaspoon oregano
- 1 tablespoon dill
- 1/4 cup bread crumbs
- 1/4 cup chicken stock
- About 3.5 tablespoon butter
- 2 cup baby carrot

Directions:

1. First of all, please make sure you've all the ingredients available. Peel the baby carrot and sprinkle it with the salt.
2. Now combine the dill, oregano, & paprika. Stir the mixture.
3. Put the baby carrot in the instant pot & add chicken stock.
4. Close the instant pot lid and cook the dish properly at the pressure mode for about 10 to 15 minutes.
5. This step is important. Then strain the chicken stock from the instant pot.
6. Then sprinkle the baby carrot with the spices & add butter.
7. Stir the vegetables gently to not damage them.
8. Now sauté the baby carrots for about 5 to 10 minutes more.
9. One thing remains to be done. After this, put the vegetables on the serving plate & sprinkle the dish with the breadcrumbs.
10. Finally serve the dish warm.

This never goes out of style.

224.   Quick Delicious Spicy Cabbage

I am interested!!

Ingredients:

- 1 cabbage
- About 1.5 teaspoon cornstarch
- 1/4 cup grated carrots
- 3/4 cup water
- 1/4 teaspoon red pepper flakes
- About 2.5 tablespoons apple cider vinegar
- 1/4 teaspoon cayenne
- 1/2 teaspoon granulated sugar
- 11/2 teaspoons sesame oil

Directions:

1. First of all, please make sure you've all the ingredients available. Cut the cabbage into wedges then place in a pressure cooker pot.
2. Now pour sesame oil over the cabbage wedges then select the menu to sauté. Stir until brown.
3. Add grated carrots into the pot then season the vegetables with cayenne, sugar, apple cider vinegar, & red pepper flakes.

4. This step is important. Pour water over the vegetables then cover the pressure cooker properly.
5. Then select the menu to high then set the time for about 5 to 10 minutes.
6. Once the beep sounds, naturally release the pressure cooker.
7. When the pressure cooker is cooler, open the lid then take the vegetables out from the pot.
8. Now arrange the cooked cabbage & carrot on a serving dish. Set aside.
9. Take about 1/4 cup of the liquid then mix with cornstarch.
10. One thing remains to be done. Return the mixture into the pot then bring to a simmer until the liquid become thick.
11. Finally pour the sauce over the cooked cabbage & carrots and serve warm.

Good days!!

Snacks and appetizers

225. Wonderful Delicious Meatballs.

Can you make it? Yes, why not?

Ingredients:

- 7 oz. tomato sauce
- 1/2 tbsp. Worcestershire sauce
- About 1.5 tbsp. olive oil
- 1/2 cup. water
- 1/2 yellow onion, chopped
- A pinch of salt and black pepper
- 1/2 pound. beef, ground
- About 4.5 tbsp. rice
- 1 garlic clove, minced

Directions:

1. First of all, please make sure you've all the ingredients available. Set your instant pot on sauté mode, add the oil & heat it up.
2. Then add half of the garlic and onion, stir and cook properly for about 2 to 5 minutes.
3. Add water, Worcestershire sauce & tomato sauce, stir and bring to a simmer.
4. Now meanwhile, in a bowl, mix beef with rice, pepper, salt, the rest of the garlic & onion and stir well.
5. One thing remains to be done. Shape meatballs out of this mix, add them to your instant pot, cover pot, and cook properly on HIGH for about 15 to 20 minutes.
6. Finally transfer meatballs on a platter & serve as an appetizer.

Now that's something!!

226. Elegant Warm Chicken Wings.

Funny but definitely yummy!!

Ingredients:

- 1 tbsp. brown sugar
- About 2.5 tbsp. butter
- A pinch of salt
- 3 oz. water
- About 1 tbsp. Worcestershire sauce
- 1 and 1/2 pounds chicken wings pieces
- 2 tbsp. cayenne pepper sauce

Directions:

1. First of all, please make sure you've all the ingredients available. Put the water in your instant pot, add the trivet, add chicken wings, cover pot, & cook properly on HIGH for about 5 to 10 minutes.
2. Now in a bowl, mix butter with Worcestershire sauce, pepper sauce, sugar and salt & whisk really well.
3. One thing remains to be done. Brush chicken pieces with this mix, spread them on a lined baking sheet, introduce in the oven at 390 to 400 degrees F and roast for about 5 to 10 minutes.
4. Finally serve as an appetizer.

Life of a legend begins here.

227.   Rich Chili Chicken Wings
This is epic. Take a look!!

Ingredients:

- 1/4 cup Butter
- 6 ounces Water
- 1 pound Chicken Wings
- About 2.5 tbsp Hot Sauce
- 1/2 tbsp Worcestershire Sauce

- 1/2 tbsp Sugar

Directions:

1. First of all, please make sure you've all the ingredients available. Pour the water into the IP & lower the trivet.
2. Now arrange the wings on the trivet & close the lid.
3. Close the lid and cook properly on HIGH for about 5 to 10 minutes,
4. Do a quick pressure release.
5. Then whisk together the remaining ingredients & brush over the wings.
6. One thing remains to be done. Cook properly on SAUTE until sticky.
7. Finally serve & enjoy!

Something is defintely different.

228.   Titanic Crab meat rounds

Dreams are good!! So dream about this one or else make it...

Ingredients:

- 1 egg yolk
- 1 tablespoon parsley
- About 1.5 teaspoon minced garlic
- 1 teaspoon salt
- 1 teaspoon butter
- About 1.5 tablespoon chives

- 12 oz. crab meat
- 1 teaspoon semolina

Directions:

1. First of all, please make sure you've all the ingredients available. Chop the crab meat into the tiny pieces & add minced garlic.
2. Then add egg yolk and salt.
3. After this, add chives and semolina.
4. Sprinkle the crabmeat mixture with the parsley.
5. This step is important. Stir it well till you get smooth mass.
6. Now dip the hands in the water & make the balls with the help of the wet hands.
7. Flatten the crab meatballs to make them flat.
8. Toss the butter in the instant pot.
9. Then add the crab meat rounds in the instant pot.
10. One thing remains to be done. Sauté the meal for about 2 to 5 minutes from the each side.
11. Finally dry the cooked crab meat rounds with the help of the paper towel.

Freshness loaded!!

229. Tasty Mouthwatering Potato Wedges.

Grab it!!

Ingredients:

- About 1.5 tsp. onion powder
- 3 quarts sunflower oil+ 2 tbsp.
- 1 cup. water
- A pinch of salt and black pepper
- 2 big potatoes, cut into medium wedges
- 1⁄2 tsp. garlic powder
- A pinch of cayenne pepper
- 1⁄2 cup. buttermilk
- 1⁄2 tsp. oregano, dried
- 1 cup. flour
- About 3.5 tbsp. cornstarch
- A pinch of baking soda

Directions:

1. First of all, please make sure you've all the ingredients available. Put the water in your instant pot, add some salt and the baking soda, stir & place the steamer basket inside.
2. Now in a bowl, mix onion powder with garlic powder, pepper, salt, oregano and cayenne and stir.
3. This step is important. Add potatoes, toss them well, add them to the pot, cover pot, and cook properly on HIGH for about 2 to 5 minutes.
4. In a bowl, mix cornstarch with flour and stir.
5. Then in another bowl, mix buttermilk with a pinch of baking soda & whisk.
6. Drain potato wedges, dredge them in flour mix & then dip them in buttermilk.

7.   One thing remains to be done. Heat up a large pan with 3 quarts water over medium high heat, add potato wedges, cook them properly for about 2 to 5 minutes and transfer them to paper towels.

8.   Finally drain grease, transfer wedges to a bowl & serve them as a snack.

Astonishing!!

230.   Yummy IP Honey Chicken.

Looking forward to healthy life.

Ingredients:

- 1 garlic clove, minced
- About 1.5 tsp. smoked paprika
- 2 pound. chicken wings pieces
- 1/2 cup. ketchup
- 2 tbsp. bourbon
- 1/2 tbsp. liquid smoke
- 2 tbsp. onion, chopped
- 1 and 1/2 tbsp. honey
- 3 tbsp. water
- A pinch of cayenne pepper
- A pinch of salt and black pepper
- About 3.5 tbsp. brown sugar

Directions:

1.   First of all, please make sure you've all the ingredients available. In your instant pot, mix ketchup with smoke, sugar, garlic, onion, bourbon, pepper, water, paprika, salt, cayenne and honey, whisk well, set on sauté mode & simmer for a few minutes.

2.   Then add chicken wings, toss, cover pot, & cook properly on HIGH for about 5 to 10 minutes.

3.   One thing remains to be done. Now transfer chicken wings to a lined baking sheet, introduce in the oven at 390 to 400 degrees F and roast for about 5 to 10 minutes.

4.   Finally serve as an appetizer.

Prepare yourself for this…

231.   Unique Boiled Peanuts

We all are legends in some ways.

Ingredients:

- 1/2 pound Raw Peanuts
- 1 tsp Cajun Seasoning
- About 2.5 tbsp Salt

Directions:

1.   First of all, please make sure you've all the ingredients available. Clean the peanuts & place inside the Instant Pot.

2.   Then sprinkle with the spices & add enough water to cover them.

3.   Close the lid and set the IP to MANUAL.

4.   Now cook properly for about 65 to 70 minutes on HIGH.

5.   One thing remains to be done. Do a quick pressure release.

6.   Finally serve & enjoy!

Total Time: 80 to 90 Minutes

Serves: 2

Royal taste…

232. Ultimate Instant pot soft chicken wings

Your friends and family are waiting. Hurry!!

Ingredients:

- 1 teaspoon onion powder
- About 1.5 teaspoon sesame seeds
- 1/2 teaspoon garlic powder
- 1 teaspoon olive oil
- 4 chicken wing
- About 1.5 teaspoon ground celery root

Directions:

1. First of all, please make sure you've all the ingredients available. Combine the onion powder & garlic powder together.
2. Then add ground celery root & sesame seeds.
3. Stir the spices well.
4. This step is important. Sprinkle the chicken wings with the spices & poach the meat.
5. Now sprinkle the chicken wings with the olive oil.
6. Put the cooked chicken wings in the instant pot.
7. One thing remains to be done. Close the lid & cook the dish properly at the pressure mode for about 20 to 25 minutes.
8. Finally when the chicken wings are cooked – serve them immediately.

Let's dive in…

233. Iconic Delicious Italian Mussels.

Sincere efforts will be awesome.

Ingredients:

- 2 tbsp. olive oil
- About 1.5 tbsp. red pepper flakes
- 20 oz. canned tomatoes (Chopped)
- 3 tbsp. onion (Chopped)
- 1 and 1⁄2 pounds mussels, scrubbed
- 1 jalapeno peppers (Chopped)
- 1 garlic cloves (Minced)
- About 2.5 tbsp. balsamic vinegar
- A pinch of salt
- 2 tbsp. basil (Chopped)
- 2 tbsp. chicken broth

Directions:

1. First of all, please make sure you've all the ingredients available. Set your instant pot on sauté mode, add the oil, heat it up, add onion and

garlic, stir & cook properly for about 2 to 5 minutes.

2. Then add tomatoes, jalapeno, vinegar, chicken broth, pepper flakes and salt, stir and simmer for about 2 to 5 minutes more.

3. One thing remains to be done. Now add mussels, stir, cover and cook properly on High for about 2 to 5 minutes.

4. Finally discard unopened mussels, divide them between 2 bowls and serve with basil sprinkled on top.

Supreme level.

234.   Awesome Pasta Salad Appetizer.

Make it quickly.

Ingredients:

- About 4.5 tbsp. mayonnaise
- 1⁄2 tsp. Worcestershire sauce
- 2 tbsp. sour cream
- 4 bacon slices, cooked and crumbled
- 2 tbsp. red onion (Chopped)
- 2 cups. water
- 1⁄2 tsp. sugar
- About 1 tsp. lemon juice
- 1 tsp. apple cider vinegar
- 2 oz. cheddar cheese (Grated)
- 5 oz. peas
- A pinch of salt and black pepper
- 1⁄2 pound. gemelli pasta

Directions:

1. First of all, please make sure you've all the ingredients available. Now in your instant pot, mix pasta with a pinch of salt and water, cover pot,

and cook properly on HIGH for about 2 to 5 minutes.

2. One thing remains to be done. Drain pasta and transfer to a bowl.

3. Finally add peas, red onion, pepper, bacon, mayo, sour cream, lemon juice, Worcestershire sauce, salt, sugar, vinegar and cheddar cheese, toss well & serve as an appetizer.

Silently, you were waiting for this one. Don't lie… ?

235.   Super Swedish Party Meatballs

I know, this is amazing!!

Ingredients:

- About 1.5 can Mushroom Soup
- 8 ounces cooked and frozen Swedish Meatballs
- 1/2 cup Sour Cream

Directions:

1. First of all, please make sure you've all the ingredients available. Whisk together the mushroom soup & sour cream into the Instant Pot.

2. Now place the meatballs inside & close the lid.

3. Set the Instant Pot to MANUAL.

4. Then cook properly on HIGH for about 10 to 15 minutes.

5. One thing remains to be done. Do a natural pressure release.

6. Finally serve & enjoy!

I was waiting for this one.

236.   Delightful Stuffed pork rolls

Tasty dish just one step away!!

Ingredients:

- 8 oz. pork fillets
- 4 oz. ham
- About 1.5 tablespoon mayo sauce
- 1 teaspoon garlic sauce
- 2 garlic cloves
- 1 teaspoon paprika
- About 1.5 tablespoon pistachio
- 1/2 teaspoon cilantro

Directions:

1. First of all, please make sure you've all the ingredients available. Beat the pork filets.
2. Now combine the garlic sauce, pistachio, mayo sauce, and paprika.
3. Add cilantro.
4. Chop the garlic cloves & mix up the mixture.
5. This step is important. Slice the ham.
6. Then take the pork fillets & spread them with the pistachio mass.
7. Add the sliced ham & roll the meat.
8. After this, put the pork rolls in the instant pot & close the lid.

9. Now cook the pork rolls properly at the pressure mode for about 30 to 35 minutes.
10. One thing remains to be done. When the pork rolls are done – cool them little.
11. Finally serve the dish & enjoy!

There it is.

237. Fantastic Easy Chicken Salad.

Used to eat this one a lot.

Ingredients:

- Salt and black pepper to the taste
- About 1.5 tbsp. balsamic vinegar
- 1 chicken breast, skinless and boneless
- 2 tbsp. olive oil
- 3 cups. water
- 2 garlic cloves, minced
- About 1.5 tbsp. mustard
- Mixed salad greens
- A handful cherry tomatoes, halved
- 1 tbsp. honey

Directions:

1. First of all, please make sure you've all the ingredients available. In a bowl, mix 2 cups. water with salt to the taste & chicken, toss a bit and keep in a cold place for 1 hour
2. Then add the rest of the water to your instant pot, add the steamer

basket, drain chicken and add to the pot, cover, cook properly on HIGH for about 5 to 10 minutes, transfer to a cutting board, cool down, cut into thin strips, add to a bowl and mix with tomatoes & salad greens,

3. One thing remains to be done. Now in a bowl, mix garlic with pepper, salt, mustard, honey, vinegar and olive oil & whisk very well.

4. Finally drizzle this vinaigrette over chicken salad, toss, divide between appetizer plates & serve.

Looking forward to this one!!

238. Great Crispy Tasty Chicken.

Ironic in taste…

Ingredients:

* 1 cup. water
* About 2.5 tbsp. butter
* 6 chicken thighs
* 1 yellow onion (Chopped)
* 2 tbsp. olive oil
* A pinch of rosemary (Chopped)
* 2 eggs, whisked
* A pinch of salt and black pepper
* 1 and 1/2 cups. panko bread crumbs
* 1 cup. flour
* About 4.5 garlic cloves (Minced)

Directions:

1. First of all, please make sure you've all the ingredients available. In your instant pot, mix garlic with onion, rosemary & water and stir.

2. Then put the steamer basket in your instant pot, add chicken thighs, cover pot, and cook properly on HIGH for about 5 to 10 minutes.

3. This step is important. Meanwhile, heat up a pan with 2 tbsp. oil, 2 tbsp. butter and panko, stir & cook properly for a couple of minutes.

4. Pat dry chicken thighs and season them with salt and pepper.

5. Now coat chicken with flour, dip in eggs, coat in panko & place on a lined baking sheet.

6. One thing remains to be done. Introduce in the oven at 390 to 400 degrees F and bake for about 5 to 10 minutes.

7. Finally arrange on a platter & serve as an appetizer.

Arrive in style with this recipe.

239. Great Scotch Eggs

The speed matters…

Ingredients:

* About 1/4 pound ground Chorizo
* 1 cup Water
* About 1.5 tbsp Oil
* 2 Hardboiled Eggs

Directions:

1. First of all, please make sure you've all the ingredients available. Peel the eggs.

2. Now flatten out the chorizo & cut into two equal pieces.

3. Wrap each egg in chorizo.

4. This step is important. Heat the oil in the IP on SAUTE.
5. Then add the wrapped eggs & cook properly until browned.
6. Pour the water over.
7. Close the lid and set the IP to MANUAL.
8. Now cook properly on HIGH for about 5 to 10 minutes.
9. One thing remains to be done. Do a quick pressure release.
10. Finally serve & enjoy!

Total Time: 20 to 25 Min

Serves: 2

Cooking level infinite....

240. Awesome Fancy-Event Oysters

When you're fantastic, this is best!!

Ingredients:

- 1 cup Water
- 8 Oysters
- About 2.5 tbsp melted Butter

Directions:

1. First of all, please make sure you've all the ingredients available. Clean the oysters well & place inside the Instant Pot.
2. Then pour the water over them.
3. Close and seal the lid & set the IP to MANUAL.
4. This step is important. Cook the oysters properly on HIGH for about 2 to 5 minutes.

5. Now let the pressure come down naturally.
6. Place on a serving platter.
7. One thing remains to be done. Drizzle with melted butter.
8. Finally enjoy!

Total Time: 15 to 20 Min

Serves: 2

Don't forget this one...

241. Happy Scalloped Potatoes

Classic style...

Ingredients:

- 1/4 tsp Salt
- About 2.5 tbsp Sour Cream
- 2 tbsp Milk
- 1/2 tbsp chopped Chives
- 1 cup Chicken Broth
- About 1.5 tbsp Potato Starch
- 2 Potatoes (Sliced)

Directions:

1. First of all, please make sure you've all the ingredients available. Combine all of the ingredients in your Instant Pot/
2. Then close the lid and set to MANUAL.
3. Cook the potatoes properly on HIGH for about 5 to 10 minutes.
4. Now do a quick pressure release.
5. One thing remains to be done. Set the IP to SAUTE and cook properly for additional 2 to 5 minutes.
6. Finally serve & enjoy!

Now you're happy…?

242.   Lucky MustArd egg halves

Always the upper hand…

Ingredients:

- 4 eggs
- About 1 teaspoon butter
- 1 cup water
- 1/2 teaspoon salt
- 4 oz. Parmesan
- About 1.5 teaspoon paprika
- 1 tablespoon mustard

Directions:

1. First of all, please make sure you've all the ingredients available. Pour the water in the instant pot and add eggs.
2. Now after this, close the lid & cook the eggs properly at the pressure mode for about 5 to 10 minutes.
3. Meanwhile, combine the paprika, salt, and butter together.
4. This step is important. Grate Parmesan cheese.
5. When the eggs are boiled – chill them well and peel.

6. Then after this, cut the eggs into the halves & remove the egg yolks.
7. Add the egg yolks to the butter mixture.
8. Add the mustard and grated cheese.
9. One thing remains to be done. Churn the mixture well & fill the egg white halves with the mustard mass.
10. Finally serve the dish.

Yeah, it is a vintage recipe.

243.   Vintage Baby Back Ribs Dish.

Magical, isn't it?

Ingredients:

- 2 tsp. chili powder
- About 1 tsp. fennel seeds, ground
- 2 carrots (Chopped)
- 1 rack baby back ribs
- 1 tsp. cinnamon powder
- 3 drops liquid smoke
- A pinch of salt and black pepper
- A pinch of cayenne pepper
- About 1.5 tsp. garlic powder
- 1 tsp. onion powder
- 2 tbsp. brown sugar
- 1/2 tsp. cumin seeds

For the sauce:

- 3 garlic cloves (Minced)
- About 1.5 tbsp. brown sugar

- 1 yellow onion (Chopped)
- 2 tbsp. mustard
- 1/8 cup. maple syrup
- About 2.5 tbsp. apple cider vinegar
- 1⁄2 cup. water
- 1/8 cup. honey
- 1 cup. ketchup

Directions:

1. First of all, please make sure you've all the ingredients available. In a bowl, mix ribs with carrots, liquid smoke and toss.
2. Then add 2 tbsp. brown sugar, chili powder, a pinch of salt, black pepper, garlic powder, onion powder, cinnamon powder, cumin seeds, fennel seeds and cayenne & toss really well.
3. This step is important. In another bowl, mix onion with garlic, vinegar, ketchup, water, maple syrup, honey, mustard and 1 tbsp. sugar and whisk really well.
4. Now add this to your instant pot, add ribs, cover pot, & cook properly on HIGH for about 25 to 30 minutes.
5. Transfer ribs to a platter and leave aside.
6. One thing remains to be done. Turn your instant pot on SAUTÉ mode again & simmer sauce for a few minutes until it thickens.
7. Finally serve your ribs with the sauce on the side.

Now the wait is over for hungry people.

244.   Best Home Made Italian Dip.

Awesomeness fully loaded…

Ingredients:

- 1 pound. beef roast, cut into medium chunks
- 3 oz. beef stock
- 1 tbsp. Italian seasoning
- About 2.5 tbsp. water
- 4 oz. pepperoncini peppers

Directions:

1. First of all, please make sure you've all the ingredients available. Now in your instant pot, mix beef with seasoning, stock, water and pepperoncini peppers, cover pot, and cook properly on HIGH for about 55 to 60 minutes.
2. Finally shred meat using 2 forks, stir your dip & serve it with sandwiches.

Mystery with this recipe or rather a chemistry with it.

245.   Nostalgic Buttery Lobster Tails

Speed defines it…

Ingredients:

- 2 tbsp Butter, melted
- 3/4 cup Water
- About 1/2 cup White Wine
- 2 Lobster Tails

Directions:

1. First of all, please make sure you've all the ingredients available. Cut the lobster tails in half & place in the steamer basket.

2. Then combine the water & wine in the Instant Pot and lower the basket.
3. This step is important. Close the lid and set the pot to MANUAL.
4. Cook the lobster properly for about 2 to 5 minutes on LOW.
5. Now do a natural pressure release.
6. One thing remains to be done. Drizzle with butter & serve.
7. Finally enjoy!

Jaw dropping!!

246. Mighty Bacon-Wrapped Carrots

Legends are born in…

Ingredients:

- 3 ounces Bacon
- 1/4 cup Chicken Stock
- About 1/2 tsp Paprika
- 1 tbsp Olive Oil
- About 1/2 tsp White Pepper
- 1/3 pound Carrots

Directions:

1. First of all, please make sure you've all the ingredients available. Sprinkle the carrots with pepper & paprika.
2. Now wrap them in bacon.
3. Heat the oil in your IP on SAUTE.
4. This step is important. Cook the carrots properly until the bacon becomes crispy on all sides.
5. Then pour the broth over and close the lid.

6. Cook properly on HIGH for about 2 to 5 minutes.
7. One thing remains to be done. Do a quick pressure release.
8. Finally serve & enjoy!

Sizzle your taste buds…

247. Funny Boiled peanuts

Don't forget this one…

Ingredients:

- About 1 tablespoon salt
- 1 cup peanuts
- 2 cups chicken stock

Directions:

1. First of all, please make sure you've all the ingredients available. Wash the peanuts carefully & put it in the instant pot.
2. Now do not peel the peanuts.
3. Sprinkle the peanuts with the salt & add chicken stock.
4. Then stir the peanut gently & close the lid.
5. One thing remains to be done. Cook the peanut for about 70 to 75 minutes at the slow cooker mode.
6. Finally cool the peanuts well & serve them.

Amazing cooking starts here…

248. Energetic Zucchini Soup (VEG)

Being rich is a plus point ?

Ingredients:

- 1 large onion - coarsely chopped
- Salt and pepper - to taste
- 2 cloves garlic - crushed
- About 1.5 tsp dried basil
- 2 small potatoes (1/2 lb) - cut in 1/2" cubes
- 2 large carrots - cut in 1/2" slices
- 1 tbsp minced fresh basil - or
- 4 large zucchini (2 lbs) - cut in 1" slices
- 4 cups vegetable stock - or bouillon
- About 2.5 tbsp extra virgin olive oil

Directions:

1. First of all, please make sure you've all the ingredients available. Heat the oil in the pressure cooker. sauté the onions & garlic for about 2 minutes.
2. Then add the potatoes & sauté for another 2 to 5 minutes.
3. This step is important. Add the remaining ingredients & stir to blend.
4. Lock the lid in place & over high heat bring to HIGH pressure.
5. Now adjust the heat to maintain high pressure & cook properly for about 5 to 10 minutes.
6. One thing remains to be done. Let the pressure drop naturally or use a quick-release method.

7. Finally remove the lid, tilting it away from you too & pepper to taste.

When you're fantastic, this is best!!

249. Charming Light Chicken Soup

Being a legend.

Ingredients:

- 1/2 cup chopped carrots
- 2 cups chicken broth
- 1/2 cup potato cubes
- About 2.5 teaspoon fried shallot
- 1 tablespoon chopped leek
- 2 tablespoons chopped onion
- 1/2 teaspoon salt
- About 1 teaspoon pepper
- 1/4 teaspoon nutmeg
- 1/2 lb. chicken thighs

Directions:

1. First of all, please make sure you've all the ingredients available. Place chicken thighs, chopped carrots, & potato cubes in the pressure cooker pot.
2. Now add onion, salt, pepper, and nutmeg into the pot then pour chicken broth over the thighs. Stir well.
3. This step is important. Cover the pressure cooker with the lid & seal properly.
4. Select the menu to high and set the time to about 15 to 20 minutes.

5. Then when the beeps sounds, naturally release the pressure cooker then open the lid.
6. One thing remains to be done. Add chopped leek into the pot then cook uncover for approximately 5 to 10 minutes.
7. Finally transfer the hot soup to a serving bowl then sprinkle fried shallots on top.

Being super is a matter of recipe... ?

250.   Reliable Wholesome Tomato Soup

Feast for you!!

Ingredients:

- 2 medium onions (Chopped)
- About 3 to 4 Fresh basil leaves, as garnish
- 2 medium carrots, skin peeled and chopped
- 3 large garlic cloves, finely chopped
- 1/2 cup tofu puree
- 2 cups of chopped ripe tomatoes
- 1 tablespoon sugar
- Black pepper, as needed
- About 2.5 tablespoons tomato paste
- 1 cup veggie broth
- Kosher salt
- 2 tablespoons extra virgin olive oil

Directions:

1. First of all, please make sure you've all the ingredients available. Preheat the pot by selecting 'Saute'.
2. Now pour in the oil. Once hot, add carrots & onions.
3. Cook properly for about 2 to 5 minutes or until onions become tender.
4. This step is important. Toss in the garlic & stir until fragrant.
5. Then pour in tomato paste, sugar, chopped tomatoes, broth, pepper and salt, stir and secure the lid.
6. Select Manual and cook properly on High for about 20 to 25 minutes.
7. Now once done, release pressure naturally & open lid.
8. One thing remains to be done. Pour in the tofu puree, & blend the mix (using immersion blender if you have one) to get a creamy soup.
9. Finally garnish with torn basil leaves. Serve hot.

Show time!!

251.   Dashing Texas Chili

Wow, just wow!!

Ingredients:

- 1 1/2 tsp oil
- Pepper
- Juice of a lime
- lbs beef chuck, cut in cubes
- About 2.5 tbsp masa harina

- 14 oz can tomatoes, crushed
- 1 1/2 tsp kosher salt
- 1/2 cup coffee
- 1 tsp oregano
- About 1.5 tbsp cumin
- 1 diced medium onion
- 1/4 cup chili powder
- 1/4 tsp kosher salt
- 1 chipotle en adobo, minced, with sauce
- 2 minced garlic cloves
- Salt

Directions:

1. First of all, please make sure you've all the ingredients available. Heat oil in cooker on medium high. Sprinkle beef with salt.
2. Now brown beef in a few batches, making sure not to overcrowd the cooker.
3. Brown only on one side & remove with slotted spoon.
4. Place the onions in cooker & season with salt.
5. This step is important. Sauté until soft, & scrape up the browned bits off the pot.
6. Then mix in garlic and chipotle, sauté one minute.
7. Push mixture to the sides and place the chili powder, oregano, and cumin in the hole.
8. Allow to cook until fragrant & then mix into the onions.
9. Now pour in coffee, & scrape the pot again.
10. Add the remaining ingredients, & meat, into the pot.
11. Stir everything together, & make sure the meat is well coated.
12. Then lock and seal the lid set to high pressure. Cook properly for about 30 to 35 minutes.
13. Allow pressure to release naturally. Carefully remove the lid.
14. This is optional.
15. Now if you can, allow the chili to cool & refrigerate overnight.
16. Scrap off the fat, and then bring in back to simmer.
17. Then remove a cup of the liquid from the pot.
18. One thing remains to be done. Mix in lime juice & masa harina.
19. Finally pour back into the pot & combine. Mix in salt to taste. Serve and enjoy.

Be amazed ?

252. Perfect French Onion Cream Soup

For those who are not ordinary, try this one.

Ingredients:

- About 2.5 large yellow onions, chopped finely
- 1 1/4 cups Gruyere cheese
- Kosher salt
- One French bread loaf, cut into 1 inch slices, lightly toasted
- Fresh black pepper powder
- About 1.5 teaspoon sugar

- 3 fresh thyme sprigs
- 3/4 cup dry white wine
- 2 cups of chicken or beef broth
- 2 tablespoons butter

Directions:

1. First of all, please make sure you've all the ingredients available. Select 'Sauté' & preheat the Instant Pot.
2. Now once hot, add the butter.
3. Throw in the onions and sauté. Let it cook properly for about 5 to 10 minutes.
4. Add pepper, salt and sugar & stir slowly until onions turn lightly golden.
5. This step is important. Pour wine, & stir well to scrape bits from bottom of the pot.
6. Then cook & boil until most of the wine gets evaporated.
7. Pour broth, pepper, salt, thyme and close lid.
8. Cook on Manual option under HIGH pressure for about 10 to 15 minutes.
9. Now once done, quickly release pressure. Set the oven on Broil.
10. One thing remains to be done. Serve soup in bowls, with toasted bread slices & garnish with cheese.
11. Finally place the bowls in broiler in over for about 5 to 10 minutes or less until cheese melts. Serve hot.

Uber fantastic!!

253.   Pinnacle Lamb Stew
Cooking level infinite....

Ingredients:

- 2 cups beef broth or chicken broth
- Salt and pepper to taste
- About 1.5 tablespoon flour
- 1 tablespoon fresh parsley
- 1/4 cup red wine
- 1 tablespoon olive oil
- 1 tablespoon tomato sauce
- 2 cloves garlic (Minced)
- 7 ounces can diced tomatoes
- 1/2 cup green beans
- 1/2 cup peas
- About 1.5 bay leaf
- 2 stalks celery, sliced into 1/2 inch pieces
- 1 medium onion (Sliced)
- 2 small carrots, peeled, sliced
- 3/4 pound lamb stew meat, cubed

Directions:

1. First of all, please make sure you've all the ingredients available. Mix flour, salt & pepper in a bowl and sprinkle over the lamb chops.
2. Now press 'Sauté' button. Add oil. When the oil heats, add lamb chops & cook properly until brown.
3. Remove with a slotted spoon and set aside.
4. This step is important. Add onions and garlic & sauté until translucent.
5. Add red wine.
6. Press 'Adjust' button twice & simmer until it reduces to half its quantity.
7. Then add rest of the ingredients except parsley & stir. Press 'Cancel' button.
8. Close the lid. Press 'Stew' button and set timer for about 15 to 20 minutes.

9. One thing remains to be done. When the timer goes off, let the pressure release naturally.
10. Finally ladle into bowls. Add parsley & serve.

Long way to go…

254. Crazy Creamy Tomato Soup (VEG)

Deserved!!

Ingredients:

- 2 medium onions (Chopped)
- 1/2 cup Parmesan cheese, grated (optional)
- 2 medium carrots, skin peeled and chopped
- 3 large garlic cloves, finely chopped
- About 3 to 4 Fresh basil leaves, as garnish
- 2 cups of chopped ripe tomatoes
- 1 tbsp sugar
- 1/2 cup heavy cream
- About 2.5 tbsp tomato paste
- 1 cup vegetable broth(or chicken)
- Salt and black pepper, as needed
- 3 tbsp extra virgin olive oil

Directions:

1. First of all, please make sure you've all the ingredients available. Preheat the pot by selecting SAUTE.
2. Now pour in the oil. Once hot, add carrots and onions.
3. Cook properly for about 5 to 10 minutes or until onions become tender.
4. Toss in the garlic and stir until fragrant.
5. This step is important. Pour in tomato paste, chopped tomatoes, sugar, broth, pepper and salt, mix & secure the lid.
6. Then select MANUAL and cook properly on HIGH for about 20 to 25 minutes.
7. Once done, release pressure naturally and open lid.
8. Pour in the cream, & puree the mix (using an immersion blender if you have one) to get a creamy soup.
9. One thing remains to be done. Garnish with torn basil leaves & cheese.
10. Finally serve hot.

Be super

255. King sized Lentil Bisque

The speed matters…

Ingredients:

- 2 tablespoons olive oil
- Fresh parsley for serving
- About 2.5 tablespoons shallots (Diced)
- 1/2 cup coconut milk
- 2 teaspoons flour
- 2 tablespoons dry white wine
- 1 cup apple, peeled and diced
- 3 cups vegetable stock

- 1 teaspoon lemon zest
- About 1.5 teaspoon lemon juice
- 1/2 teaspoon curry powder
- 1 cup vegetable juice
- 1/2 teaspoon cinnamon
- 1 teaspoon salt
- 1 teaspoon coarse ground black pepper
- 1 cup dry lentils, rinsed

Directions:

1. First of all, please make sure you've all the ingredients available. Add the olive oil to the pressure cooker & turn on the sauté or brown setting.
2. Then add in the shallots & sauté for about 2 to 5 minutes.
3. Sprinkle the shallots with flour and stir.
4. Add the white wine & let reduce for about 2 to 5 minutes.
5. This step is important. Add in the lentils and apples.
6. Now season with the lemon zest, curry powder, lemon juice, cinnamon, salt and black pepper.
7. Combine the vegetable juice & vegetable stock and add them to the pressure cooker.
8. Close and seal the pressure cooker.
9. Then cook properly on high for about 15 to 20 minutes.
10. Use the quick release valve to release the steam & take one half of the soup mixture & place it in a blender with the coconut milk. Blend until smooth.
11. One thing remains to be done. Add the blender mixture back into the rest of the soup.

12. Finally serve immediately, garnished with fresh parsley, if desired.

Mystery is unveiled!!

256. Mighty Cream of Cauliflower with Potato
Being lucky is definitely better.

Ingredients:

- About 1.5 large onion (Chopped)
- 1/2 cup vegan cheese, grated and divided
- 5 large garlic cloves, finely mashed
- 4 cups of cauliflower florets
- 1.5 cups soy / almond milk
- 2 cups Yukon Gold Potatoes, skin removed and cubed into bit size pieces
- Black pepper, as needed
- 2 cups veggie broth
- About 2.5 tablespoons extra virgin olive oil
- Kosher salt

Directions:

1. First of all, please make sure you've all the ingredients available. Select the Saute and preheat the Instant Pot.
2. Then pour in the oil. Once hot, add garlic & onion and cook properly for about 5 to 10 minutes.

3. This step is important. Add potatoes, broth, cauliflower, salt and pepper and close lid.
4. Press Manual and cook properly on High for about 10 to 15 minutes.
5. Now once done, release pressure naturally & open lid.
6. Check if vegetables are very soft.
7. One thing remains to be done. Pour milk, & puree the mix to get a creamy soup.
8. Finally adjust the salt & serve warm.

If you're a legend, then make this one.

257. Nostalgic White Bean Chili

Something is special!!

Ingredients:

- pinch cayenne
- 2 cup chicken (Diced)
- 1 1/2 tsp cumin
- 7 oz diced tomatoes
- 1 cup chicken stock
- About 2.5 oz mild green chilies
- 1 1/2 cup great northern beans
- 2/3 cup onion (Diced)
- About 1/2 tsp paprika

Directions:

1. First of all, please make sure you've all the ingredients available. Combine everything in the pot.
2. Now lock & seal lid.

3. One thing remains to be done. Then set to soup for about 10 to 15 minutes.
4. Finally carefully release pressure.

Be unique, be extraordinary...

258. Best Cream of Cauliflower with Potato

Stupidly simple...

Ingredients:

- About 1.5 large onion (Chopped)
- 1 cup Cheddar cheese, grated and divided
- 5 large garlic cloves, finely mashed
- 1.5 cups full fat milk
- 4 cups of cauliflower florets
- 2 cups Yukon Gold Potatoes, skin removed and cubed into bite-sized pieces
- Black pepper, as needed
- 3 cups chicken/veggie broth
- Kosher salt
- About 2.5 tablespoons extra virgin olive oil

Directions:

1. First of all, please make sure you've all the ingredients available. Select the Saute and preheat the Instant Pot.

2. Then pour the oil. Once hot, add garlic & onion and cook properly for about 5 to 10 minutes.

3. Add potatoes, cauliflower broth, salt & pepper and close lid.

4. This step is important. Press Manual and cook properly on High for about 10 to 15 minutes.

5. Now once done, release pressure naturally & open the lid.

6. Check if vegetables are very soft.

7. One thing remains to be done. Pour cream, and puree the mix to get a creamy soup.

8. Finally adjust thickness of soup & pour more or less broth as required.

Oh yeah!

259. Vintage Boeuf Bourguignon

Good luck!!

Ingredients:

- 1/3 cup beef broth
- Salt to taste
- 1 pound beef chuck roast or round roast, cubed
- About 2.5 tablespoons parsley, chopped to garnish
- 3/4 cup red wine (Divided)
- 1 medium carrot, cubed
- 1/2 tablespoon tomato paste
- 1 small onion, thinly sliced
- 1 stalk celery (Diced)
- 1 bay leaf
- 2 sprigs fresh thyme
- About 1.5 clove garlic (Minced)
- 1 cup mushrooms (Sliced)
- 3 ounces thick cut bacon, cubed

Directions:

1. First of all, please make sure you've all the ingredients available. Press 'Sauté' button. Press 'Adjust' button once. Add bacon & sauté until crisp.

2. Now remove with a slotted spoon & set aside on paper towels.

3. Discard most of the fat. Add beef.

4. Season with salt and pepper. Cook properly until golden brown.

5. This step is important. Remove with a slotted spoon and set aside.

6. Then add onions & sauté until brown.

7. Add carrots and celery & sauté for a couple of minutes.

8. Add half the wine & broth.

9. Now scrape the bottom of the pan to remove any brown bits that are stuck to the bottom of the pot.

10. Add rest of the ingredients except bacon & stir.

11. Close the lid. Press 'Stew' button and set timer for about 15 to 20 minutes.

12. Now when the timer goes off, let the pressure release naturally.

13. One thing remains to be done. Ladle into soup bowls.

14. Finally garnish with parsley & serve with crusty baguette.

I've always loved them. Plus they can be eaten anytime!!

260. Lucky Beef and Green Bean Soup

Astonishing!!

Ingredients:

- 3 medium parsnips, finely chopped
- About 1.5 tsp dried marjoram
- 2 onions (Chopped)
- 4 cloves garlic (Minced)
- 1 tsp salt
- 25 ounces canned tomatoes (Diced)
- 1 1/2 pounds boneless beef bottom round, diced
- About 1/4 tsp ground black pepper
- 1 cup carrots (Diced)
- 4 1/2 cups beef broth
- 20 ounces green beans, trimmed and cut into small pieces

Directions:

1. First of all, please make sure you've all the ingredients available. First, combine the broth, parsnip, beef, garlic, onion, salt, carrots, tomatoes, marjoram, & black pepper in a cooker.
2. Now lock the lid onto the pot.
3. Cook properly for about 15 to 20 minutes under HIGH pressure.
4. This step is important. Use the quick-release method to drop the pressure.
5. Unlock and open the pot.
6. Then stir in the green beans.
7. One thing remains to be done. Seal the lid & wait for about 2 to 5 minutes to warm up and blanch the beans.
8. Finally serve hot with croutons of choice.

Grab it!!

261. Happy White Bean and Fennel Stew

Freshness loaded!!

Ingredients:

- About 2.5 tablespoons olive oil
- 4 cups vegetable stock
- 1 cup yellow onion (Diced)
- 2 cups sweet potato, cubed
- 1 cup fennel (Sliced)
- 1 teaspoon salt
- About 1.5 tablespoon lemon juice
- 1 teaspoon pepper
- 1 sprig fresh rosemary
- 4 cups vegetable stock
- 1 bay leaf
- 1/4 cup sherry
- 1 cup dried cannellini beans, soaked overnight and rinsed

Directions:

1. First of all, please make sure you've all the ingredients available. Place

the olive oil in the pressure cooker & set on the sauté or brown setting.

2. Now add in the onion and fennel.

3. Sauté until just tender, approximately 2 to 5 minutes.

4. Season with pepper, salt, rosemary and bay leaf.

5. This step is important. Add in the sherry and let reduce for about 2 to 5 minutes.

6. Pour the vegetable stock into the pressure cooker.

7. Then close and seal the pressure cooker.

8. Set to high and cook properly for about 15 to 20 minutes.

9. Now use the quick release to release the steam & add in the sweet potato and lemon juice.

10. One thing remains to be done. Close the pressure cooker and bring the pressure back up to high.

11. Finally cook properly for an additional 5 to 10 minutes, or until the beans are tender.

Dreams are good!! So dream about this one or else make it…

262. Great Asian Corn Chowder
Something is defintely different.

Ingredients:

- 2 tablespoons extra virgin olive oil
- 2 tablespoons chopped fresh parsley
- About 1.5 onion, finely chopped
- Ground black pepper, to taste
- 1 red bell pepper, finely chopped, seeds removed
- 4 garlic cloves, grated
- Kosher salt
- 1 tablespoon sesame oil
- 1/2 teaspoon smoked paprika
- Pinch of red pepper flakes
- Juice of one medium lime
- 11/2 cups vegetable broth
- 11/2 cups light coconut milk
- About 1.5 tablespoons soy sauce
- 4 corn ears, shucked

Directions:

1. First of all, please make sure you've all the ingredients available. Select Sauté.

2. Now remove corn from cob and set aside.

3. Pour in the oil, add pepper, onion & sauté for about 5 to 10 minutes until wilted.

4. This step is important. Next add in sesame oil, red pepper flakes & garlic.

5. Then sauté for about 5 to 10 minutes.

6. Mix in the corn and broth, stir & close with lid.

7. Cook properly on Manual at HIGH pressure for about 5 to 10 minutes.

8. Now turn off the pot. Let depressurize naturally.

9. Pour coconut milk, soy sauce, lime juice, salt and pepper.

10. One thing remains to be done. Stir and use an immersion blender to puree into a creamy mix.

11. Finally serve with a garnish of parsley.

This is epic. Take a look!!

263. Fantastic Tomato Soup
Life of a legend begins here.

Ingredients:

- Pepper
- 14 Oz Crushed Tomatoes
- 1 1/2 Tsp Agave
- About 2.5 Garlic Cloves
- 14 Oz Whole Tomatoes
- 1 1/2 Tsp Basil
- 1 Vegetarian Bouillon Cube
- 1 1/2 Cup Water
- About 1.5 Tbsp Oats
- 1/4 Cup Cashew Pieces
- Salt

Directions:

1. First of all, please make sure you've all the ingredients available. Add everything, except for the first 3 ingredients, into the pot.
2. Then cook properly for about 5 to 10 minutes & carefully release pressure.
3. One thing remains to be done. Now put mixture in a blender & blend until it's smooth.
4. Finally mix in pepper, agave, & salt to taste.

Funny but definitely yummy!!

264. Delightful Wholesome Tomato Soup

Now that's something!!

Ingredients:

- 2 medium onions (Chopped)
- 1/2 cup Parmesan cheese, grated (optional)
- 2 medium carrots, skin peeled and chopped
- About 3 to 4 Fresh basil leaves, as garnish
- 3 large garlic cloves, finely chopped
- 2 cups of chopped ripe tomatoes
- 1/2 cup heavy cream
- 1 tablespoon sugar
- About 2.5 tablespoons tomato paste
- Black pepper, as needed
- 1 cup chicken or vegetable broth
- Kosher salt
- 3 tablespoons extra virgin olive oil

Instructions:

1. First of all, please make sure you've all the ingredients available. Preheat the pot by selecting 'Saute'.
2. Then pour the oil. Once hot, add carrots and onions.
3. Cook properly for about 5 to 10 minutes or until onions become tender.

4. This step is important. Toss in the garlic and stir until fragrant.
5. Pour tomato paste, chopped tomatoes, sugar, broth, pepper and salt, stir and secure the lid.
6. Now select Manual & cook properly on High for about 20 to 25 minutes.
7. Once done, release pressure naturally & open lid.
8. One thing remains to be done. Pour the cream, & puree the mix (using an immersion blender if you have one) to get a creamy soup.
9. Finally garnish with torn basil leaves & cheese. Serve hot.

Can you make it? Yes, why not?

265. Super German Style Pork Stew

Good days!!

Ingredients:

- 3/4 cup apple juice
- Pepper to taste
- 1/2 pound potatoes (Diced)
- 1 jar (12 ounces) mushroom gravy
- Salt to taste
- About 1.5 teaspoon caraway seeds
- 1 pound pork shoulder, boneless, cubed

Directions:

1. First of all, please make sure you've all the ingredients available. Press 'Sauté' button. Add oil and heat.

2. Then press 'Adjust' button once.
3. Add pork to the pot & sauté until brown. Drain excess fat.
4. Add rest of the ingredients & stir.
5. Now close the lid. Press 'Meat/Stew' button & set timer for about 40 to 45 minutes.
6. One thing remains to be done. When the timer goes off, let the pressure release naturally.
7. Finally ladle into bowls & serve hot.

I am interested!!

266. Awesome Minestrone Soup (S&F)

This never goes out of style.

Ingredients:

- 1 quart beef broth
- About 1 tsp sea salt
- 25 ounces canned tomatoes, crushed
- 1/4 tsp ground black pepper
- 1 cup carrots, trimmed and thinly sliced
- 2 potatoes (Diced)
- 1 1/4 pounds ground beef
- 1/2 celery stalks (Chopped)
- About 2.5 cloves garlic (Minced)
- 1 1/4 cups cooked beans
- 1 cup onions (Chopped)

Directions:

1. First of all, please make sure you've all the ingredients available. Then

add the ingredients to your Instant Pot & stir to combine.

2. One thing remains to be done. Put the lid on; choose MANUAL and HIGH pressure for about 25 to 30 minutes.

3. Finally serve warm & enjoy.

Now be a legend!!

267. Iconic Sweet Peanut Stew

Simple yet fantastic!!

Ingredients:

- 2 tablespoons olive oil
- 1/2 cup fresh cilantro (Chopped)
- About 2.5 tablespoons shallots (Diced)
- 2 cloves garlic, crushed and minced
- 1 teaspoon salt
- 1/2 cup peanuts (Chopped)
- 1 teaspoon black pepper
- About 2.5 teaspoons crushed red pepper flakes
- 3 cups fresh spinach, torn
- 4 cups vegetable stock
- 1/2 cup chunky natural peanut butter
- 2 cups fresh pineapple, chunked
- 1 cup brown rice

Directions:

1. First of all, please make sure you've all the ingredients available. Place the olive oil in a pressure cooker & turn on the sauté or brown setting.

2. Now add in the shallots, salt, garlic, black pepper and crushed red

pepper flakes. Sauté for about 2 to 5 minutes.

3. Add in the rice, vegetable stock and peanut butter.

4. This step is important. Cover and seal the pressure cooker.

5. Then cook properly on high for about 15 to 20 minutes.

6. Using the quick release, open the pressure cooker & release the steam.

7. Add in the pineapple and spinach. Cover and bring the pressure back up to low.

8. Now continue to cook properly for about 2 to 5 minutes.

9. One thing remains to be done. Use the natural release method to release the steam.

10. Finally serve garnished with chopped peanuts & fresh cilantro.

It is a brand new day.... Ever listened to this one!!

268. Ultimate Leek Broccoli Cream Soup

Awesome, isn't it?

Ingredients:

- 3 large leeks, cleaned and diced
- 1/2 cup grated vegan cheese or more, as required
- About 4.5 garlic cloves (Chopped)
- 4 cups broccoli florets
- 1 cup milk (soy / almond / coconut)
- 3 cups vegetable broth
- Kosher salt

176

- About 4.5 tablespoons all purpose flour
- Ground black pepper
- 3 Pinches of red pepper flakes
- 2 tablespoons olive oil

Directions:

1. First of all, please make sure you've all the ingredients available. Select the Saute & heat the pot.
2. Now add in 1 tablespoon oil. Once hot & melted, add in garlic, leeks, and sauté for about 5 to 10 minutes until leeks are soft.
3. Add in broth, pepper, broccoli, salt and red pepper flakes.
4. This step is important. Stir and close the lid.
5. Cook properly on Manual at HIGH pressure for about 5 to 10 minutes.
6. Then add rest of the oil in a saucepan.
7. Once hot, tip flour into saucepan. Stir well.
8. Remove pressure naturally, spread the grated cheese & mix.
9. Now add the milk and flour mix.
10. With an immersion blender, puree everything up.
11. One thing remains to be done. Check seasonings, set to Sauté & reheat the soup before serving.
12. Finally serve with more cheese.

Luxury tasty dish for you!!

269.   Unique Chicken Noodle Soup
Get ready to make it my way!!

Ingredients:

- Pepper
- 1 chicken breast
- Salt
- 1/4 lb carrots (Sliced)
- 1 1/2 tsp chicken bouillon
- 3 cup water
- About 1.5 celery stalk
- 1/4 onion (Chopped)
- Small potato
- 1/2 bag kluski noodles

Directions:

1. First of all, please make sure you've all the ingredients available. Add onion, carrot, potato, celery, and chicken to pot.
2. Then pour in the water and bouillon.
3. This step is important. Lock and seal lid. Set to soup for about 35 to 40 minutes.
4. Carefully release pressure.
5. Now remove chicken & shred.
6. One thing remains to be done. Place chicken back into soup mix.
7. Finally sprinkle with pepper & salt.

The best combo ever!!

270.   Yummy Quick Matzo Ball Soup
Something is new here!!

Ingredients:

- 1/4 teaspoon baking powder
- 2 small celery stalks (Chopped)
- About 1.5 teaspoon Kosher salt
- 1/2 teaspoon black pepper
- 1 small carrot (Chopped)
- 1/4 teaspoon ground nutmeg
- 2 medium eggs
- 2 cups water (Divided)
- 4 cups chicken broth
- About 2.5 tablespoons vegetable oil
- 1 chicken breast, bone in, skin on
- 2 bay leaves
- 3/4 heaped cup matzo meal

Directions:

1. First of all, please make sure you've all the ingredients available. Mix together the matzo meal, pepper, a pinch of salt, nutmeg and baking powder in a medium bowl.
2. Now crack the eggs in another bowl, pour 1/2 cup water & oil.
3. Whisk well and transfer into the previous bowl of matzo meal.
4. This step is important. Stir well until it looks like a moist oatmeal mix.
5. (If not, add more meal and stir).
6. Then let this mixture chill for about 40 to 45 minutes.
7. Take your instant pot and add chicken, remaining water, broth, a bit salt and cook properly on Manual at HIGH pressure for about 5 to 10 minutes.
8. Once done, press Cancel and release naturally (5 to 10 minutes).
9. Now discard bay leaves and shred the chicken pieces using 2 forks and remove the bones.
10. One thing remains to be done. Make 1-inch balls out of the chilled matzo mix.
11. Finally add the balls, celery, carrot, seasonings into the pot, select Manual and cook again on HIGH for about 10 to 15 minutes.

A little work here but will be worth it.

271. Tasty Root Stew

Try it…

Ingredients:

- 1 medium onion (Chopped)
- Salt to taste
- 1 turnip (Chopped)
- 1 large carrot (Chopped)
- About 1 tablespoon apple cider vinegar
- 1 parsnip (Chopped)
- 1 cup fresh spinach (Chopped)
- 1 cup butternut squash, cubed
- Freshly powdered black pepper
- 1/2 can chickpeas, drained, rinsed
- 2 tablespoons golden raisins
- 1 cup vegetable broth
- 1/4 teaspoon ground ginger
- About 1.5 teaspoon ground cumin
- A pinch saffron
- 1/2 teaspoon ground coriander
- 1/2 teaspoon cayenne pepper
- 1 Yukon gold potato (Chopped)

Directions:

1. First of all, please make sure you've all the ingredients available. Add all the ingredients except spinach into instant pot.
2. Now close the lid. Press 'Meat/Stew' button & set timer for about 15 to 20 minutes.
3. When the timer goes off, quick release excess pressure.
4. Then add spinach & stir.
5. One thing remains to be done. Cover and set aside for about 10 to 15 minutes.
6. Finally ladle into bowls & serve immediately.

This is different, isn't it?

272. Titanic Spiced Tunisian Chickpea Soup

Yeah, this is a new variation.

Ingredients:

- About 2.5 tablespoons olive oil
- Lemon wedges for garnish
- 1 cup sweet yellow onion (Diced)
- Fresh parsley for garnish
- 1 cup green bell pepper (Sliced)
- 1 cup acorn squash, cubed
- 4 cups vegetable stock
- 2 cups canned crushed tomatoes, with liquid
- About 1.5 teaspoon curry powder
- 1 teaspoon black pepper
- 1/2 teaspoon cinnamon
- 1/2 teaspoon coriander
- 1 teaspoon salt
- 1 cup dry chickpeas

Directions:

1. First of all, please make sure you've all the ingredients available. Place the olive oil in a pressure cooker & turn on the sauté or brown setting.
2. Now add in the onion and bell pepper & sauté for about 2 to 5 minutes.
3. Next, add in the acorn squash followed by the tomatoes with liquid.
4. This step is important. Season the mixture with cinnamon, curry powder, coriander, salt and black pepper.
5. Then add the vegetable stock & cover and seal the pressure cooker.
6. Set to high and cook properly for about 15 to 20 minutes.
7. One thing remains to be done. Use the natural release method to release the steam from the pressure cooker.
8. Finally serve the soup garnished with parsley & lemon wedges.

Classic, isn't it?

273. Rich French Onion Cream Soup

Different yet fantastic in many ways.

Ingredients:

- About 2.5 medium yellow onions, chopped finely
- 1/2 cup vegan cheese
- Kosher salt
- One French bread loaf, cut into 1 inch slices, lightly toasted
- Fresh black pepper powder
- About 1.5 teaspoon sugar
- 3 fresh thyme sprigs
- 3/4 cup dry white wine
- 2 cups veggie broth
- 1 tablespoon olive oil

Directions:

1. First of all, please make sure you've all the ingredients available. Select 'Sauté' and preheat the Instant Pot.
2. Now once hot, add the oil.
3. Throw in the onions and sauté.
4. Let it cook for about 5 to 10 minutes.
5. This step is important. Add pepper, salt and sugar & stir slowly until onions turn light golden.
6. Then pour wine, and stir well to scrape bits from bottom of the pot.
7. Cook and boil until most of the wine gets evaporated.
8. Pour broth, pepper, salt, thyme and close lid.
9. Now cook properly on Manual option under HIGH pressure for about 10 to 15 minutes.
10. Once done, quickly release pressure.
11. Set the oven on Broil.
12. One thing remains to be done. Serve soup in bowls, with toasted bread slices and garnish with cheese.
13. Finally place the bowls in broiler in over for about 5 to 10 minutes or less until cheese melts. Serve hot.

Yeah, direct from the heaven; yeah?

274.   Elegant Curried Chicken Soup

What's so typical or different here?

Ingredients:

- 1 cup basmati rice
- 1 tbsp olive oil
- About 2.5 tbsp cilantro
- 1 1/2 cup diced, cooked chicken
- 1 cup diced onion
- 1/2 tsp sucanat
- 1 tbsp sriracha
- 1 tbsp peanut butter
- 3/4 cup coconut milk
- 1 cup sliced carrot
- 3/4 tbsp lemongrass
- About 1 tsp salt
- 2 cup chicken broth
- 1 1/2 cup sliced bell pepper
- 1 tbsp soy sauce
- 1 1/2 tsp curry powder
- 2 tsp minced garlic
- lime wedges
- 1 1/2 tsp minced ginger

Directions:

1. First of all, please make sure you've all the ingredients available. Set to sauté and heat oil. Cook onions, pepper, and carrot until soft.
2. Then add ginger, curry, and garlic.
3. This step is important. Let cook until fragrant.
4. Add lemongrass, broth, & salt and allow to boil. Add in chicken.
5. Now mix in milk sucanat, soy sauce, sriracha, and peanut butter.
6. One thing remains to be done. Lock and seal lid and cook properly for about 2 to 5 minutes.
7. Finally quick release. Serve with cilantro, rice, and lime wedge.

Best combo ever... Don't you agree?

275. Wonderful Ham and Split Pea Soup

Someone is definitely ready for this.

Ingredients:

- 1/2 lb. split peas, dried
- About 1.5 teaspoon thyme
- 1/2 lb. ham bone
- 1/2 diced onion
- 1 diced carrot
- About 1.5 diced celery rib
- 4 cups water

Directions:

1. First of all, please make sure you've all the ingredients available. Fill up the pressure cooker with water and all the ingredients, making sure that the cooker never gets over half full.
2. Then place the lid on top of the cooker & then bring it to high pressure and cook the meal properly for about 20 to 25 minutes.
3. Let it release the steam naturally.
4. Now take the meat out & take it off the bone.
5. One thing remains to be done. Shred it up before placing back into the soup.
6. Finally add more salt if you like & serve warm.

Ready in about 20 to 25 minutes

Servings 2

Good recipe!!

276. Quick Easy Peasy Pea Soup

Lucky!!

Ingredients:

- 1 1/2 cups green split peas
- About 1 teaspoon freshly ground black pepper
- 2 cup chopped carrots
- 2 large garlic cloves (Minced)
- 2 cups veggie broth

- 1 medium onion (Chopped)
- About 1.5 teaspoon olive oil

Directions:

1. First of all, please make sure you've all the ingredients available. Select Saute & preheat your Instant Pot.
2. Then pour in the oil.
3. Once hot, throw in the chopped onion & garlic and saute for about 2 to 5 minutes or until fragrant.
4. This step is important. Add the carrots, peas, and broth.
5. Now stir well & secure the lid.
6. Select Manual and cook properly for about 5 to 10 minutes on High Pressure.
7. One thing remains to be done. Allow the pressure to release naturally.
8. Finally mix in the freshly ground black pepper & blend the soup using an immersion blender until you get the desired texture.

Preparation Time: 5 to 10 minutes

Pressure Time: 5 to 10 minutes

Servings: 2

Yes, this is famous!!

277. Awesome Butternut Squash and Sage Soup

Wow, that's cute!!

Ingredients:

- 6 fresh sage leaves
- About 1/2 teaspoon nutmeg
- 1 medium yellow onion, chopped
- 1 large celery stalk, chopped
- 3/4 cup tofu puree
- 4 medium garlic cloves, finely chopped
- 2 cups butternut squash deseeded, skin removed and diced into small cubes
- Ground black pepper
- 3 cups veggie broth
- About 1 teaspoon baking soda
- Kosher salt
- 1 tablespoon extra virgin oil

Directions:

1. First of all, please make sure you've all the ingredients available. Preheat the Pot with the 'Sauté' option. Pour oil.
2. Now once hot, add in the sage leaves.
3. Cook until crispy and drain onto paper towel.
4. Add onions and sauté until translucent, then add garlic and celery and stir well for about 5 to 10 minutes until fragrant.
5. This step is important. Add squash, broth, baking soda, salt and pepper and stir well. Secure the lid.
6. Then select Manual and cook properly on HIGH for about 20 to 25 minutes.
7. Once done, quickly release pressure.

8. Pour tofu puree, sprinkle nutmeg & use an immersion blender to puree the whole mix.
9. One thing remains to be done. Now adjust consistency by pouring more broth, check seasonings & adjust accordingly.
10. Finally garnish with crispy sage & serve.

Preparation Time: 15 to 20 minutes

Pressure Time: 20 to 25 minutes

Servings: 2

Fresh start with something new!!

278.   Legendary Kale and Sweet Potato Soup

Try this my way!!

Ingredients:

- 2 medium onions (Chopped)
- 1 cup kale, washed, drained, stemmed and chopped
- About 4.5 garlic cloves (Minced)
- Ground black pepper
- 2 large white potatoes or sweet potatoes, skin peeled, washed and cut into bite size cubes
- Kosher salt
- 4 cups veggie broth
- About 2.5 tablespoons extra virgin oil

Directions:

1. First of all, please make sure you've all the ingredients available. Preheat the Instant Pot using 'Sauté'.
2. Now Pour oil. Once hot, add the onions & garlics and sauté until fragrant.
3. Add potatoes, broth, salt and pepper and stir well.
4. This step is important. Secure the lid.
5. Then select Manual and cook properly on HIGH for about 10 to 15 minutes.
6. Select Cancel, and let the pressure release naturally.
7. One thing remains to be done. Mash with a masher & then use an immersion blender to blend until creamy.
8. Finally use Sauté option, add kale & cook properly for about 5 to 10 minutes. Serve.

Preparation Time: 20 to 25 minutes

Pressure Time: 10 to 15 minutes

Servings: 2

Baking does the trick!!

279.   Excellent Sweet n Spicy Carrots

I don't know about you, but I include this one everytime I get a chance.

Ingredients:

- 4 medium carrots, skin peeled and sliced into bite sized (~1-inch) pieces
- Sea salt and black pepper powder, to taste
- About 1.5 tablespoon vegan butter
- 1/4 teaspoon cayenne pepper
- About 1.5 tablespoon maple syrup
- 11/2 cup tap water
- 1/2 teaspoon ground cumin

Directions:

1. First of all, please make sure you've all the ingredients available. Pour the water into your Instant Pot.
2. Then place a steam rack on top. Distribute the carrot slices on the rack.
3. Secure the lid, select 'Steam' and cook properly for about 5 to 10 minutes on high pressure.
4. This step is important. Once cooked, release the pressure quickly.
5. Now remove the steam rack & water from the pot and let it dry.
6. Hit the 'Saute' and let the pot dry.
7. Pour in the butter. Once hot & melted, add the steamed carrots, stir well, add the ground cumin & cayenne powder.
8. Then sprinkle salt and pepper & stir everything up.
9. One thing remains to be done. Pour in the syrup and hit the 'Cancel'.
10. Finally stir continuously & coat. Let cool a bit and serve.

Preparation Time: 5 to 10 minutes

Pressure Time: 5 to 10 minutes

Servings: 2

I repeat… Try it if you want to. No regrets. Right!!

280.   Fantastic Cauliflower and Broccoli Salad

Why not??

Ingredients:

- 1 small head broccoli, chopped into florets
- About 1.5 small head cauliflower, chopped into florets
- 2 oranges, peeled, deseeded, thinly sliced

For Dressing:

- Zest of half an orange, grated
- 1/3 cup extra virgin olive oil
- 1/2 hot pepper, thinly sliced
- 3 anchovies
- Pepper to taste
- About 1.5 tablespoons capers

- Salt to taste
- Juice of half an orange

Directions:

1. First of all, please make sure you've all the ingredients available. Add cauliflower & broccoli to the instant pot.
2. Then add 1/2 cup water.
3. Close the lid. Press 'Steam' button & set timer for about 5 to 10 minutes. Drain & add to a serving bowl.
4. Now add orange and toss.
5. One thing remains to be done. Whisk dressing ingredients in a bowl & pour over salad.
6. Finally toss well and serve.

Leave a mark!!

281.   Great Carrot and Pumpkin Stew

Spice up!!

Ingredients:

- About 1.5 onion (Chopped)
- 1 cup vegetable broth
- 4 carrots, peeled (Chopped)
- 2 cups chicken broth
- 1 tsp salt
- About 1.5 tsp black pepper
- 2 tbsp olive oil
- 1/2 tsp cumin powder
- 3-4 garlic cloves (Minced)
- 1 cup pumpkin (Chopped)

Directions:

1. First of all, please make sure you've all the ingredients available. In the Instant Pot add pumpkin, carrots, salt, chicken broth, onion, oil, vegetable broth, garlic, cumin powder, and black pepper. Mix well.
2. Then cover pot with lid and leave to cook properly on SLOW cook mode for about 60 to 65 minutes.
3. Transfer to blender & blend till puree.
4. One thing remains to be done. Now pour stew into serving bowls & serve hot.
5. Finally serve and enjoy.

Prep + Cooking Time: 70 to 75 minutes

Servings: 2

What do you think? ?

282.   Happy Coconut, Kidney bean, Corn, and Lime Nacho Bowls (V, VG)

What makes this the best? Check it out for yourself!!

Ingredients:

- 8fl oz coconut milk

- Enough vegan corn chips for two people (I'll leave that up to your discretion!)
- 1 tin corn kernels, drained
- About 1.5 onion, finely chopped
- Large handful of fresh coriander, roughly chopped
- 4 garlic cloves, finely chopped
- 1 tsp ground paprika
- 1 avocado, sliced
- 1 tsp chili powder
- About 1.5 tsp ground cumin
- 1 lettuce
- Salt and pepper, to taste
- 2 juicy limes, halved
- 1 tin red kidney beans, drained

Directions:

1. First of all, please make sure you've all the ingredients available. Place the beans, coconut milk, corn, garlic, pepper, onion, paprika, chili, cumin, salt, and zest of one lime into your Instant Pot, stir to combine.
2. Then secure the lid onto the pot & press the BEAN/CHILLI button and adjust the time to about 25 to 30 minutes.
3. Once the pot beeps, quick-release the pressure, remove the lid, and stir the mixture.
4. One thing remains to be done. Now place a generous serving of the bean mixture onto a wide bowl or plate, place a pile of lettuce to one side of the plate or bowl, add some avocado slices, a handful of chopped cilantro, 2 lime halves, & a handful of corn chips onto the plate (yup, it's a lot!).

5. Finally one thing left to do: devour! Preferably with a Margarita.

Time: approximately 30 to 35 minutes

Just got better!!

283.   Lucky Veggie Burgers (V)

Got the idea!!

Ingredients:

- 2 slices of cheddar (or any other melt-friendly cheese)
- About 2.5 large Portobello mushrooms, finely chopped
- 1 onion, finely chopped
- Tomato
- About 3.5 garlic cloves, finely chopped
- 1/2 cup corn kernels (tinned, frozen, or fresh)
- 1/2 cup grated mozzarella cheese
- Lettuce
- 1 egg
- Salt and pepper, to taste
- Herbs and spices of your choice
- Mayonnaise
- Olive oil
- 2 burger buns
- Mustard
- 1 tin chickpeas, drained

Directions:

1. First of all, please make sure you've all the ingredients available. Mash the chickpeas in a bowl until they resemble a paste with a few lumps and chunks.
2. Then add the mushroom pieces, mozzarella, garlic, onion, corn, egg, salt, and pepper to the bowl & stir to combine.
3. Now you can add any herbs & spices you like. Personally, I like paprika and chili (my usual spice duo!), but fresh parsley and thyme would be great too.
4. This step is important. Drizzle some olive oil into your Instant Pot & press the SAUTE button, keep the temperature at NORMAL.
5. Now shape your patty mixture into burgers (don't worry if it's rather sticky or difficult to shape, rugged patties are the best patties).
6. Place the patties into the hot pot & fry on both sides until golden and crispy.
7. Then to warm the buns, you can slice them in half & lay them sliced-side down in the Instant Pot on the SAUTE function once the patties have finished cooking.
8. The buns will soak up some of the yummy oil and flavors leftover from the patties.
9. One thing remains to be done. Spread the buns with mustard & mayo, place a patty on top, then load up with lettuce, cheese, tomato, and any other tasty fillings you like (ahem, pickles…).
10. Finally eat messily & enjoy!

Time: approximately 25 to 30 minutes

Relax and enjoy this recipe!!

284.   Vintage Simple Artichokes With Cashew Dips

Try this one if you're hungry!!

Ingredients:

For Artichoke:

- 4 large garlic cloves, thinly sliced
- About 2.5 tablespoons freshly chopped thyme
- 1 cup water/veggie stock
- 4 small-medium artichokes, trimmed and cleaned

For Dipping:

- 1/4 cup water
- Pinch of salt
- 2 garlic cloves
- About 2.5 tablespoons lemon juice
- 1/2 teaspoon apple cider vinegar
- 1/2 teaspoon lemon zest
- 1/2 cup cashew, soaked for 2 hours

Directions:

1. First of all, please make sure you've all the ingredients available. Open up the cleaned artichoke & insert the garlic slices in-between the leaves.
2. Now pour the stock & herbs in your Instant Pot.
3. Place a steamer rack on top.
4. This step is important. Place the artichokes on the rack.
5. Make sure the stem side is faced up.
6. Then secure the lid. Select Manual & cook properly for about 5 to 10 minutes on High Pressure.
7. Meanwhile, combine all the dipping ingredients & blend in a blender until super smooth.
8. Set aside in a small cup.
9. Now allow the pressure to release naturally.
10. Remove the lid and check if the artichokes are well-cooked.
11. One thing remains to be done. If not cook properly for about 2 to 5 more minutes.
12. Finally dip & serve.

Preparation Time: 5 to 10 minutes

Pressure Time: 10 to 15 minutes

Servings: 2

Make me remember the good old days!!

285. Best Artichokes with Cashew Dips

Luxury in its own class!!

Ingredients:

For Artichoke:

- 4 large garlic cloves, thinly sliced
- About 2.5 tablespoons freshly chopped thyme
- 1 cup water/veggie stock
- 4 small-medium artichokes, trimmed and cleaned

For Dipping:

- 1/4 cup water
- Pinch of salt
- 2 garlic cloves
- 1/2 teaspoon apple cider vinegar
- About 2.5 tablespoons lemon juice
- 1/2 teaspoon lemon zest
- 1/2 cup cashew, soaked for 2 hours

Directions:

1. First of all, please make sure you've all the ingredients available. Open up the cleaned artichoke & insert the garlic slices in-between the leaves.
2. Then pour the stock & herbs in your Instant Pot.
3. Place a steamer rack on top.
4. Place the artichokes on the rack.

5. This step is important. Make sure the stem side is faced up.
6. Now secure the lid. Select Manual & cook properly for about 5 to 10 minutes on High Pressure.
7. Meanwhile, combine all the dipping ingredients & blend in a blender until super smooth. Set aside in a small cup.
8. Then allow the pressure to release naturally.
9. Remove the lid and check if the artichokes are well-cooked.
10. One thing remains to be done. If not cook properly for about 2 to 5 more minutes.
11. Finally dip and serve.

Preparation Time: 5 to 10 minutes

Pressure Time: 10 to 15 minutes

Servings: 2

Healthy is a new trend these days!! ? Always I guess…

286. Nostalgic Italian Cannellini and Mint Salad

Stunner!!

Ingredients:

- 1 bay leaf
- About 1.5 teaspoon Italian seasoning
- 2 cloves garlic (Mashed)
- Pepper to taste
- 1 tablespoon vinegar
- Salt to taste
- About 1.5 tablespoon mint (Chopped)

- 1 tablespoon olive oil
- 1/2 cup dry cannellini beans, soaked in water

Directions:

1. First of all, please make sure you've all the ingredients available. Add beans along with water, garlic & bay leaf to the instant pot.
2. Now close lid. Press 'Manual' button & set timer for about 5 to 10 minutes.
3. One thing remains to be done. Then drain water & transfer into a bowl.
4. Finally add rest of the ingredients, toss well & serve.

Super awesome plus unique!!

287. Mighty Steamed Broccoli (S&F)

Iconic recipe of my list!!

Ingredients:

- 2/3 cup water
- About 2.5 pounds broccoli
- Salt and pepper to taste

Directions:

1. First of all, please make sure you've all the ingredients available. Place water into the bottom of your Instant Pot, & you can measure it out with the cup provided.

2. Now chop your broccoli into florets & place it on the steamer rack.

3. Place the lid on your Instant Pot & set the valve to sealing and press STEAM for about 2 to 5 minutes.

4. Then once it has started, it will beep when done.

5. One thing remains to be done. Once it has cooled down from keep warm mode you can get it out.

6. Finally serve seasoned with salt & pepper.

Prep + Cooking Time: 5 to 10 minutes

Servings: 2

Well it is a Grandma's recipe!!

288.   King sized Corn, Mango, and Toasted Seed Tacos (V)

Happiness has finally arrived!!

Ingredients:

- Handful of fresh coriander, finely chopped
- 1 fresh mango, peeled, flesh cut into small chunks
- Olive oil
- About 1.5 onion, finely chopped
- 1 avocado (Sliced)
- 1 tin corn kernels, drained
- 1 tin black beans, drained
- 4 tbsp refried beans (store bought, I like the ones with the adobo chili!)
- Salt and pepper, to taste
- About 2.5 tbsp pumpkin seeds
- 2 tbsp sunflower seeds
- 4 flour tortillas (2 each)
- 1/2 cup (4fl oz) plain yogurt

Directions:

1. First of all, please make sure you've all the ingredients available. Prepare the crema by mixing the yogurt & coriander together (easy!).

2. Now drizzle some olive oil into your Instant Pot and add the onion, pepper, black beans, corn, salt, & about 4 floz of water.

3. Secure the lid onto the pot & press the MANUAL button, cook properly on HIGH for about 10 to 15 minutes.

4. This step is important. As the beans and corn are cooking, heat a small frying pan without any oil & toast the seeds until they are fragrant & beginning to turn golden.

5. Then once the pot beeps, quick-release the pressure & remove the lid, stir the corn and bean mixture.

6. If you want to heat your tortillas, do it now by throwing them in the pan you used to toast the seeds & heat until they start to puff up.

7. Now lay the tortillas on a board & spread thinly with refried beans.

8. Pile some of the corn & bean mixture on top (yup, 2 layers of beans!).

9. One thing remains to be done. Add some avocado slices, then the mango (lots), sprinkle the toasted seeds on top, then drizzle with crema.

10. Finally serve with sangria for 2!

Time: approximately 25 to 30 minutes

Whenever you want a great recipe!!

289.   Crazy Ramen Noodle Salad with Tofu, Peanuts and Avocado (V, VG)

How is it? Only one way to find out...

Ingredients:

- Olive oil
- 1/4 cup roasted, salted peanuts
- 5 oz firm tofu, cut into small cubes
- About 1.5 tsp sesame oil
- 1 avocado, cut into chunks
- 1 tbsp soy sauce
- 2 blocks of ramen (or 3 if you want a larger meal)
- About 1.5 tsp Sriracha (chili sauce, or use 1tsp ground chili)

Directions:

1.   First of all, please make sure you've all the ingredients available. Place the ramen noodle blocks into a bowl & cover with boiling water, cover the bowl & leave the noodles to cook as you prepare the rest (if your brand of noodle specifies different cooking methods then just follow those).

2.   Then drizzle some olive oil into the Instant Pot & press the SAUTE button, keep the temperature at NORMAL.

3.   Place the tofu, soy sauce, sesame oil, & Sriracha into the hot pot and stir to coat and combine, sauté for about 5 to 10 minutes or until the tofu is golden and starting to char.

4.   Now drain the cooked noodles & add them to the pot, stir to combine and coat in sauce & seasoning.

5.   One thing remains to be done. Transfer the contents of the pot into a salad bowl and place the peanuts, avocado chunks, & any other additions you like on top (coriander, grated carrot, lime, extra chilli, cucumber pickles would all be great additions).

6.   Finally this salad is just as good when served cold.

Time: approximately 15 to 20 minutes

I can eat them all day!!

290.   Pinnacle Quick Mushroom Asparagus Veggies

Different take on this one...

Ingredients:

- 3/4 cup crimini mushrooms (Sliced)
- Salt, to taste
- 2 garlic cloves (Minced)
- About 1.5 teaspoon lemon zest
- 1/4 cup veggie stock
- 6 oz (170 gm) asparagus, bottoms discarded, cut into bite sized pieces
- About 1.5 tablespoon lemon juice
- 5 oz (140 gm) sugar snap peas, fiber removed, cut in halves
- 1 teaspoon olive oil

Directions:

1. First of all, please make sure you've all the ingredients available. Select Saute and preheat your Instant Pot.
2. Then pour the oil. Once hot, add the mushrooms & cook properly for about 2 to 5 minutes.
3. Add the minced garlic and cook for a minute.
4. This step is important. Pour the veggie stock.
5. Secure the lid and cook properly for about 2 to 5 minutes on High Pressure.
6. Now release the pressure quickly and remove the lid.
7. Add the cut asparagus.
8. Put back the lid and cook properly for about 2 to 5 minutes in Low Pressure.
9. Remove the lid and add the sugar snap peas.
10. Then put back the lid and allow to sit for about 2 to 5 minutes.
11. One thing remains to be done. Sprinkle the lemon juice and zest.
12. Finally adjust the seasoning & serve.

Preparation Time: 5 to 10 minutes

Pressure Time: 2 to 5 minutes

Servings: 2

Grandfather of Recipes!!

291.   Perfect Desi Aloo Gobi
I am actually popular among my friends for eating this one a lot.

Ingredients:

- 1 head of cauliflower (Quartered)
- 1 teaspoon of grated ginger
- About 1.5 teaspoon olive oil
- 1/2 cup red onion, finely chopped
- 1/2 teaspoon of chili powder
- 1 1/2 cups of water
- 3 garlic clove (Minced)
- 1/2 teaspoon turmeric
- About 1 teaspoon salt
- 3/4 teaspoon garam masala
- 1/2 teaspoon ground coriander
- 14 oz. (400 gm) potatoes, peeled and chopped

Direction:

1. First of all, please make sure you've all the ingredients available. Pour 2 cups of water in the Instant Pot & place the steamer basket.

192

2. Now distribute the sliced cauliflowers in the basket.

3. Close the lid, select Manual and cook properly for about 2 to 5 minutes on Low Pressure.

4. Do a quick pressure release. Remove the basket & allow to cool. Set aside

5. This step is important. Remove the water from the pot. Select Sauté & pour in the oil.

6. Then once hot, add the ginger, chopped onions, & garlic and saute for about 2 to 5 minutes until fragrant. Add 1/2 cup water and stir.

7. Add the spices, chopped potatoes, and remaining 1 cup water. Stir.

8. Secure the lid, select Manual & cook properly on High Pressure for about 5 to 10 minutes.

9. Now meanwhile, slice the steamed cauliflower into bit sized bits.

10. Once the IP is done cooking, allow the pressure to release naturally.

11. Then remove the lid, & add in the sliced cauliflower.

12. One thing remains to be done. Mix well with a spoon.

13. Finally serve over rice.

Preparation Time: 5 to 10 minutes

Pressure Time: 2 to 5 minutes

Servings: 2

So, what's your opinion?

292. Dashing Tofu Salad

Yeah, you can make it in your free time...

Ingredients:

- 1 cup cooked elbow pasta
- Salt to taste
- About 1.5 medium tomato (Chopped)
- 1 small green bell pepper (Chopped)
- About 1.5 apple (Chopped)
- 1/2 cup tofu (Chopped)
- 1 cups chickpeas, rinsed, soaked in water overnight, drained

For the dressing:

- 1 tablespoon honey
- About 1.5 teaspoon dried oregano
- Salt to taste
- Pepper powder to taste
- 1 clove garlic (Minced)
- About 1 teaspoon red chili flakes
- 4 teaspoons apple cider vinegar

Directions:

1. First of all, please make sure you've all the ingredients available. Add the chickpeas & salt to the instant pot.

2. Then add enough water to cover the chickpeas (2 inches above the chick peas).

3. Close the lid. Press 'Manual' button & timer for about 20 to 25 minutes.

4. Now drain and transfer into a large bowl and cool.

5. One thing remains to be done. Meanwhile, whisk together all the ingredients of the dressing in a bowl & set aside.

6. Finally add rest of the ingredients. Pour dressing on top & toss well.

Supremacy defined!!

293. Reliable Lentil and Veggie Soup

Looking forward to this one!!

Ingredients:

- 6 small potatoes, diced (see note above)
- 1 bay leaf
- 3 large carrots (Sliced)
- About 1 tsp thyme
- 3 cups chopped broccoli
- 1 cup dry lentils
- 1/2 tsp paprika
- 2 quarts of water
- 1 tsp salt
- About 1.5 tsp garlic powder
- 1/2 tsp black pepper
- 1 tsp onion powder
- 1 cup diced onions

Directions:

1. First of all, please make sure you've all the ingredients available. Add all of the chopped veggies to a large pot on medium heat.
2. Now i like to do this as I'm cutting them but if you pre-cut them you can do it all at once.
3. Add the dry lentils, careful to sort them for debris. I found a stick in mine.
4. Then add the water and all of the seasonings & cover with a lid.
5. Bring to a simmer and allow to simmer for about 30 to 35 minutes.
6. One thing remains to be done. Check soup, make sure the carrots & potatoes are soft.
7. Finally remove the bay leaf & serve.

Prep + Cooking Time: 5 to 10 minutes

Servings: 2

Ironic in taste…

294. Charming Feta and Olive Spaghetti with Rosemary Ricotta (V)

Arrive in style with this recipe.

Ingredients:

- 30fl oz vegetable stock (enough to just cover the spaghetti)
- 3 oz feta cheese, crumbled or cut into small chunks
- 10 black olives, stones removed, cut into small chunks
- 3 garlic cloves, finely chopped
- About 1.5 tsp chopped fresh rosemary
- 1/2 tsp chili flakes
- Pepper, to taste
- 7 oz dried spaghetti
- About 3.5 oz ricotta cheese

Directions:

1. First of all, please make sure you've all the ingredients available. Place the spaghetti, chili, olives, stock, garlic, and pepper (I don't add extra salt yet as the feta and olives are salty) into your Instant Pot and make sure the spaghetti is submerged in liquid.
2. Then secure the lid onto the pot & press the MANUAL button, cook properly at a high pressure at 5 to 10 minutes.
3. Once the pot beeps, quick-release the pressure & remove the lid, stir the pasta.
4. One thing remains to be done. Now add the rosemary, ricotta, & feta to the pot and stir to combine, the pasta will be thick & creamy.
5. Finally taste to check if you need to add pepper, any extra salt, or chili if you want some heat.

Time: approximately 15 to 20 minutes

Classic style…

295. Energetic Tangy Ladies' Finger

Now you're happy…?

Ingredients:

- 1/2 cup finely chopped onion
- Salt and black pepper, to taste
- 10 oz (300 gm) ladies' finger (Okra), sliced into 1/2 inch pieces
- 1 cup diced tomato
- About 1/2 teaspoon cayenne pepper
- 1 tablespoon ginger, freshly grated
- About 1.5 teaspoon olive oil

Directions:

1. First of all, please make sure you've all the ingredients available. Select Saute and preheat your Instant Pot.
2. Now pour the oil. Once hot, add the chopped onion & sauté for about 2 to 5 minutes or until fragrant.
3. Select Cancel. Add the sliced okra, ginger, tomatoes, and cayenne. Stir well.
4. Then secure the lid and cook properly for about 2 to 5 minutes on High Pressure.
5. One thing remains to be done. Do a quick release & remove the lid.
6. Finally transfer the content to a bowl, adjust the seasonings and serve.

Always the upper hand…

296. Funny Quick Mushroom Asparagus Veggies

Yeah, it is a vintage recipe.

Ingredients:

- 3/4 cup crimini mushrooms (Sliced)
- Salt, to taste
- 2 garlic cloves (Minced)
- About 1.5 teaspoon lemon zest
- 1/4 cup veggie stock
- 1 tablespoon lemon juice
- 6 oz (170 gm) asparagus, bottoms discarded, cut into bite sized pieces
- 5 oz (140 gm) sugar snap peas, fiber removed, cut in halves
- About 1.5 teaspoon olive oil

Directions:

1. First of all, please make sure you've all the ingredients available. Select Saute and preheat your Instant Pot.
2. Now pour in the oil. Once hot, add the mushrooms & cook properly for about 2 to 5 minutes.
3. Add the minced garlic & cook for a minute.
4. This step is important. Pour in the veggie stock. Secure the lid & cook properly for about 2 to 5 minutes on High Pressure.
5. Then release the pressure quickly & remove the lid.
6. Add the cut asparagus.
7. Put back the lid and cook properly for about 2 to 5 minutes in Low Pressure.
8. Remove the lid & add the sugar snap peas.
9. Now put back the lid & allow to sit for about 2 to 5 minutes.
10. One thing remains to be done. Sprinkle the lemon juice and zest.
11. Finally adjust the seasoning & serve.

Preparation Time: 2 to 5 minutes

Pressure Time: 2 to 5 minutes

Servings: 2

Magical, isn't it?

297. Scrumptious Butterfly Pasta

Now the wait is over for hungry people.

Ingredients:

- 2 cloves garlic, smashed
- Pepper to taste
- About 1 teaspoon oregano
- 2 fresh hot chili pepper (Chopped)
- Salt to taste
- 2 cups tomato puree
- About 1.5 tablespoon olive oil
- 16 ounces farfalle pasta

Directions:

1. First of all, please make sure you've all the ingredients available. Press 'Sauté'. Add oil and garlic & sauté until light brown.
2. Then add rest of the ingredients & enough water to cover the pasta and stir.
3. Press 'Cancel' button.

4. One thing remains to be done. Now close the lid. Press 'Manual' button & set timer for about 2 to 5 minutes.
5. Finally when the timer goes off, quick release excess steam.

Awesomeness fully loaded...

298. Nostalgic Veggie Spaghetti

Mystery with this recipe or rather a chemistry with it.

Ingredients:

- 1 cup water
- 1/4 cup pistachios, shell removed
- Sea salt and black pepper powder, to taste
- About 2.5 tbsp butter
- 2 large garlic cloves, finely chopped
- 2 tbsp basil leaves, freshly chopped
- 1/2 tbsp lime juice
- About 4.5 tbsp parmesan cheese, grated
- 1 pound (16 oz. / 450 gm) spaghetti squash, halved, deseeded, fibrous innards removed

Directions:

1. First of all, please make sure you've all the ingredients available. Pour water into the Instant Pot & place the squash halves, cut-side facing up.
2. Now secure the lid, select MANUAL & cook properly for about 5 to 10 minutes on HIGH pressure.
3. In the meantime, heat a medium skillet on stove top.

4. This step is important. Once hot, add the pistachios & sauté for about 2 to 5 minutes or until toasted.
5. Remove from the skillet & aside.
6. Then pour 1 tablespoon butter (in the same skillet).
7. Once hot and melted, sauté garlic for about a minute until lightly golden.
8. Turn off the stove and keep aside.
9. Now release the pressure of the Instant Pot once it is done cooking.
10. Remove the squash & drain out the water.
11. Carefully separate the squash strands from the peel using a fork.
12. One thing remains to be done. Transfer the strands into a large mixing bowl, mix the cooked garlic, remaining tablespoon butter, lime juice & grated parmesan.
13. Finally sprinkle salt and pepper, top with toasted pistachios & freshly chopped basil. Serve.

Prep + Cooking Time: 15 to 20 minutes

Servings: 2

Speed defines it...

299. Best Southern Delight

Jaw dropping!!

Ingredients:

- 1 large white onion, diced
- Salt and pepper, to taste
- 2 cups sliced (1-inch pieces) okra
- 1 cup corn kernels
- About 2.5 tablespoon freshly chopped cilantro
- 1/4 cup veggie stock
- 1 cup ripe tomatoes, freshly diced
- About 1.5 teaspoon olive oil

Directions:

1. First of all, please make sure you've all the ingredients available. Select Saute and preheat your Instant Pot.
2. Then pour the oil. Once hot, add the chopped onion and saute for about 2 to 5 minutes or until fragrant.
3. Add the sliced okra. Stirring continuously, cook properly for a minute.
4. This step is important. Stir in the corn and veggie stock.
5. Now distribute the tomatoes on top (without stirring).
6. Secure the lid and cook properly for about 2 to 5 minutes on High Pressure.
7. Do a quick release when done.
8. One thing remains to be done. Remove the lid & transfer the contents to a serving bowl.
9. Finally adjust the seasonings & serve.

Preparation Time: 5 to 10 minutes

Pressure Time: 2 to 5 minutes

Servings: 2

Legends are born in...

300.   Vintage Tangy Ladies' Finger

Sizzle your taste buds...

Ingredients:

- 1/2 cup finely chopped onion
- Salt and black pepper, to taste
- 10 oz (300 gm) ladies' finger (Okra), sliced into 1/2 inch pieces
- 1 cup diced tomato
- About 1/2 teaspoon cayenne pepper
- 1 tablespoon ginger, freshly grated
- About 1.5 teaspoon olive oil

Directions:

1. First of all, please make sure you've all the ingredients available. Select Saute and preheat your Instant Pot.
2. Then pour in the oil. Once hot, add the chopped onion & saute for 2 minutes or until fragrant.
3. Select Cancel. Add the sliced okra, ginger, tomatoes, & cayenne. Stir well.

4. Now secure the lid and cook properly for about 2 to 5 minutes on High Pressure.
5. One thing remains to be done. Do a quick release & remove the lid.
6. Finally transfer the content to a bowl, adjust the seasonings and serve.

Preparation Time: 5 to 10 minutes

Pressure Time: 2 to 5 minutes

Servings: 2

Don't forget this one…

301. Lucky Southern Delight

Amazing cooking starts here…

Ingredients:

- 1 large white onion (Diced)
- Salt and pepper, to taste
- 2 cups sliced (1-inch pieces) okra
- 1 cup corn kernels
- About 2.5 tablespoons freshly chopped cilantro
- 1/4 cup veggie stock
- 1 cup ripe tomatoes, freshly diced
- About 1.5 teaspoon olive oil

Directions:

1. First of all, please make sure you've all the ingredients available. Select Sauté & preheat your Instant Pot.
2. Then pour in the oil. Once hot, add the chopped onion & saute for about 2 to 5 minutes or until fragrant.
3. Add the sliced okra. Stirring continuously, cook for a minute.
4. This step is important. Stir in the corn & veggie stock.
5. Distribute the tomatoes on top (without stirring).
6. Now secure the lid and cook properly for about 2 to 5 minutes on High Pressure.
7. Do a quick release when done.
8. One thing remains to be done. Remove the lid & transfer the contents to a serving bowl.
9. Finally adjust the seasonings & serve.

Being rich is a plus point ?

302. Happy Spicy Kale

When you're fantastic, this is best!!

Ingredients:

- 1 medium onion (Diced)
- Salt and pepper, to taste
- About 1.5 medium capsicum (Diced)
- 2 large garlic cloves (Minced)
- 1 medium bunch marrow-stem kale, destemmed and sliced
- 1/2 teaspoon ground fenugreek
- 3/4 cup water/veggie stock
- About 1.5 teaspoon berbere spice
- 1 tablespoon olive oil

Directions:

1. First of all, please make sure you've all the ingredients available. Select Saute and preheat your Instant Pot.
2. Then pour in the oil. Once hot, add the diced onion & sauté for about 2 to 5 minutes or until fragrant.
3. This step is important. Add the diced capsicum, garlic, and all the spices.
4. Stir and cook properly for about 20 to 30 seconds.
5. Now scrape the bottom & pour in the veggie stock.
6. Throw in the kale and secure the lid.
7. One thing remains to be done. Select Manual and cook properly for about 5 to 10 minutes on Low Pressure.
8. Finally adjust the seasonings & serve warm.

Preparation Time: 5 to 10 minutes

Pressure Time: 10 to 15 minutes

Servings: 2

Being a legend.

303.   Great Steamed Garlic Soybeans

Being super is a matter of recipe… ?

Ingredients:

- 2 cups fresh soybeans / edamame, in their pods
- Kosher salt and black pepper, to taste
- About 1.5 teaspoon extra virgin olive oil
- 1 tablespoon soy sauce
- About 4.5 large garlic cloves, finely chopped
- 11/2 cup tap water

Directions:

1. First of all, please make sure you've all the ingredients available. Pour the water into your Instant Pot. Place a steam rack on top.
2. Then add in the edamame and secure the lid.
3. This step is important. Select 'Steam' and cook properly for about 2 to 5 minutes at high pressure.
4. In the meantime, heat a small skillet, pour in the oil and saute garlic for about 2 to 5 minutes until lightly golden (not brown).

5. Now turn off the heat, sprinkle the salt & stir in the sauce.
6. One thing remains to be done. Once the edamame is done cooking, release the pressure quickly.
7. Finally transfer the cooked edamame with garlic mixture into a medium bowl & mix.

Preparation Time: 5 to 10 minutes

Pressure Time: 2 to 5 minutes

Servings: 2

Feast for you!!

Thanks for reading my book.

Made in the USA
Columbia, SC
17 July 2018